MAKING SENSE OF CHANGE MANAGEMENT

Praise for *Making Sense of Change Management*

'I commend it highly. It has a good coverage of relevant theoretical work while at the same time giving plenty of practical examples. It is written in an accessible style that engages the reader and it is full of useful ideas without being overly prescriptive or formulaic.'
Philip Sadler, author of a number of acclaimed business titles and former chief executive of Ashridge Business School

'I really enjoyed this book. I like the straightforward approach, the inclusion of the author's opinion and the insight provided by the case studies. This book will be very useful for those business managers in my organisation who need to prepare themselves for tackling major organizational change.'
Andy Houghton, Head of Organization Development, Retail Direct, Royal Bank of Scotland Group

'There has long been a need for a readable, practical but theoretically under-pinned book on Change which recognised a multiplicity of perspectives. By combining the behavioural, humanistic, organizational and cognitive perspectives and by helping the reader make sense of what each perspective brings to understanding Change, this book should help students and practitioners. By linking in work on personality tests such as MBTI the book breaks new ground from a practitioner point of view not least because these tests are widely used in practice. I thoroughly recommend it.'
Professor Colin Carnall, Associate Dean, Executive Programme, Warwick Business School, University of Warwick

'If you're interested in successfully managing and leading change, then read this book! It not only covers change from both the individual and organisational perspective, but also increases the number of options available to you.'
Judi Billing, Director of IDeA Leadership Academy, Improvement & Development Agency

'Change is a huge thing wherever you work. The key is to make change happen, and make it happen well – with everyone on side, and everyone happy. This book provides an extremely stimulating and accessible guide to doing just that. There are a few people at the Beeb who could do with this. I'll definitely be placing copies on a couple of desks at White City.'
Nicky Campbell, Presenter Radio Five Live and BBC1's *Watchdog*

'This book is a great resource for managers thrown into the midst of change, who need to gain understanding of what happens when you try to make significant changes in a business, and how best to manage people through it. The authors have tackled a complex topic in a lively and engaging way, leading readers through the maze of theory available and offering just the right amount of practical advice.'
Andy Newall, Organisational Effectiveness Director, Allied Domecq plc

'This impressive book on change is an essential read for any professional manager who is serious about getting to grips with the important issues of making change happen.'
Dr Jeff Watkins, MSc Course Director, Management Research Centre,
University of Bristol

'This practical handbook, combining contemporary management theory with very practical suggestions, is an indispensable tool for any manager involved in change processes. And aren't we all …'
Adriaan Vollebergh, Director, Multi Products Mainland Europe & Ireland
Corus Metal Services Europe

'This is a book which lives up to its title. By combining a guide to the ideas of key thinkers on change and useful tips for making change happen, it really does provide a toolkit to help us to make sense of change. It is useful to see a focus on the individual, team and organisational levels, and in particular, on the role of the leader in the change process. It is written in a way that makes the book interesting to read both at length as well as to dip into.'
Richard McBain, Director of Studies Distance Learning MBA, Henley Management College

MAKING SENSE OF CHANGE MANAGEMENT

A Complete Guide to the Models, Tools
& Techniques of Organizational Change

Esther Cameron & Mike Green

KOGAN
PAGE

London and Sterling, VA

First published in Great Britain and the United States in 2004 by Kogan Page Limited
Reprinted 2004 (twice), 2005

120 Pentonville Road
London N1 9JN
UK
www.kogan-page.co.uk

22883 Quicksilver Drive
Sterling VA 20166–2012
USA

© Esther Cameron and Mike Green, 2004

ISBN 0 7494 4087 2

British Library Cataloguing-in-Publication Data

A CIP record for this book is available from the British Library.

Library of Congress Cataloging-in-Publication Data

Cameron Esther,
   Making sense of change management : a complete guide to the models,
tools and techniques of organizational change / Esther Cameron and Mike Green
      p. cm.
Includes bibliographical references and index
   ISBN 0-7494-4087-2
   1. Organizational change--Management. 2. Teams in the
workplace--Management. 3. Reengineering (Management) 4. Information
technology--Management. I. Green, Mike, 1959- II. Title.
HD58.8.C317 2004
658.4'06--dc22
                              2003026220

Typeset by Saxon Graphics Ltd, Derby
Printed and bound in Great Britain by Bell & Bain, Glasgow

Contents

Acknowledgements

We want to start by acknowledging the many people in organizations with whom we have worked over the years. You are all in here in some shape or form! We have worked with many generous, courageous and inspiring managers of change who we thank for the privilege of working alongside them to make real change happen. Without these experiences the book would be a dry catalogue of theory, devoid of life and character.

Then of course there are our colleagues who challenge and support us every day as we reflect on our work, and make decisions about what to do next. Particular thanks go from Mike to Andy Holder, Mhairi Cameron, Philip Darley and Tim Hockridge, who probably do not know how much they are appreciated, and to colleagues and MBA students at Henley Management College for a never-ending supply of ideas and challenges. Esther wants to specially acknowledge Anne-Marie Saunders and Alex Clark for their wisdom, humour and friendship, and their generosity in sharing their expertise. Many of their ideas and thoughts are embedded in this book. Also, thanks go to Esther's learning set who have been a source of strength throughout the last few years, and who really boosted the leadership chapter in particular. Thanks too to Bill Critchley for his ideas on linking metaphor and change, which form the bedrock of the organizational change chapter.

Really special thanks go to Ailsa Cameron for her wonderful pictures, which soften the pages so beautifully.

We also want to thank from the bottom of our hearts the hard-working reviewers who squeezed the time out of their busy agendas to read draft versions of these chapters. Special thanks go to Louise Overy, Steve Summers, Duncan Cameron, Mervyn Smallwood, Peter Hyson and Richard Lacey for their timely and thoughtful suggestions throughout the iterative process of writing the book.

Our families have helped too by being very patient and supportive. So love and thanks to Jane, Lewin, Oliver and Brigit. Love, and thanks too to Duncan, Ailsa, Ewan and Katka.

We want to thank each other too. We have learnt a lot from this rich and sometimes rocky process of writing a book together. We do not always see things the same way, and we do not work from an identical set of assumptions about change, so the book is the culmination of much healthy airing of views. Let's hope we are still writing, talking and enjoying each other's company many years from now.

Esther Cameron
Mike Green

The Myers-Briggs Type Indicator and MBTI are registered trademarks of Consulting Psychologists Press. Anyone interested in knowing more about Myers-Briggs should contact Consulting Psychologists Press in the US (800-624-1765) and OPP in the UK (08708-728727).

Introduction

I balance on a wishing well that all men call the world.
We are so small between the stars, so large against the sky,
and lost amongst the subway crowd I try and catch your eye.

L Cohen

This book is about making sense of change management. The world we live in continues to change at an intense rate. Not a day goes by, it seems, without another important discovery or boundary-pushing invention in the scientific fields. The economics of globalization seems to dominate much of our political and corporate thinking, while the shadow side of globalization – refugees, exploitation, terrorism and the like – develops at an equally alarming pace.

The rate of change and discovery outpaces our individual ability to keep up with it. The organizations we work in or rely on to meet our needs and wants are also changing dramatically, in terms of their strategies, their structures, their systems, their boundaries and of course their expectations of their staff and their managers.

WHO THIS BOOK IS AIMED AT

Making Sense of Change Management is aimed at anyone who wants to begin to understand why change happens, how change happens and what needs to be done to make change a more welcoming concept. In particular we hope that leaders and managers in organizations might appreciate a book that does not give them the one and only panacea, but offers insights into different frameworks and ways of approaching change at an individual, team and organizational level.

We are mindful of the tremendous pressures and priorities of practising managers –in either the private or public sector – and *Making Sense of Change Management* is our attempt at making their lives that little bit easier. It is also our attempt at convincing them that addressing the issues that cause change to be so poorly managed in organizations will lead not only to more satisfying experiences for them, but to more fulfilling lives for their staff.

Students of learning – be they MBA or MSc programme members, or individuals who just want to do things better – will hopefully find some models, tools and techniques which bridge the gap between the purely academic and the more pragmatic aspects of management theory and practice. The intention is to help them to make sense of the changes that they will undergo, initiate and implement.

THE BASIC CONTENT OF THE BOOK

We focus our attention on individual, team and organizational change with good reason. Many readers will be grappling with large-scale change at some point, which might be departmental, divisional or whole organizational change. Whatever the level or degree of organizational change, the people on the receiving end are individual human beings. It is they who will ultimately cause the change to be a success or a failure. Without looking at the implications of change on individuals we can never really hope to manage large-scale change effectively.

In addition, one of the themes of organizational life over recent years has been the ascendancy of the team. Much of today's work is organized through teams and requires team collaboration and team working for it to succeed. Very little has been written about the role of teams in organizational change, and we have attempted to offer some fresh ideas mixed with some familiar ones.

A thread running through the book is the crucial role of leadership. If management is all about delivering on current needs, then leadership is all about inventing the future. There is a specific chapter on leadership, but you will find the importance of effective leadership arising throughout.

In some respects the chapters on individual, team and organizational change, together with the chapter on leadership of change are freestanding and self-contained. However we have also included application chapters where we have chosen a number of types of change, some of which, no doubt, will be familiar to you. These chapters aim to provide guidelines, case studies and learning points for those facing specific organizational challenges. Here the individual, team and organizational aspects of the changes are integrated into a coherent whole.

WHY EXPLORE DIFFERENT APPROACHES TO CHANGE

Managers in today's organizations face some bewildering challenges. Paul Evans (2000) says that 21st century leadership of change issues is not simple; he sees modern leadership as a balancing act. He draws our attention to the need for leaders to accept the challenge of navigating between opposites. Leaders have to balance a track record of success with the ability to admit mistakes and meet failure well. They also have to balance short term and long term goals, be both visionary and pragmatic, pay attention to global and local issues and encourage individual accountability at the same time as enabling team work.

It is useful to note that while some pundits encourage leaders to lead rather than manage, Paul Evans is emphasizing the need for leaders to pay attention to both management and leadership. See the box for a list of paradoxes that managers at Lego are asked to manage.

THE 11 PARADOXES OF LEADERSHIP THAT HANG ON THE WALL OF EVERY LEGO MANAGER

- To be able to build a close relationship with one's staff, and to keep a suitable distance.
- To be able to lead, and to hold oneself in the background.
- To trust one's staff, and to keep an eye on what is happening.
- To be tolerant, and to know how you want things to function.
- To keep the goals of one's department in mind, and at the same time to be loyal to the whole firm.
- To do a good job of planning your own time, and to be flexible with your schedule.
- To freely express your view, and to be diplomatic.
- To be a visionary, and to keep one's feet on the ground.
- To try to win consensus, and to be able to cut through.
- To be dynamic, and to be reflective.
- To be sure of yourself, and to be humble.

Source: Evans (2000)

We believe that anyone interested in the successful management of change needs to develop the ability to handle such paradoxes. Throughout this book we offer a range of ideas and views, some of which are contradictory. We would urge you to try to create a space within yourself for considering a variety of perspectives. Allow your own ideas and insights to emerge, rather than looking for ideas that you agree with, and discarding those you do not care for. It is highly probable that there is some merit in everything you read in this book!

With so many choices and so many dynamic tensions in leadership, how does a manager learn to navigate his or her way through the maze? We have developed a straightforward model of leadership that acts as a strong reminder to managers that they need to balance three key dimensions. See Figure 0.1.

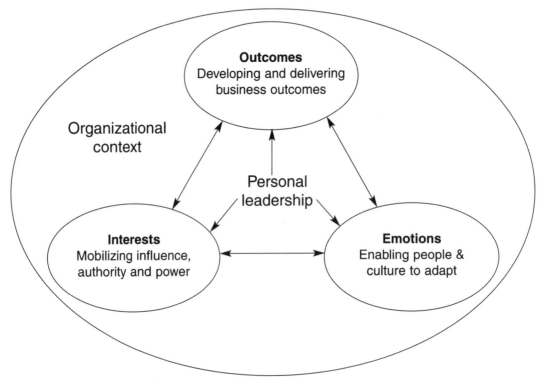

Figure 0.1 Three dimensions of leadership
Source: developed by Mike Green, Andy Holder and Mhairi Cameron

Managers usually learn to focus on outcomes and tangible results very early on in their careers. This book is a reminder that although outcomes are extremely important, the leader must also pay attention to underlying emotions, and to the world of power and influence, in order to sustain change and achieve continued success in the long term. Leaders of change need to balance their efforts across all three dimensions of an organizational change:

- outcomes: developing and delivering clear outcomes;
- interests: mobilizing influence, authority and power;
- emotions: enabling people and culture to adapt.

Leaders are at the centre of all three. They shape, direct and juggle them. One dimension may seem central at any time: for example, developing a strategy. However, leadership is about ensuring that the other dimensions are also kept in view. The three balls must always be juggled successfully.

In our experience, if you as leader or manager of change are unaware of what is happening (or not happening) in each of the three dimensions then you will have 'taken your eye off the ball'. Your chances of progressing in an effective way are diminished.

The early chapters of this book give the reader some underpinning theory and examples to illustrate how people initiate change and react to change at an individual level, when in teams, or when viewed as part of a whole organization. This theory will help managers to understand what is going on, how to deal with it and how to lead it with the help of others.

The later chapters take real change situations and give specific tips and guidelines on how to tackle these successfully from a leadership point of view.

OVERVIEW OF STRUCTURE

We have structured the book principally in two parts.

Part One, 'The underpinning theory', comprises four chapters and aims to set out a wide range of ideas and approaches to managing change. Chapter 1 draws together the key theories of how individuals go through change. Chapter 2 compares different types of team, and examines the process of team development and also the way in which different types of team contribute to the organizational change process. Chapter 3 looks at a wide range of approaches to organizational change, using organizational metaphor to show how these are interconnected and related. Chapter 4 examines leadership of change, the role of visionary leadership, the roles that leaders play in the change process and the competencies that a leader needs to become a successful leader of change.

These chapters enable the reader to develop a broader understanding of the theoretical aspects of individual, team and organizational change, and to learn more about a variety of perspectives on how best to be a leader of change. This lays firm foundations for anyone wanting to learn about new approaches to managing change with a view to becoming more skilled in this area.

Part Two, 'The applications', focuses on specific change scenarios with a view to giving guidelines, hints and tips to those involved in these different types of change process. These chapters are illustrated with case studies and make reference to the models and methods discussed in Part One. Chapter 5 looks at organizational restructuring, why it goes wrong, and how to get it right. Chapter 6 tackles mergers and acquisitions by categorizing the different types of activity and examining the learning points resulting from research into this area. Chapter 7 examines cultural change by describing some diverse case studies and extracting the learning points, and Chapter 8 attempts to shed some light on IT-based process change, why it so often goes awry and what organizations can do to improve on this.

Please do not read this book from beginning to end in one sitting. It is too much to take in. We recommend that if you prefer a purely pragmatic approach you should start by reading Part Two. You will find concrete examples and helpful guidelines. After that, you might like to go back into the theory in Part One to understand the choices available to you as a leader of change.

Likewise, if you are more interested in understanding the theoretical underpinning of change, then read Part One first. You will find a range of approaches together with their associated theories of change. After that, you might like to read Part Two to find out how the theory can be applied in real situations.

MESSAGE TO READERS

We wish you well in all your endeavours to initiate, adapt to and survive change. We hope the book provides you with some useful ideas and insights, and we look forward to hearing about your models, approaches and experiences, and to your thoughts on the glaring gaps in this book. We are sure we have left lots of important things out!

Do e-mail us at estherandmike@makingsenseofchange.com with your comments and ideas, or visit us at www.makingsenseofchange.com.

Part One

The underpinning theory

All appears to change when we change.
Henri Amiel

Individual change is at the heart of everything that is achieved in organizations. Once individuals have the motivation to do something different, the whole world can begin to change. The conspiracy laws in the UK recognize this capacity for big change to start small. In some legal cases, the merest nod or a wink between two people seems to be considered adequate evidence to indicate a conspiratorial act. In some respects this type of law indicates the incredible power that individuals have within them to challenge existing power strongholds and alter the way things are done.

However, individuals are to some extent governed by the norms of the groups they belong to, and groups are bound together in a whole system of groups of people that interconnect in various habitual ways. So the story is not always that simple. Individuals, teams and organizations all play a part in the process of change, and leaders have a particularly onerous responsibility: that is, making all this happen.

We divided this book into two parts so that readers could have the option either to start their journey through this book by first reading about the theory of change, or to begin by reading about the practical applications. We understand that people have different preferences. However, we do think that a thorough grounding in the theory is useful to help each person to untangle and articulate his or her own assumptions about how organizations work, and how change occurs. Do you for instance think that organizations can be changed by those in leadership positions to reach a predetermined end state, or do you think that people in organizations need to be collectively aware of the need for change before they can begin to adapt? Assumptions can be dangerous things when not explored, as they can restrict your thinking and narrow down your options.

Part One comprises four chapters. These have been chosen to represent four useful perspectives on change: individual change, team change, organizational change and leading change. Chapter 1 draws together the four key approaches to understanding individual change. These are the behavioural, cognitive, psychodynamic and humanistic psychology approaches. This chapter also looks at the connection between personality and change, and how to enable change in others when you are acting in a managerial role.

Chapter 2 identifies the main elements of team and group theory that we believe are useful to understand when managing change. This chapter compares different types of team, looks at the area of team effectiveness, and examines the process of team development. The composition of the team and the effect this has on team performance are also examined, as well as the way in which different types of team contribute to the organizational change process.

Chapter 3 looks at a wide range of approaches to organizational change, using organizational metaphor to show how these are interconnected and related. Familiar and unfamiliar models of the change process are described and categorized by metaphor to enable the underpinning assumptions to be examined, and we give our views on how useful these various models are to leaders of change.

Chapter 4 examines the leadership of change. We start by looking at the variety of leadership roles that arise from using different assumptions about how organizations work. The need for visionary leadership, the characteristics of successful leaders and some thoughts on the need for a different sort of leadership in the 21st century are all aired. The chapter also examines how communities of leaders can work together to make change happen, and what styles and skills are required of a leader, including the need for emotional competencies. The phases of a change process are looked at in order to illuminate the need for different leadership actions and attention during the different phases of change, and the importance of self-knowledge and self-awareness is highlighted.

Individual change

INTRODUCTION

This chapter draws together the key theories of how individuals go through change, using various models to explore this phenomenon. The aims of this chapter are to give managers and others experiencing or implementing change an understanding of the change process and how it impacts individuals, and strategies to use when helping people through change to ensure results are achieved.

This chapter covers the following topics, each of which takes a different perspective on individual change:

- Learning and the process of change – in what ways can models of learning help us understand individual change?

- The behavioural approach to change – how can we change people's behaviour?

- The cognitive approach to change – how change can be made attractive to people and how people can achieve the results that they want.

- The psychodynamic approach to change – what's actually going on for people.

- The humanistic psychology approach to change – how can people maximize the benefits of change?

- Personality and change – how do we differ in our responses to change?

- Managing change in self and others – if we can understand people's internal experience and we know what changes need to happen, what is the best way to effect change?

As the box points out, a key point for managers of change is to understand the distinction between the changes being managed in the external world and the concurrent psychological transitions that are experienced internally by people (including managers themselves).

FOOD FOR THOUGHT

It was the ancient Greek philosopher, Heraclitus, who maintained that you never step into the same river twice. Of course most people interpret that statement as indicating that the river – that is, the external world – never stays the same, is always changing: constant flux, in Heraclitus's words again. However there is another way of interpreting what he said. Perhaps the 'you' who steps into the river today is not the same 'you' who will step into the river tomorrow. This interpretation – which might open up a whole can of existential and philosophical worms – is much more to do with the inner world of experience than with the external world of facts and figures.

Immediately therefore we have two ways of looking at and responding to change: the changes that happen in the outside world and those changes that take place in the internal world. Often though, it is the internal reaction to external change that proves the most fruitful area of discovery, and it is often in this area that we find the reasons external changes succeed or fail.

In order to demonstrate this, we will draw on four approaches to change. These are the behavioural, the cognitive, the psychodynamic and the humanistic psychological approaches, as shown in Figure 1.1.

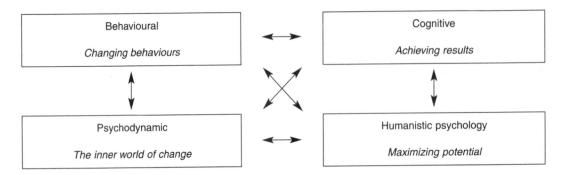

Figure 1.1 Four approaches to individual change

We will also look at Edgar Schein's analysis of the need to reduce the anxiety surrounding the change by creating psychological safety. This is further illuminated by discussion of the various psychodynamics that come into play when individuals are faced with change, loss and renewal.

Finally we will explore tools and techniques that can be used to make the transition somewhat smoother and somewhat quicker. This will include a summary of how the Myers Briggs Type Indicator, which is used to develop personal and interpersonal awareness, can illuminate the managerial challenges at each stage of the individual change process. But first we will begin our exploration though by looking at how individuals learn.

LEARNING AND THE PROCESS OF CHANGE

Buchanan and Huczynski (1985) define learning as 'the process of acquiring knowledge through experience which leads to a change in behaviour'. Learning is not just an acquisition of knowledge, but the application of it through doing something different in the world.

Many of the change scenarios that you find yourself in require you to learn something new, or to adjust to a new way of operating, or to unlearn something. Obviously this is not always the case – a company takes over your company but retains the brand name, the management team and it is 'business as usual' – but often in the smallest of changes you need to learn something new: your new boss's likes and dislikes, for example.

A useful way of beginning to understand what happens when we go through change is to take a look at what happens when we first start to learn something new. Let us take an example of driving your new car for the first time. For many people the joy of a new car is tempered by the nervousness of driving it for the first time. Getting into the driving seat of your old car is an automatic response, as is doing the normal checks, turning the key and driving off. However, with a new car all the buttons and control panels might be in different positions. One can go through the process of locating them either through trial and error, or perhaps religiously reading through the driver's manual first. But that is only the beginning, because you know that when you are actually driving any manner of things might occur that will require an instantaneous response: sounding the horn, flashing your lights, putting the hazard lights on or activating the windscreen wipers.

All these things you would have done automatically but now you need to think about them. Thinking not only requires time, it also requires a 'psychological space' which it is not easy to create when driving along at your normal speed. Added to this

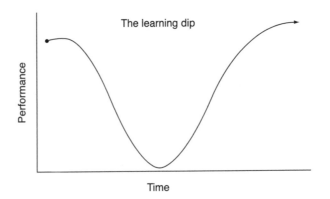

Figure 1.2   The learning dip

is the nervousness you may have about it being a brand new car and therefore needing that little bit more attention so as to avoid any scrapes to the bodywork.

As you go through this process, an external assessment of your performance would no doubt confirm a reduction in your efficiency and effectiveness for a period of time. And if one were to map your internal state your confidence levels would most likely dip as well. Obviously this anxiety falls off over time. This is based on your capacity to assimilate new information, the frequency and regularity with which you have changed cars, and how often you drive.

Conscious and unconscious competence and incompetence

Another way of looking at what happens when you learn something new is to view it from a Gestalt perspective. The Gestalt psychologists suggested that people have a worldview that entails some things being in the foreground and other things being in the background of their consciousness.

To illustrate this, the room where I am writing this looks out on to a gravel path which leads into a cottage garden sparkling with the sun shining on the frost-covered shrubs. Before I chose to look up, the garden was tucked back into the recesses of my consciousness. (I doubt whether it was even in yours.) By focusing attention on it I brought it into the foreground of my consciousness. Likewise all the colours in the garden are of equal note, until someone mentions white and I immediately start to notice the snowdrops, the white narcissi and the white pansies. They have come into my foreground.

Now in those examples it does not really matter what is fully conscious or not. However in the example of driving a new car for the first time something else is happening. Assuming that I am an experienced driver, many of the aspects of driving, for me, are unconscious. All of these aspects I hopefully carry out competently. So perhaps I can drive for many miles on a motorway, safe in the knowledge that a lot of the activities I am performing I am actually doing unconsciously. We might say I am unconsciously competent. However, as soon as I am in the new situation of an unfamiliar car I realize that many of the things I took for granted I cannot now do as well as before. I have become conscious of my incompetence. Through some trial and error and some practice and some experience I manage – quite consciously – to become competent again. But it has required focus and attention. All these tasks have been in the forefront of my world and my consciousness. It will only be after a further period of time that they recede to the background and I become unconsciously competent again(Figure 1.3).

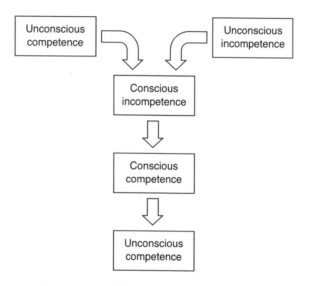

Figure 1.3   Unconscious competence

Of course there is another cycle: not the one of starting at unconscious competence, but one of starting at unconscious incompetence! This is where you do not know what you do not know, and the only way of realizing is by making a mistake (and reflecting upon it), or when someone kind enough and brave enough tells you. From self-reflection or from others' feedback your unconscious incompetence becomes conscious, and you are able to begin the cycle of learning.

Kolb's learning cycle

David Kolb (1984) developed a model of experiential learning, which unpacked how learning occurs, and what stages a typical individual goes through in order to learn. It shows that we learn through a process of doing and thinking. (See Figure 1.4.)

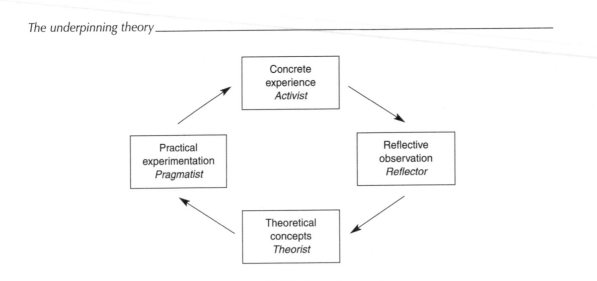

Figure 1.4   Kolb's learning cycle

Following on from the earlier definition of learning as 'the process of acquiring knowledge through experience which leads to a change in behaviour', Kolb saw this as a cycle through which the individual has a concrete experience. The individual actually does something, reflects upon his or her specific experience, makes some sense of the experience by drawing some general conclusions, and plans to do things different in the future. Kolb would argue that true learning could not take place without someone going through all stages of the cycle.

In addition, research by Kolb suggested that different individuals have different sets of preferences or styles in the way they learn. Some of us are quite activist in our 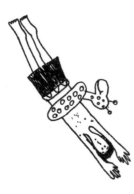 approach to learning. We want to experience what it is that we need to learn. We want to dive into the swimming pool and see what happens (immerse ourselves in the task). Some of us would like to think about it first! We like to reflect, perhaps on others' experience before we take action. The theorists might like to see how the act of swimming relates to other forms of sporting activity, or investigate how other mammals take the plunge. The pragmatists amongst us have a desire to relate what is happening to their own circumstances. They are interested in how the act of swimming will help them to achieve their goals.

Not only do we all have a learning preference but also the theory suggests that we can get stuck within our preference.

FOOD FOR THOUGHT

If you were writing a book on change and wanted to maximize the learning for all of your readers perhaps you would need to:

- encourage experimentation (activist);
- ensure there were ample ways of engendering reflection through questioning (reflector);
- ensure the various models were well researched (theorist);
- illustrate your ideas with case studies and show the relevance of what you are saying by giving useful tools, techniques and applications (pragmatist).

So activists may go from one experience to the next one, not thinking to review how the last one went or planning what they would do differently. The reflector may spend inordinate amounts of time conducting project and performance reviews, but not necessarily embedding any learning into the next project. The theorist can spend a lot of time making connections and seeing the bigger picture by putting the current situation into a wider context, but they may not actually get around to doing anything. Pragmatists may be so intent on ensuring that it is relevant to their job that they can easily dismiss something that does not at first appear that useful.

STOP AND THINK!

Q 1.1   A new piece of software arrives in the office or in your home. How do you go about learning about it?

- Do you install it and start trying it out? (Activist)
- Do you watch as others show you how to use it? (Reflector)
- Do you learn about the background to it and the similarities with other programmes? (Theorist)
- Do you not bother experimenting until you find a clear purpose for it? (Pragmatist)

THE BEHAVIOURAL APPROACH TO CHANGE

The behavioural approach to change, as the name implies, very much focuses on how one individual can change another individual's behaviour using reward and punishment, to achieve intended results. If the intended results are not being achieved then an analysis of the individual's behaviour will lead to an understanding of what is contributing to success and what is contributing to non-achievement. In order to elicit

the preferred behaviour the individual must be encouraged to behave that way, and discouraged from behaving any other way. This approach has its advantages and disadvantages.

For example, an organization is undergoing a planned programme of culture change, moving from being an inwardly focused bureaucratic organization to a flatter and more responsive customer oriented organization. Customer facing and back office staff will all need to change the way they behave towards customers and towards each other to achieve this change. A behavioural approach to change will focus on changing the behaviour of staff and managers. The objective will be behaviour change, and there will not necessarily be any attention given to improving processes, improving relationships or increasing involvement in goal setting. There will be no interest taken in how individuals specifically experience that change.

This whole field is underpinned by the work of a number of practitioners. The names of Pavlov and Skinner are perhaps the most famous. Ivan Pavlov noticed while researching the digestive system of dogs that when his dogs were connected to his experimental apparatus and offered food they began to salivate. He also observed that, over time, the dogs started to salivate when the researcher opened the door to bring in the food. The dogs had learnt that there was a link between the door opening and being fed. This is now referred to as classical conditioning.

CLASSICAL CONDITIONING

Unconditioned stimulus (food) leads to an unconditioned response (salivation).
 If neutral stimulus (door opening) and unconditioned stimulus (food) are associated, neutral stimulus (now a conditioned stimulus) leads to unconditioned response (now a conditioned response).

Pavlov (1928)

Further experimental research led others to realize that cats could learn how to escape from a box through positive effects (rewards) and negative effects (punishments). Skinner (1953) extended this research into operant conditioning, looking at the effects of behaviours, not just at the behaviours themselves. His experiments with rats led him to observe that they soon learnt that an accidental operation of a lever led to there being food provided. The reward of the food then led to the rats repeating the behaviour.

Using the notion of rewards and punishments, four possible situations arise, as demonstrated in Table 1.1.

Table 1.1   Rewards and punishments

Actions	Positive	Negative
Addition	**Positive reinforcement** Pleasurable and increases probability of repeat behaviour	**Punishment** Unpleasant (for example, an electric shock) leading to decrease in repeat behaviour
Subtraction	**Extinction** Avoidance of an unpleasant stimulus increases the likelihood of repeat behaviour	**Negative reinforcement** Removal of a pleasant stimulus decreases the likelihood of repeat behaviour

STOP AND THINK!

Q 1.2   What rewards and what punishments operate in your organization?

How effective are they in bringing about change?

So in what ways may behaviourism help us with individuals going through change? In any project of planned behaviour change a number of steps will be required:

- **Step 1:** The _identification_ of the behaviours that impact performance.

- **Step 2:** The _measurement_ of those behaviours. How much are these behaviours currently in use?

- **Step 3:** A _functional analysis_ of the behaviours – that is, the identification of the component parts that make up each behaviour.

- **Step 4:** The generation of a _strategy of intervention_ – what rewards and punishments should be linked to the behaviours that impact performance.

- **Step 5:** An _evaluation_ of the effectiveness of the intervention strategy.

Reinforcement strategies

When generating reward strategies at Step 4 above, the following possibilities should be borne in mind:

Financial reinforcement

Traditionally financial reinforcement is the most explicit of the reinforcement mechanisms used in organizations today, particularly in sales oriented cultures. The use of bonus payments, prizes and other tangible rewards is common. To be effective the financial reinforcement needs to be clearly, closely and visibly linked to the behaviours and performance that the organization requires.

A reward to an outbound call centre employee for a specific number of appointments made on behalf of the sales force would be an example of a reinforcement closely linked to a specified behaviour. A more sophisticated system might link the reward to not only the number of appointments but also the quality of the subsequent meeting and also the quality of the customer interaction.

An organization-wide performance bonus unrelated to an individual's contribution to that performance would be an example of a poorly linked reinforcement.

Non-financial reinforcement

Non-financial reinforcement tends to take the form of feedback given to an individual about performance on specific tasks. The more specific the feedback is, the more impactful the reinforcement can be. This feedback can take both positive and negative forms. This might well depend on the organizational culture and the managerial style of the boss. This feedback perhaps could take the form of a coaching conversation, where specific effective behaviours are encouraged, and specific ineffective behaviours are discouraged and alternatives generated.

Social reinforcement

Social reinforcement takes the form of interpersonal actions: that is, communications of either a positive or negative nature. Praise, compliments, general recognition, perhaps greater (or lesser) attention can all act as a positive reinforcement for particular behaviours and outcomes. Similarly social reinforcement could also take the form of 'naming and shaming' for ineffective performance.

Social reinforcement is not only useful for performance issues, but can be extremely useful when an organizational culture change is underway. Group approval or disapproval can be a determining factor in defining what behaviours are acceptable or unacceptable within the culture. New starters in an organization often spend quite some time working out which behaviours attract which reactions from bosses and colleagues.

Motivation and behaviour

The pure behaviourist view of the world, prevalent in industry up to the 1960s, led to difficulties with motivating people to exhibit the 'right' behaviours. This in turn led researchers to investigate what management styles worked and did not work.

In 1960 Douglas McGregor published his book *The Human Side of Enterprise*. In it he described his Theory X and Theory Y, which looked at underlying management assumptions about an organization's workforce, as demonstrated in Table 1.2.

Theory X was built on the assumption that workers are not inherently motivated to work, seeing it as a necessary evil and therefore needing close supervision. Theory Y stated that human beings generally have a need and a desire to work, and given the right environment are more than willing to contribute to the organization's success. McGregor's research appeared to show that those managers who exhibited Theory Y beliefs were more successful in eliciting good performance from their people.

Table 1.2   Theory X and Theory Y

Theory X assumptions	Theory Y assumptions
People dislike work	People regard work as natural and normal
They need controlling and direction	They respond to more than just control or coercion, for example recognition and encouragement
They require security	
They are motivated by threats of punishment	They commit to the organization's objectives in line with the rewards offered
They avoid taking responsibility	
They lack ambition	They seek some inner fulfilment from work
They do not use their imagination	Given the right environment people willingly accept responsibility and accountability
	People can be creative and innovative

Source: McGregor (1960)

Frederick Herzberg also investigated what motivated workers to give their best performance. He was an American clinical psychologist who suggested that workers have two sets of drives or motivators: a desire to avoid pain or deprivation (hygiene factors) and a desire to learn and develop (motivators). (See Table 1.3.) His work throughout the 1950s and 1960s suggested that many organizations provided the former but not the latter.

An important insight of his was that the hygiene factors did not motivate workers, but that their withdrawal would demotivate the workforce.

Table 1.3 Herzberg's motivating factors

Hygiene factors	Motivators
Pay	Achievement
Company policy	Recognition
Quality of supervision/management	Responsibility
Working relations	Advancement
Working conditions	Learning
Status	The type and nature of the work
Security	

Source: adapted from Herzberg (1968)

STOP AND THINK!

Q 1.3 What are the underlying assumptions built into the behaviourist philosophy, and how do they compare to McGregor's theories?

Q 1.4 In a change programme based on the behaviourist approach, what added insights would Herzberg's ideas bring?

Q 1.5 If one of your team members is not good at giving presentations, how would you address this using behaviourist ideas?

Summary of behavioural approach

If you were to approach change from a behaviourist perspective you are more likely to be acting on the assumption of McGregor's Theory X: the only way to motivate and align workers to the change effort is through a combination of rewards and punishments. You would spend time and effort ensuring that the right reward strategy and performance management system was in place and was clearly linked to an individual's behaviours. Herzberg's ideas suggest that there is something more at play than reward and punishment when it comes to motivating people. That is not to say that the provision of Herzberg's motivators cannot be used as some sort of reward for correct behaviour.

THE COGNITIVE APPROACH TO CHANGE

Cognitive psychology developed out of a frustration with the behaviourist approach. The behaviourists focused solely on observable behaviour. Cognitive psychologists were much more interested in learning about developing the capacity for language and a person's capacity for problem solving. They were interested in things that happen within a person's brain. These are the internal processes which behavioural psychology did not focus on.

Cognitive theory is founded on the premise that our emotions and our problems are a result of the way we think. Individuals react in the way that they do because of the way they appraise the situation they are in. By changing their thought processes, individuals can change the way they respond to situations.

> _People control their own destinies by believing in and acting on the values and beliefs that they hold._
>
> R Quackenbush, Central Michigan University

Much groundbreaking work has been done by Albert Ellis on rational-emotive therapy (Ellis and Grieger, 1977) and Aaron Beck on cognitive therapy (1970). Ellis emphasized:

> [T]he importance of 1) people's conditioning themselves to feel disturbed (rather than being conditioned by parental and other external sources); 2) their biological as well as cultural tendencies to think 'crookedly' and to needlessly upset themselves; 3) their uniquely human tendencies to invent and create disturbing beliefs, as well as their tendencies to upset themselves about their disturbances; 4) their unusual capacity to change their cognitive, emotive and behavioural processes so that they can: a) choose to react differently from the way they usually do; b) refuse to upset themselves about almost anything that may occur, and c) train themselves so that they can semi-automatically remain minimally disturbed for the rest of their lives. (Ellis, in Henrik, 1980)

> _If you keep doing what you're doing you'll keep getting what you get._
>
> Anon

Beck developed cognitive therapy based on 'the underlying theoretical rationale that an individual's affect (moods, emotions) and behaviour are largely determined by the way in which he construes the world; that is, how a person thinks determines how he feels and reacts' (A John Rush, in Henrik, 1980).

Belief system theory emerged principally from the work of Rokeach through the 1960s and 1970s. He suggested that an individual's self concept and set of deeply held values were both central to that person's beliefs and were his or her primary determinant. Thus individuals' values influence their beliefs, which in turn influence their attitudes. Individuals' attitudes influence their feelings and their behaviour.

Out of these approaches has grown a way of looking at change within individuals in a very purposeful way. Essentially individuals need to look at the way they limit themselves through adhering to old ways of thinking, and replace that with new ways of being.

This approach is focused on the results that you want to achieve, although crucial to their achievement is ensuring that there is alignment throughout the cause and effect chain. The cognitive approach does not refer to the external stimuli and the responses to the stimuli. It is more concerned with what individuals plan to achieve and how they go about this.

Achieving results

Key questions in achieving results in an organizational context, as shown in Figure 1.5, are:

- Self concept and values: what are my core values and how do they dovetail with those of my organization?

- Beliefs and attitudes: what are my limiting beliefs and attitudes and with what do I replace them?

- Feelings: what is my most effective state of being to accomplish my goals and how do I access it?

- Behaviour: what specifically do I need to be doing to achieve my goals and what is my first step?

- Results: what specific outcomes do I want and what might get in the way?

Self concept & values ⇨ Beliefs ⇨ Attitudes ⇨ Feelings ⇨ Behaviour ⇨ Results

Figure 1.5 Achieving results

Setting goals

The cognitive approach advocates the use of goals. The assumption is that the clearer the goal, the greater the likelihood of achievement. Consider the following case study. Graduates at Yale University in the United States were surveyed over a period of 20 years. Of those surveyed, 3 per cent were worth more than the other 97 per cent put together. There were no correlations with parental wealth, gender or ethnicity. The only difference between the 3 per cent and the 97 per cent was that the former had clearly articulated and written goals, and the latter grouping did not. (This is perhaps just an apocryphal story, as the details of this case study are much quoted on many 'positive thinking' Web sites but we have been unable to trace the research back to where it should have originated at Yale.)

However, research undertaken by one of the authors (Green, 2001) into what makes for an outstanding sales person suggests that in the two key areas of business focus and personal motivation, goals-setting looms large. The outstanding sales people had clearer and more challenging business targets that they set themselves. These were coupled with very clear personal goals as to what the sales person wanted to achieve personally with the rewards achieved by business success.

This is further backed up by research conducted by Richard Bandler and John Grinder (1979), creators of neuro-linguistic programming, who found that the more successful psychotherapists were those who were able to get their clients to define exactly what wellness looked like. This in turn led to the idea of a 'well-formed outcome' which enabled significantly better results to be achieved by those who set clear goals as opposed to those with vague goals. The goals themselves were also more ambitious.

Making sense of our results

The cognitive approach suggests we pay attention to the way in which we talk to ourselves about results. For example, after a particularly good performance one person might say things such as, 'I knew I could do it, I'll be able to do that again.' Another person might say something like, 'That was lucky, I doubt whether I'll be able to repeat that.' Likewise after a poor or ineffective performance our first person might say something like, 'I could do that a lot better next time', while the second person might say, 'I thought as much, I knew that it would turn out like this.'

Once we have identified our usual way of talking to ourselves we can look at how these internal conversations with ourselves limit us, then consider changing the script.

FOOD FOR THOUGHT

Reflect upon a time when you did not achieve one of your results.
What did you say to yourself?
What was your limiting belief?
What is the opposite belief?
What would it be like to hold the new belief?
How might your behaviour change as a result?
What results would you achieve as a consequence?

Techniques for change

The cognitive approach has generated numerous techniques for changing the beliefs of people and thereby improving their performance. These include the following.

Positive listings

Simply list all the positive qualities you have, such as good feelings, good experiences, good results, areas of skills, knowledge and expertise. By accepting that these are all part of you, the individual, you can reinforce all these positive thoughts, feelings and perceptions, which then lead to enhanced beliefs.

Affirmations

An affirmation is a positive statement describing the way that you want to be. It is important that the statement is:

- Personal: '**I** am always enthusiastic when it comes to work!' It is you who this is about, and it is as specific as you can make it.

- Present tense: '**I am always** enthusiastic when it comes to work!' It is not in the future, it is right now.

- Positive: 'I am always **enthusiastic** when it comes to work!' It describes a positive attribute, not the absence of a negative attribute.

- Potent: 'I am always **enthusiastic** when it comes to **work**!' Use words that mean something to you.

Try writing your own affirmation. Put it on a card and read it out 10 times a day. As you do so, remember to imagine what you would feel, what you would see, what you would hear if it were true.

Visualizations

Visualizations are very similar to affirmations but focus on a positive, present mental image. Effective visualizations require you to enter a relaxed state where you imagine a specific example of the way you want to be. You imagine what you and others would see, what would be heard and what would be felt. Using all your senses you imagine yourself achieving the specific goal. You need to practise this on a regular basis.

Reframing

Reframing is a technique for reducing feelings and thoughts that impact negatively on performance. You get daunted when going in to see the senior management team? Currently you see them looming large, full of colour, vitality and menacing presence? Imagine them in the boardroom, but this time see them all in grey. Maybe shrink them in size, as you would a piece of clip art in a document that you are word processing. Turn down their volume so they sound quite quiet. Run through this several times and see what effect it has on your anxiety.

Pattern breaking

Pattern breaking is a technique of physically or symbolically taking attention away from a negative state and focusing it on a positive. Take the previous example of going into the boardroom to meet the senior management team (or it could be you as the senior manager going out to meet the staff and feeling a little awkward). You find you have slipped into being a bit nervous, and catch yourself. Put your hand in the shape of a fist to your mouth and give a deep cough, or at an appropriate moment clap your hands firmly together and say, 'Right, what I was thinking was ...'. Once you've done the distraction, you can say to yourself, 'That wasn't me. This is me right now.'

Detachment

This is a similar technique with the same aim. Imagine a time when you did not like who you were. Perhaps you were in the grip of a strong negative emotion. See yourself in that state, then imagine yourself stepping outside or away from your body, leaving all that negativity behind and becoming quite calm and detached and more rational. When you next catch yourself being in one of those moods, try stepping outside of yourself.

Anchoring and resource states

These are two techniques where you use a remembered positive experience from the past which has all the components of success. For example, remember a time in the past where you gave an excellent presentation. What did you see? What did you hear? What did you feel? Really enter into that experience, then pinch yourself and repeat a word that comes to mind. Rerun the experience and pinch yourself and say the word. Now try it the other way pinch yourself and say the word – and the experience should return. Before your next presentation, as you go into the room reconnect to the positive experience by pinching yourself and saying the word. Does it work? If it does not, simply try something else.

Rational analysis

Rational analysis is a cognitive technique *par excellence*. It is based on the notion that our beliefs are not necessarily rational: 'I could never do that' or 'I'm always going to be like that'. Rational analysis suggests you write down all the reasons that is incorrect. You need to be specific and not generalize (for example, 'I'm always doing that' – *always?*). You need to set measurable criteria, objectively based, and you need to use your powers of logic. By continuously proving that this is an irrational belief you will eventually come to disbelieve it.

STOP AND THINK!

Q 1.6 What might the main benefits be of a cognitive approach?

Q 1.7 What do you see as some of the limitations of this approach?

Summary of cognitive approach

The cognitive approach builds on the behaviourist approach by putting behaviour into the context of beliefs, and focusing more firmly on outcomes. Many cognitive techniques are used in the field of management today, particularly in the coaching arena. This approach involves focusing on building a positive mental attitude and some stretching goals, backed up by a detailed look at what limiting beliefs produce behaviour that becomes self-defeating.

A drawback of the cognitive approach is the lack of recognition of the inner emotional world of the individual, and the positive and negative impact that this can have when attempting to manage change. Some obstacles to change need to be worked through, and cannot be made 'OK' by reframing or positive talk.

THE PSYCHODYNAMIC APPROACH TO CHANGE

The idea that humans go through a psychological process during change became evident due to research published by Elizabeth Kubler-Ross (1969). The word 'psychodynamic' is based on the idea that when facing change in the external world, an individual can experience a variety of internal psychological states. As with the behavioural and cognitive approaches to change, research into the  psychodynamic approach began not in the arena of organizations, but for Kubler-Ross in the area of terminally ill patients. Later research showed that individuals going through changes within organizations can have very similar experiences, though perhaps less dramatic and less traumatic.

The Kubler-Ross model

Kubler-Ross published her seminal work _On Death and Dying_ in 1969. This described her work with terminally ill patients and the different psychological stages that they went through in coming to terms with their condition. Clearly this research was considered to have major implications for people experiencing other types of profound change.

Kubler-Ross realized that patients – given the necessary conditions – would typically go through five stages as they came to terms with their prognosis. The stages were denial, anger, bargaining, depression and finally acceptance.

Denial

People faced with such potentially catastrophic change would often not be able to accept the communication. They would deny it to themselves. That is, they would not actually take it in, but would become emotionally numb and have a sense of disbelief. Some would argue that this is the body's way of allowing people to prepare themselves for what is to follow. On a more trivial scale, some of us have experienced the numbness and disbelief when our favourite sports team is defeated. There is little that we can do but in a sense 'shut down'. We do not want to accept the news and expose ourselves to the heartache that that would bring.

Anger

When people allow themselves to acknowledge what is happening they enter the second stage, typically that of anger. They begin to ask themselves questions like, 'Why me?', 'How could such a thing happen to someone like me? If only it had been someone else', 'Surely it's the doctors who are to blame – perhaps they've misdiagnosed' (back into denial). 'Why didn't they catch it in time?'

Anger and frustration can be focused externally, but for some of us it is ourselves we blame. Why did we not see it coming, give up smoking? 'It's always me who gets into trouble.'

In some ways we can see this process as a continuation of our not wanting to accept the change and of wanting to do something, anything, other than fully believe in it. Anger is yet another way of displacing our real feelings about the situation.

Bargaining

When they have exhausted themselves by attacking others (or themselves) people may still want to wrest back some control of the situation or of their fate. Kubler-Ross saw bargaining as a stage that people would enter now.

For those who themselves are dying, and also for those facing the death of a loved one, this stage can be typified by a conversation with themselves. Or if they are religious, this may be a conversation with God, which asks for an extension of time. 'If I promise to be good from now on, if I accept some remorse for any ills I have committed, if I could just be allowed to live to see my daughter's wedding, I'll take back all the nasty things I said about that person if you'll only let them live.'

Once again we can see this stage as a deflection of the true gravity of the situation. This is bargaining, perhaps verging on panic. The person is desperately looking around for something, anything, to remedy the situation. 'If only I could get it fixed or sorted everything would be all right.'

Depression

When it becomes clear that no amount of bargaining is going to provide an escape from the situation, perhaps the true momentousness of it kicks in. How might we react? Kubler-Ross saw her patients enter a depression at this stage. By depression we mean a mourning or grieving for loss, because in this situation we will be losing all that we have ever had and all those we have ever known. We shall be losing our future, we shall be losing our very selves. We are at a stage where we are ready to give up on everything. We are grieving for the loss that we are about to endure.

For some, this depression can take the form of apathy or a sense of pointlessness. For others it can take the form of sadness, and for some a mixture of intense emotions and disassociated states.

Acceptance

Kubler-Ross saw many people move out of their depression and enter a fifth stage of acceptance. Perhaps we might add the word 'quiet' to acceptance, because this is not necessarily a happy stage, but it is a stage where people can in some ways come to terms with the reality of their situation and the inevitability of what is happening to them. People have a sense of being fully in touch with their feeling about the situation, their hopes and fears, their anxieties. They are prepared.

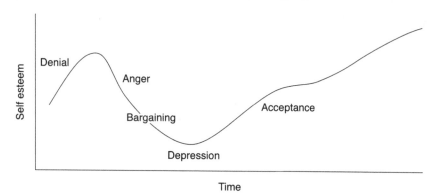

Figure 1.6   The process of change and adjustment
Source: based on Kubler-Ross (1969)

Further clinical and management researchers have added to Kubler-Ross's five stages, in particular Adams, Hayes and Hopson (1976) as follows and as illustrated in Figure 1.7:

- **Relief:** 'At least I now know what's happening now, I had my suspicions, I wasn't just being paranoid.'

- **Shock and/or surprise:** really a subset of denial but characterized by a sense of disbelief.

- **Denial:** total non-acceptance of the change and maybe 'proving' to oneself that it is not happening and hoping that it will go away.

- **Anger:** experiencing anger and frustration but really in an unaware sort of way, that is, taking no responsibility for your emotions.

- **Bargaining:** the attempt to avoid the inevitable.

- **Depression:** hitting the lows and responding (or being unresponsive) with apathy or sadness.

- **Acceptance:** the reality of the situation is accepted.

- **Experimentation:** after having been very inward looking with acceptance, the idea arrives that perhaps there are things 'out there'. 'Perhaps some of these changes might be worth at least thinking about. Perhaps I might just ask to see the job description of that new job.'

- **Discovery:** as you enter this new world that has changed there may be the discovery that things are not as bad as you imagined. Perhaps the company was telling the truth when it said there would be new opportunities and a better way of working.

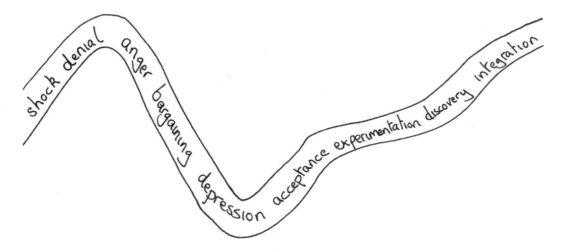

Figure 1.7 Adams, Hayes and Hopson's (1976) change curve

Virginia Satir model

Virginia Satir, a family therapist, developed her model (Satir *et al*, 1991) after observing individuals and families experience a wide range of changes. Her model not only has a number of stages but also highlights two key events that disturb or move an individual's experience along: the foreign element and the transforming idea (Figure 1.8).

She describes the initial state as one of maintaining the status quo. We have all experienced periods within our lives – at home or at work – where day to day events continue today as they have done in previous days, and no doubt will be the same tomorrow. It may be that the organization you are working in is in a mature industry with well established working practices which need little or no alteration. This is a state in which if you carry on doing what you are doing, you will continue to get what you are getting. The situation is one of relative equilibrium where all parts of the system are in relative harmony. That is not to say, of course, that there is no dissatisfaction. It is just that no one is effecting change.

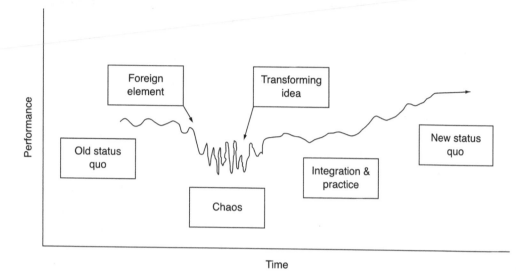

Figure 1.8   Satir's model

This changes when something new enters the system. Satir calls it a 'foreign element' in the sense that a factor previously not present is introduced. As with the examples from the two previous models it might be the onset of an illness, or in the world of work, a new chief executive with ideas about restructuring. Whatever the nature of this foreign element, it has an effect.

A period of chaos ensues. Typically this is internal chaos. The world itself may continue to function but the individual's own perceived world might be turned upside down, or inside out. He or she may be in a state of disbelief – denial or emotional numbness – at first, not knowing what to think or feel or how to act. Individuals may resist the notion that things are going to be different. Indeed they may actually try to redouble their efforts to ensure that the status quo continues as long as possible, even to the extent of sabotaging the new ideas that are forthcoming. Their support networks, which before had seemed so solid, might now not be trusted to help and support the individual. They may not know who to trust or where to go for help.

During this period of chaos, we see elements of anger and disorganization permeating the individual's world. Feelings of dread, panic and despair are followed by periods of apathy and a sense of pointlessness. At moments like this it may well seem like St John of the Cross's _Dark Night of the Soul_ (2003) when all hope has vanished.

But it is often when things have reached their very worst that from somewhere – usually from within the very depths of the person – the germ of an idea or an insight occurs. In terms of the Kubler-Ross model the individual is coming to terms with the reality of the situation and experiencing acknowledgement and acceptance. He or she has seen the light, or at least a glimmer of hope. An immense amount of work may still need to be done, but the individual has generated this transforming idea, which spreads some light on to the situation, and perhaps shows him or her a way out of the predicament.

Once this transforming idea has taken root, the individual can begin the journey of integration. Thus this period of integration requires the new world order to be assimilated into the individual's own world.

Imagine a restructuring has taken place at your place of work. You have gone through many a sleepless night worrying what job you may end up in, or whether you will have a role at the end of the change. The jobs on offer do not appeal at all to you at first ('Why didn't they ask me for my views when they formulated the new roles?' 'If they think I'm applying for that they have another think coming!'). However as the chief executive's thinking is made clearer through better communications, you grudgingly accept that perhaps he did have a point in addressing the complacency within the firm. Then perhaps one day you wake up and feel that maybe you might just have a look at that job description for the job in Operations. You have never worked in that area before and you have heard a few good things about the woman in charge.

You begin to accept the idea of a new role and 'try it on for size'. Perhaps at first you are just playing along, but soon it becomes more experimentation and more of an exploration. As time moves on the restructure is bedded into the organization, roles and responsibilities clarified, new objectives and ways of working specified and results achieved. A new status quo is born. The scars are still there perhaps but they are not hurting so much.

Gerald Weinberg (1997), in his masterly book on change, but with a title that might not appeal to everyone (*Quality Software Management, Volume 4: Anticipating Change*) draws heavily on the Satir model and maps on to it the critical points that can undermine or support the change process. (See Figure 1.9.) Weinberg shows that if the change is not planned well enough, or if the receivers of change consciously or unconsciously decide to resist, the change effort will falter.

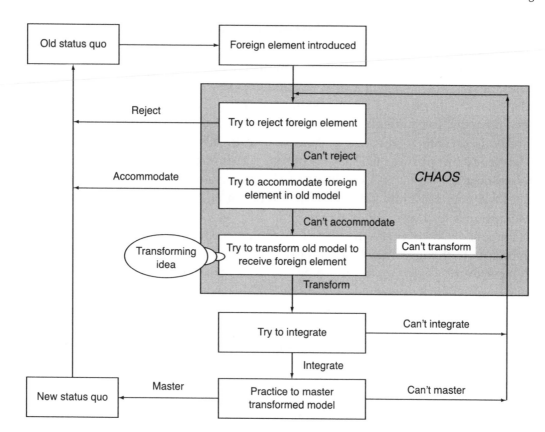

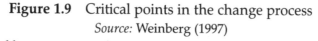

Figure 1.9   Critical points in the change process
Source: Weinberg (1997)

Summary of psychodynamic approach

The psychodynamic approach is useful for managers who want to understand the reactions of their staff during a change process and deal with them. These models allow managers to gain an understanding of why people react the way they do. It identifies what is going on in the inner world of their staff when they encounter change.

As with all models, the ones we have described simplify what can be quite a complex process. Individuals do not necessarily know that they are going through different phases. What they may experience is a range of different emotions (or lack of emotion), which may cluster together into different groupings which could be labelled one thing or another. Any observer, at the time, might see manifestations of these different emotions played out in the individual's behaviour.

Research suggests that these different phases may well overlap, with the predominant emotion of one stage gradually diminishing over time as a predominant emotion of the next stage takes hold. For example the deep sense of loss and associated despondency, while subsiding over time, might well swell up again and engulf the individual with grief, either for no apparent reason, or because of a particular anniversary, contact with a particular individual or an external event reported on the news.

Individuals will go through a process which, either in hindsight or from an observer's point of view, will have a number of different phases which themselves are delineated in time and by different characteristics. However the stages themselves will not necessarily have clear beginnings or endings, and characteristics from one stage may appear in other stages.

Satir's model incorporates the idea of a defining event – the transforming idea – that can be seen to change, or be the beginning of the change for, an individual. It may well be an insight, or waking up one morning and sensing that a cloud had been lifted. From that point on there is a qualitative difference in the person undergoing change. He or she can see the light at the end of the tunnel, or have a sense that there is a future direction.

Key learnings here are that everyone to some extent goes through the highs and lows of the transitions curve, although perhaps in different times and in different ways. It is not only perfectly natural and normal but actually an essential part of being human.

STOP AND THINK!

Q 1.8   Think of a current or recent change in your organization.

- Can you map the progress of the change on to Satir's or Weinberg's model?
- At what points did the change falter?
- At what points did it accelerate?
- What factors contributed in each case?

THE HUMANISTIC PSYCHOLOGY APPROACH TO CHANGE

The humanistic psychological approach to change combines some of the insights from the previous three approaches while at the same time developing its own. It emerged as a movement in the United States during the 1950s and 1960s. The American Association of Humanistic Psychology describes it as 'concerned with topics having little place in existing theories and systems: e.g. love, creativity, self, growth ... self-actualization, higher values, being, becoming, responsibility, meaning ... transcendental experience, peak experience, courage and related concepts'.

In this section we look at how the humanistic approach differs from the behavioural and cognitive approaches, list some of the key assumptions of this approach, and look at three important models within humanistic psychology.

Table 1.4 charts some of the similarities and differences between the psychoanalytic, behavioural, cognitive and humanistic approaches. Although taken from a book more concerned with counselling and psychotherapy, it illustrates where humanistic psychology stands in relation to the other approaches.

Table 1.4   The psychoanalytic, behaviourist, cognitive and humanistic approaches

Theme	Psychoanalytic	Behaviourism	Cognitive	Humanistic
Psychodynamic approach – looking for what is behind surface behaviour	Yes	No	Yes	Yes
Action approach – looking at actual conduct of person, trying new things	No	Yes	Yes	Yes
Acknowledgement of importance of sense-making, resistance, etc	Yes	No	No	Yes
Use of imagery, creativity	No	Yes	Yes	Yes
Use in groups as well as individual	Yes	No	No	Yes
Emphasis on whole person	No	No	No	Yes
Emphasis on gratification, joy, individuation	No	No	No	Yes
Adoption of medical model of mental illness	Yes	Yes	Yes	No
Felt experience of the practitioner important as a tool for change	Yes	No	No	Yes
Mechanistic approach to client	No	Yes	Yes	No
Open to new paradigm research methods	No	No	Yes	Yes

Source: adapted from Rowan (1983)

Humanistic psychology has a number of key areas of focus:

- The importance of subjective awareness as experienced by the individual.

- The importance of taking responsibility for one's situations – or at least the assumption that whatever the situation there will be an element of choice in how you think, how you feel and how you act.

- The significance of the person as a whole entity (a holistic approach) in the sense that as humans we are not just what we think or what we feel, we are not just our behaviours. We exist within a social and cultural context.

In juxtaposition with Freud's view of the aim of therapy as moving the individual from a state of neurotic anxiety to ordinary unhappiness, humanistic psychology has 'unlimited aims … our prime aim is to enable the person to get in touch with their real self' (Rowan, 1983).

Maslow and the hierarchy of needs

Maslow did not follow the path of earlier psychologists by looking for signs of ill health and dis-ease. He researched what makes men and women creative, compassionate, spontaneous and able to live their lives to the full. He therefore studied the lives of men and women who had exhibited these traits during their lives, and in so doing came to his theory of motivation, calling it a hierarchy of needs. (See Figure 1.10.)

Figure 1.10   Maslow's hierarchy of needs
Source: Maslow (1970)

Maslow believed that human beings have an inbuilt desire to grow and develop and move towards something he called self-actualization. However in order to develop self-actualization an individual has to overcome or satisfy a number of other needs first.

One of Maslow's insights was that until the lower level needs were met an individual would not progress or be interested in the needs higher up the pyramid. He saw the first four levels of needs as 'deficiency' needs. By that he meant that it was the absence of satisfaction that led to the individual being motivated to achieve something.

Physiological needs are requirements such as food, water, shelter and sexual release. Clearly when they are lacking the individual will experience physiological symptoms such as hunger, thirst, discomfort and frustration.

Safety needs are those that are concerned with the level of threat and desire for a sense of security. Although safety needs for some might be concerned with actual physical safety, Maslow saw that for many in the western world the need was based more around the idea of psychological safety. We might experience this level of need when faced with redundancy.

Love and belonging needs are more interpersonal. This involves the need for affection and affiliation on an emotionally intimate scale. It is important here to note that Maslow introduces a sense of reciprocity into the equation. A sense of belonging can rarely be achieved unless an individual gives as well as receives. People have to invest something of themselves in the situation or with the person or group. Even though it is higher in the hierarchy than physical or safety needs, the desire for love and belonging is similar in that it motivates people when they feel its absence.

Self-esteem needs are met in two ways. They are met through the satisfaction individuals get when they achieve competence or mastery in doing something. They are also met through receiving recognition for their achievement.

Maslow postulated one final need – the need for self-actualization. He described it as 'the desire to become more and more what one is, to become everything that one is capable of becoming'. He observed that people continued to search for something else once all their other needs were being satisfied. Individuals try to become the person they believe or feel that they are capable of becoming. It is a difficult concept to put into words. Perhaps it is a longing for something to emerge from the depths of your being.

> Before his death, Rabbi Zusya said, 'In the coming world, they will not ask me, "Why were you not Moses?" They will ask me, "Why were you not Zusya?"'
>
> Martin Buber, 1961, _Tales of the Hasidim_

Self-actualization can take many forms, depending on the individual. These variations may include the quest for knowledge, understanding, peace, self-fulfilment, meaning in life, or beauty ... but the need for beauty is neither higher nor lower than the other needs at the top of the pyramid. Self-actualization needs aren't hierarchically ordered.

(Griffin, 1991)

Rogers and the path to personal growth

Carl Rogers is one of the founders of the humanistic movement. He has written extensively on the stages through which people travel on their journey towards 'becoming a person'. Rogers' work was predominately based on his observations in the field of psychotherapy. However he was increasingly interested in how people learn, how they exercise power and how they behave within organizations.

Rogers is an important researcher and writer for consultants, as his 'client-centred approach' to growth and development provides clues and cues as to how we as change agents might bring about growth and development with individuals within organizations. Rogers (1967) highlighted three crucial conditions for this to occur:

- **Genuineness and congruence:** to be aware of your own feelings, to be real, to be authentic. Rogers' research showed that the more genuine and congruent the change agent is in the relationship, the greater the probability of change in the personality of the client.

- **Unconditional positive regard:** a genuine willingness to allow the client's process to continue, and an acceptance of whatever feelings are going on inside the client. Whatever feeling the client is experiencing, be it anger, fear, hatred, then that is all right. It is saying that underneath all this the person is all right.

- **Empathic understanding:** in Rogers' words, ' it is only as I understand the feelings and thoughts which seem so horrible to you, or so weak, or so sentimental, or so bizarre – it is only as I see them as you see them, and accept them and you, that you feel really free to explore all the hidden roots and frightening crannies of your inner and often buried experience.'

Rogers continues, 'in trying to grasp and conceptualize the process of change ... I gradually developed this concept of a process, discriminating seven stages in it'. The following are the consistently recurring qualities at each stage as described by Rogers (1967):

- One:
  - an unwillingness to communicate about self, only externals;
  - no desire for change;

- – feelings neither recognized nor owned;
- – problems neither recognized nor perceived.

- Two:
  - – expressions begin to flow;
  - – feelings may be shown but not owned;
  - – problems perceived but seen as external;
  - – no sense of personal responsibility;
  - – experience more in terms of the past not the present.

- Three:
  - – a little talk about the self, but only as an object;
  - – expression of feelings, but in the past;
  - – non-acceptance of feelings; seen as bad, shameful, abnormal;
  - – recognition of contradictions;
  - – personal choice seen as ineffective.

- Four:
  - – more intense past feelings;
  - – occasional expression of current feelings;
  - – distrust and fear of direct expression of feelings;
  - – a little acceptance of feelings;
  - – possible current experiencing;
  - – some discovery of personal constructs;
  - – some feelings of self-responsibility in problems;
  - – close relationships seen as dangerous;
  - – some small risk-taking.

- Five:
  - – feelings freely expressed in the present;
  - – surprise and fright at emerging feelings;
  - – increasing ownership of feelings;
  - – increasing self-responsibility;
  - – clear facing up to contradictions and incongruence.

- Six:
  - – previously stuck feelings experienced in the here and now;
  - – the self seen as less of an object, more of a feeling;
  - – some physiological loosening;
  - – some psychological loosening – that is, new ways of seeing the world and the self;
  - – incongruence between experience and awareness reduced.

- Seven:
    - new feelings experienced and accepted in the present;
    - basic trust in the process;
    - self becomes confidently felt in the process;
    - personal constructs reformulated but much less rigid;
    - strong feelings of choice and self-responsibility.

There are a number of key concepts that emerge from Rogers' work which are important when managing change within organizations at an individual level:

- The creation of a facilitating environment, through authenticity, positive regard and empathic understanding, enabling growth and development to occur.

- Given this facilitating environment and the correct stance of the change agent, clients will be able to surface and work through any negative feelings they may have about the change.

- Given this facilitating environment and the correct stance of the change agent, there will be a movement from rigidity to more fluidity in the client's approach to thinking and feeling. This allows more creativity and risk-taking to occur.

- Given this facilitating environment and the correct stance of the change agent, clients will move towards accepting a greater degree of self-responsibility for their situation, enabling them to have more options from which to choose.

Gestalt approach to individual and organizational change

Gestalt therapy originated with Fritz Perls, who was interested in the here and now. Perls believed that a person's difficulties today arise because of the way he or she is acting today, here and now. In Perls's words:

> [T]he goal ... must be to give him the means with which he can solve his present problems and any that may arise tomorrow or next year. The tool is self-support, and this he achieves by dealing with himself and his problems with all the means presently at his command, right now. If he can be truly aware at every instant of himself and his actions on whatever level – fantasy, verbal or physical – he can see how he is producing his difficulties, he can see what his present difficulties are, and he can help himself to solve them in the present, in the here and now.
>
> (Perls, 1976)

A consultant using a Gestalt approach has the primary aim of showing clients that they interrupt themselves in achieving what they want. Gestalt is experiential, not just based on talking, and there is an emphasis on doing, acting and feeling. Gestaltists use a cycle of experience to map how individuals and groups enact their desires, but more often than not how they block themselves from completing the cycle as shown in Figure 1.11.

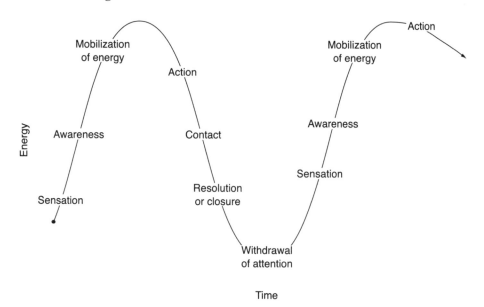

Figure 1.11   The Gestalt cycle

A favourite saying of Fritz Perls was to 'get out of your mind and come to your senses'. Gestalt always begins with what one is experiencing in the here and now. Experiencing has as its basis what one is sensing. 'Sensing determines the nature of awareness' (Perls, Hefferline and Goodman, 1951).

What we sense outside of ourselves or within leads to awareness. Awareness comes when we alight or focus upon what we are experiencing. Nevis (1998) describes it as 'the spontaneous sensing of what arises or becomes figural, and it involves direct, immediate experience'. He gives a comprehensive list of the many things that we can be aware of at any one moment, including the following:

- **What we sense:** sights, sounds, textures, tastes, smells, kinaesthetic stimulations and so on.

- **What we verbalize and visualize:** thinking, planning, remembering, imagining and so on.

- **What we feel:** happiness, sadness, fearfulness, wonder, anger, pride, empathy, indifference, compassion, anxiety and so on.

- **What we value:** inclinations, judgements, conclusions, prejudices and so on.

- **How we interact:** participation patterns, communication styles, energy levels, norms and so on.

Although your awareness can only ever be in the present, this awareness can include memory of the past, anticipation of the future, inner experience and awareness of others and the environment.

Mobilization of energy occurs as awareness is focused on a specific facet. Imagine you have to give a piece of negative feedback to a colleague. As you focus on this challenge by bringing it into the foreground, you might start to feel butterflies in your stomach, or sweaty palms. This is like using a searchlight to illuminate a specific thing and bring it into full awareness. In Nevis's terminology this brings about an 'energized concern'.

This energy then needs to be released typically by doing something, by taking action, by making contact in and with the outside world. You give the feedback.

Closure might come when the colleague thanks you for the feedback and compliments you on the clarity and level of insight. Or perhaps you have an argument and agree to disagree. You will then experience a reduction in your energy, and will complete the cycle by having come to a resolution, with the object of attention fading into the background once more. The issue of the colleague's performance becomes less important.

For real change to have occurred (either internally or out in the world) the full Gestalt cycle will need to have been experienced.

Nevis shows how the Gestalt cycle maps on to stages in managerial decision making:

Awareness
Data generation, Seeking information, Sharing information, Reviewing past performance, Environmental scanning

Energy/action
Attempts to mobilize energy and interest in ideas or proposals, Supporting ideas presented by others, Identifying and experiencing differences and conflicts of competing interests or views, Supporting own position, Seeking maximum participation

Contact
Joining in a common objective, Common recognition of problem definition, Indications of understanding, not necessarily agreement, Choosing a course of possible future action

Resolution/closure
Testing, checking for common understanding, Reviewing what's occurred, Acknowledgement of what's been accomplished and what remains to be done, Identifying the

meaning of the discussion, Generalizing from what's been learned, Beginning to develop implementation and action plans

Withdrawal
Pausing to let things 'sink in'
Reducing energy and interest in the issue
Turning to other tasks or problems
Ending the meeting.

STOP AND THINK!

Q 1.9 Use the Gestalt curve to describe how a manager moves from a concern about the team's performance to launching and executing a change initiative.

Summary of humanistic psychology approach

For the manager, the world of humanistic psychology opens up some interesting possibilities and challenges. For years we have been told that the world of organizations is one that is ruled by the rational mind. Recent studies such as Daniel Goleman's (1998) on emotional intelligence and management competence (see Chapter 4) suggest that what makes for more effective managers is their degree of emotional self-awareness and ability to engage with others on an emotional level. Humanistic psychology would not only agree, but would go one step further in stating that without being fully present emotionally in the situation you cannot be fully effective, and you will not be able to maximize your learning, or anyone else's learning.

PERSONALITY AND CHANGE

We have looked at different approaches to change, and suggested that individuals do not always experience these changes in a consistent or uniform way. However we have not asked whether people are different, and if so, whether their difference affects the way they experience change.

We have found in working with individuals and teams through change that it is useful to identify and openly discuss people's personality types. This information helps people to understand their responses to change. It also helps people to see why other people are different from them, and to be aware of how that may lead to either harmony or conflict.

The most effective tool for identifying personality type is the Myers Briggs Type Indicator (MBTI). This is a personality inventory developed by Katherine Briggs and her daughter Isabel Myers. The MBTI is based on the work of the Swiss analytical psychologist Carl Jung. The MBTI identifies eight different personality 'preferences' that we all use at different times – but each individual will have a preference for one particular combination over the others.

These eight preferences can be paired as set out below.

Where individuals draw their energy

Extraversion is a preference for drawing energy from the external world, tasks and things, whereas **Introversion** is a preference for drawing energy from the internal world of one's thoughts and feelings.

What individuals pay attention to and how they receive data and information

Sensing is concerned with the five senses and what is and has been whereas **Intuition** is concerned with possibilities and patterns and what might be.

How an individual makes decisions

Thinking is about making decisions in an objective, logical way based on concepts of right and wrong whereas **Feeling** is about making decisions in a more personal values-driven and empathic way.

What sort of lifestyle an individual enjoys

Judging is a preference for living in a more structured and organized world which is more orderly and predictable, whereas **Perceiving** is a preference for living in a more flexible or spontaneous world where options are kept open and decisions not made until absolutely necessary.

So for example, a person who has a preference for Introversion, Intuition, Thinking and Judging (an INTJ, in the jargon) will have certain characteristics. Likewise an individual with a preference for Extroversion, Sensing, Feeling and Perceiving (ESFP) will have quite different characteristics.

The MBTI has been researched and validated for over 50 years now, and people rarely move permanently from their preferred 'home' type. That is not to say that Extroverts cannot spend time reflecting and being on their own, nor Introverts spend time in large groups discussing a broad range of issues. What it means is that if you are a particular type you have particular preferences and are different from other people of different types. This means that when it comes to change, people with different preferences react differently to change, both when they initiate it and when they are on the receiving end of it.

We can group the MBTI types into four categories for ease of analysis. One group of people will be cautious and careful about change – the Thoughtful Realists (those who are introverted sensing types). A second group will generate concepts that represent how things should be – the Thoughtful Innovators (introverted intuitives). A third group will have the energy and enthusiasm to get things done – the Action Oriented Realists (extraverted sensing). Meanwhile the fourth group – the Action Oriented Innovators (extraverted intuitives) – will be wanting to move into new areas and soon! (See Table 1.5.)

Table 1.5 Myers Briggs Type Indicator types

MBTI type by Quadrant	IS Thoughtful Realist	IN Thoughtful Innovator
What they are most concerned with	Practicalities	Thoughts, ideas, concepts
How they learn	Pragmatically and by reading and observing	Conceptually by reading, listening and making connections
Where they focus their change efforts	Deciding what should be kept and what needs changing	Generating new ideas and theories
Motto	"If it isn't broke don't fix it"	"Let's think ahead"
MBTI type by Quadrant	**ES Action Oriented Realist**	**EN Action Oriented Innovator**
What they are most concerned with	Actions	New ways of doing things
How they learn	Actively and by experimentation	Creatively and with others
Where they focus their change efforts	Making things better	Putting new ideas into practice
Motto	"Let's just do it"	"Let's change it"

MANAGING CHANGE IN SELF AND OTHERS

We now look at some of the factors that arise when you as a manager are required to manage change within your organization. We will:

- Discuss individual and group propensity for change.

- Introduce the work of Edgar Schein and his suggestions for managing change.

- Describe some of the ways that change can be thwarted.

- Identify how managers or change agents can help others to change.

RESPONSES TO CHANGE

Those who let it happen.
Those who make it happen.
Those who wonder what happened.

Anon

Propensity for change

We have isolated five factors, as shown in Figure 1.12, that have an influence on an individual's response to change. As a manager of change you will need to pay attention to these five areas if you wish to achieve positive responses to change.

- The nature of the change varies. Changes can be externally imposed or internally generated. They can be evolutionary or revolutionary in nature. They can be routine or one-off. They can be mundane or transformative. They can be about expansion or contraction. Different types of change can provoke different attitudes and different behaviours.

- The consequences of the change are significant. For whose benefit are the changes seen to be (employees, customers, the community, the shareholders, the board)? Who will be the winners and who will be the losers?

- The organizational history matters too. This means the track record of how the organization has handled change in the past (or how the acquiring organization is perceived), what the prevailing culture is, what the capacity of the organization is in terms of management expertise and resources to manage change effectively, and what the future, beyond the change, is seen to hold.

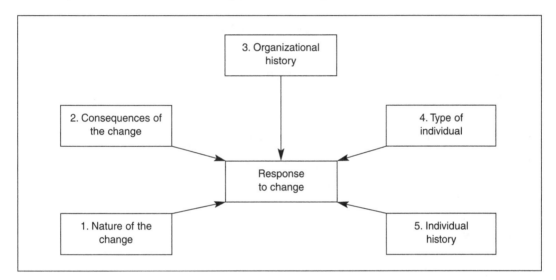

Figure 1.12   Five factors in responding to change

- The personality type of the individual is a major determining factor in how she or he responds to change. The Myers Briggs type of the individual (reviewed earlier) can give us an indication of how an individual will respond to change. People's motivating forces are also important – for example, are they motivated by power, status, money or affiliation and inclusion?

- The history of an individual can also give us clues as to how he or she might respond. By history we mean previous exposure and responses to change, levels of knowledge, skills and experience the individual has, areas of stability in his or her life and stage in his or her career. For example an individual who has previously experienced redundancy might re-experience the original trauma and upheaval regardless of how well the current one is handled. Or he or she may have acquired sufficient resilience and determination from the previous experience to be able to take this one in his or her stride.

Schein's model of transformative change

Edgar Schein has been a leading researcher and practitioner in the fields of individual, organizational and cultural change over the last 20 years. His seminal works have included *Process Consultation* and *Organizational Culture and Leadership*.

SCHEIN'S MODEL

Stage One
Unfreezing: Creating the motivation to change:
- Disconfirmation.
- Creation of survival anxiety or guilt.
- Creation of psychological safety to overcome learning anxiety.

Stage Two
Learning new concepts and new meanings for old concepts:
- Imitation of and identification with role models.
- Scanning for solutions and trial-and-error learning.

Stage Three
Refreezing: Internalizing new concepts and meanings:
- Incorporation into self-concept and identity.
- Incorporation into ongoing relationships.

Schein sees change as occurring in three stages:

- Unfreezing: creating the motivation to change.

- Learning new concepts and new meanings from old concepts.

- Internalizing new concepts and meanings.

During the initial unfreezing stage people need to unlearn certain things before they can focus fully on new learning.

Schein says that there are two forces at play within every individual undergoing change. The first force is learning anxiety. This is the anxiety associated with learning something new. Will I fail? Will I be exposed? The second, competing force is survival anxiety. This concerns the pressure to change. What if I don't change? Will I get left behind? These anxieties can take many forms. Schein lists four of the associated fears:

- Fear of temporary incompetence: the conscious appreciation of one's lack of competence to deal with the new situation.

- Fear of punishment for incompetence: the apprehension that you will somehow lose out or be punished when this incompetence is discovered or assessed.

- Fear of loss of personal identity: the inner turmoil when your habitual ways of thinking and feeling are no longer required, or when your sense of self is defined by a role or position that is no longer recognized by the organization.

- Fear of loss of group membership: in the same way that your identity can be defined by your role, for some it can be profoundly affected by the network of affiliations you have in the workplace. In the same way that the stable equilibrium of a team or group membership can foster states of health, instability caused by shifting team roles or the disintegration of a particular group can have an extremely disturbing effect.

What gets in the way of change: resistance to change

Leaders and managers of change sometimes cannot understand why individuals and groups of individuals do not wholeheartedly embrace changes that are being introduced. They often label this 'resistance to change'.

Schein suggests that there are two principles for transformative change to work: first, survival anxiety must be greater than learning anxiety, and second, learning anxiety must be reduced rather than increasing survival anxiety. Used in connection with Lewin's force field (see Chapter 3), we see that survival anxiety is a driving force and learning anxiety is a restraining force. Rather than attempting to increase the individual or group's sense of survival anxiety, Schein suggests reducing the individual's learning anxiety. Remember also that the restraining forces may well have some validity.

How do you reduce learning anxiety? You do it by increasing the learner's sense of psychological safety through a number of interventions. Schein lists a few:

- a compelling vision of the future;

- formal training;

- involvement of the learner;

- informal training of relevant family groups/teams;

- practice fields, coaches, feedback;

- positive role models;

- support groups;

- consistent systems and structures;

- imitation and identification versus scanning and trial and error.

STOP AND THINK!

Q 1.11 Think of a recent skill that you had to learn in order to keep up with external changes. This could be installing a new piece of software, or learning about how a new organization works.

- What were your survival anxieties?

- What were your learning anxieties?

- What helped you to change?

How managers and change agents help others to change

We have listed in Table 1.6 some of the interventions that an organization and its management could carry out to facilitate the change process. We have categorized them into the four approaches described earlier in this chapter.

From the behavioural perspective a manager must ensure that reward policies and performance management is aligned with the changes taking place. For example if the change is intended to improve the quality of output, then the company should not reward quantity of output. Kerr (1995) lists several traps that organizations fall into:

We hope for:
Teamwork and collaboration
Innovative thinking and risk-taking
Development of people skills
Employee involvement and empowerment
High achievement

But reward:
The best team members
Proven methods and no mistakes
Technical achievements
Tight control over operations
Another year's effort

Table 1.6   Interventions to facilitate the change process

Behavioural	Cognitive
Performance management	Management by objectives
Reward policies	Business planning and performance frameworks
Values translated into behaviours	Results based coaching
Management competencies	Beliefs, attitudes and cultural interventions
Skills training	Visioning
Management style	
Performance coaching	
360 degree feedback	
Understanding change dynamics	Living the values
Counselling people through change	Developing the learning organization
Surfacing hidden issues	Addressing the hierarchy of needs
Addressing emotions	Addressing emotions
Treating employees and managers as adults	Fostering communication and consultation
Psychodynamic	**Humanistic**

Managers and staff need to know in detail what they are expected to do and how they are expected to perform. Behaviour needs to be defined, especially when many organizations today are promoting 'the company way'.

From the cognitive perspective a manager needs to employ strategies that link organizational goals, individual goals and motivation. This will create both alignment and motivation. An additional strategy is to provide ongoing coaching through the change process to reframe obstacles and resistances.

The psychodynamic perspective suggests adapting one's managerial approach and style to the emotional state of the change implementers. This is about treating people as adults and having mature conversations with them. The psychodynamic approach enables managers to see the benefits of looking beneath the surface of what is going on, and uncovering thoughts that are not being articulated and feelings that are not being expressed. Working through these feelings can release energy for the change effort rather than manifesting as resistance to change.

Drawing on the transitions curve we can plot suitable interventions throughout the process. (See Figure 1.13.)

The humanistic psychology perspective builds on the psychodynamic ethos by believing that people are inherently capable of responding to change, but require enabling structures and strategies so to do. Healthy levels of open communication, and a positive regard for individuals and their potential contribution to the organization's goals, contribute to creating an environment where individuals can grow and develop.

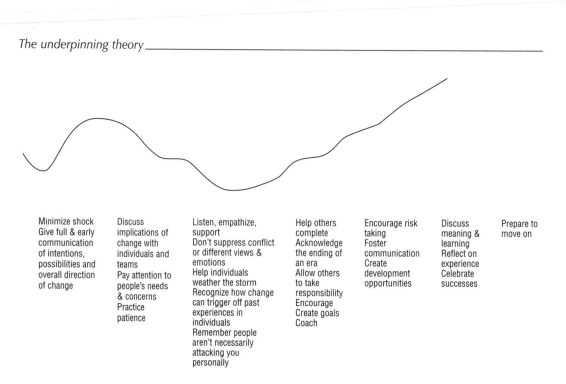

Figure 1.13 Management interventions through the change process

SUMMARY AND CONCLUSIONS

- Learning to do something new usually involves a temporary dip in performance.

- When learning something new, we focus on it and become very conscious of our performance. Once we have learnt something we become far less conscious of our performance. We are then unconsciously competent. This continues until something goes wrong, or there is a new challenge.

- There are four key schools of thought when considering individual change:
    - The behaviourist approach is about changing the behaviours of others through reward and punishment. This leads to behavioural analysis and use of reward strategies.
    - The cognitive approach is about achieving results through positive reframing. Associated techniques are goal setting and coaching to achieve results.
    - The psychodynamic approach is about understanding and relating to the inner world of change. This is especially significant when people are going through highly affecting change.
    - The humanistic psychology approach is about believing in development and growth, and maximizing potential. The emphasis is on healthy development, healthy authentic relationships and healthy organizations.

- Personality type has a significant effect on an individual's ability to initiate or adapt to change.

- The individual's history, the organization's history, the type of change and the consequence of the change are also key factors in an individual's response to change.

- Schein identified two competing anxieties in individual change: survival anxiety versus learning anxiety. Survival anxiety has to be greater than learning anxiety if a change is to happen. He advocated the need for managers to reduce people's learning anxiety rather than increase their survival anxiety.

- Each of the four approaches above leads to a set of guidelines for managers:
  - Behavioural: get your reward strategies right.
  - Cognitive: link goals to motivation.
  - Psychodynamic: treat people as individuals and understand their emotional states as well as your own!
  - Humanistic: be authentic and believe that people want to grow and develop.

2

Team change

INTRODUCTION

This chapter will look at teams, team development and change from a number of perspectives and will be asking a number of pertinent questions:

- What is a group and when is it a team?

- Why do you need teams?

- What types of organizational teams are there?

- How do you improve team effectiveness?

- What does team change look like?

- What are the leadership issues in team change?

- How do individuals affect team dynamics?

- How well do teams initiate and adapt to organizational change?

The chapter aims to enhance understanding of the nature of teams and how they develop, identify how teams perform in change situations, and develop strategies for managing teams through change and change through teams.

We open with a discussion around what constitutes a group and what constitutes a team. We will also look at the phenomena of different types of teams: for example, virtual teams, self-organizing teams and project teams.

Models of team functioning, change and development will be explored. We look at the various components of team working, and at how teams develop and how different types of people combine to make a really effective (or not) team.

We take as our basic model Tuckman's model of team development to illustrate how teams change over time. This is the forming, storming, norming and performing model. But we will add to it by differentiating between the task aspects of team development and the people aspects of team development.

Finally we look at the way in which teams can impact or react to organizational change.

WHAT IS A GROUP AND WHEN IS IT A TEAM?

There has been much academic discussion as to what constitutes a team and what constitutes a group. In much of the literature the two terms are used indistinguishably. Yet there are crucial differences, and anyone working in an organization instinctively knows when he or she is in a team and when he or she is in a group. We will attempt to clarify the essential similarities and differences. This is important when looking at change because teams and groups experience change in different ways.

Schein and Bennis (1965) suggest that a group is 'any number of people who interact with each other, are psychologically aware of each other, and who perceive themselves to be a group'. Morgan _et al_ (1986) suggest that 'a team is a distinguishable set of two or more individuals who interact interdependently and adaptively to achieve specified, shared, and valued objectives'. Sundstrom, de Meuse and Futrell (1990) define the work team as 'A small group of individuals who share responsibility for outcomes for their organizations'.

Cohen and Bailey (1997) define a team as 'a collection of individuals who are interdependent in their tasks, who share responsibility for outcomes, who see themselves and who are seen by others as an intact social entity embedded in one or more larger social systems (for example, business unit or the corporation), and who manage their relationships across organizational boundaries'.

Our own list of differentiators appears in Table 2.1.

A group is a collection of individuals who draw a boundary around themselves. Or perhaps we from the outside might draw a boundary around them and thus define them as a group. A team on the other hand, with its common purpose, is generally tighter and clearer about what it is and what its _raison d'être_ is. Its members know

Table 2.1 Differences between groups and teams

Group	Team or work group
Indeterminate size	Restricted in size
Common interests	Common overarching objectives
Sense of being part of something or seen as being part of something	Interaction between members to accomplish individual and group goals
Interdependent as much as individuals might wish to be	Interdependency between members to accomplish individual and group goals
May have no responsibilities other than a sense of belonging to the group	Shared responsibilities
May have no accountabilities other than 'contractual' ones	Individual accountabilities
A group does not necessarily have any work to do or goals to accomplish	The team works together, physically or virtually

exactly who is involved and what their goal is. Of course it turns out that we are speaking hypothetically here, as any one of us has seen teams within organizations that appear to have no sense at all of what they are really about!

Let us illustrate the difference between a team and a group by using an example. We might look into an organization and see the Finance Department. The Finance Controller heads up a Finance Management Team that leads, manages and coordinates the activities within this area. The team members work together on common goals, meet regularly and have clearly defined roles and responsibilities (usually).

Perhaps the senior management team has decreed that all the high potential managers in the organization shall be members of the Strategic Management Group. So the Finance Controller, who is on the high potential list, gets together with others at his or her level to form a collection of individuals who contribute to the overall strategic direction of the organization. Apart from gatherings every six months, this group rarely meets or communicates. It is a grouping, which might be bounded but does not have any ongoing goals or objectives that require members to work together.

STOP AND THINK!

Q 2.1 Within your working life, what teams are you a member of and to which groups do you belong?

Q 2.2 Within your personal life, what teams are you a member of and to which groups do you belong?

Q 2.3 In what ways was it easier to answer in your personal life, and in what ways more difficult?

WHY WE NEED TEAMS

Why do we need teams and team working? Casey (1993) from Ashridge Management College researched this question by asking a simple question of each team he worked with: 'Why should you work together as a team?' The simplest answer  is, 'Because of the work we need to accomplish.' Team work may be needed because there is a high volume of interconnected pieces of work, or because the work is too complex to be understood and worked on by one person.

What about managers? Do they need to operate as teams, or can they operate effectively as groups? The Ashridge-based writers say that a management team does not necessarily have to be fully integrated as a team all of the time. Nor should it be reduced to a mere collection of individuals going about their own individual functional tasks.

Casey believes that there is a clear link between the level of uncertainty of the task being handled and the level of team work needed. The greater the uncertainty is, the greater the need for team work. The majority of management teams deal with both uncertain and certain tasks, so need to be flexible about the levels of team working required. Decisions about health and safety, HR policy, reporting processes and recruitment are relatively certain, so can be handled fairly quickly without a need for much sharing of points of view. There is usually a right answer to these issues, whereas decisions about strategy, structure and culture are less certain. There is no right answer, and each course of action involves taking a risk. This means more team working, more sharing of points of view, and a real understanding of what is being agreed and what the implications are for the team.

THE TYPES OF ORGANIZATIONAL TEAMS

Robert Keidal identified a parallel between sports teams and organizational teams. He uses baseball, American football and basketball teams to show the differences.

A baseball team is like a sales organization. Team members are relatively independent of one another, and while all members are required to be on the field together, they virtually never interact together all at the same time.

Football is quite different. There are really three subteams within the total team: offense, defense, and the special team. When the subteam is on the field, every player is involved in every play, which is not the case in baseball. But the team work is centred in the subteam, not the total team.

Basketball is a different breed. Here the team is small, with all players in only one team. Every player is involved in all aspects of the game, offense and defense, and all must pass, run, shoot. When a substitute comes in, all must play with the new person.

Source: Adapted from Keidal (1984)

Many different types of team exist within organizations. Let us look at a range of

Table 2.2 Types of team

Team	Group	Work	Parallel	Project
Continuity	Variable	Stable	Stable or one-off project	Focused on project achievement
Lifespan	Variable	Unlimited	Variable	Time limited
Organizational links	Can be part of the formal and/ or informal organization	Part of management structure	Outside of normal management structure	Separate management structure
Led by	Dependent on nature and purpose of group	One manager or supervisor	Normally coordinated or facilitated	Project manager
Location	Variable	Colocated	Converge for meetings	Colocated, dispersed, virtual
Purpose	Variable	Business as usual	Maintenance function or part of change infra-structure	Change or development
Authority	Dependent on nature and purpose of group	Through the line	Depends	Via project manager and project sponsor
Focus	Communication	Task	Communication	Task

Table 2.2 _continued_

Team	Matrix	Virtual	Network	Management	Change
Continuity	Stable as a structure but fluid by project	Potential fluid	Potential fluid	Stable	Fluid
Lifespan	Unlimited	Variable	Variable	Unlimited	Variable
Organizational links	Part of management structure Dual accountability	Can be part of the management structure	More distributed across the organization	Part of management structure	Variable
Led by	Project manager and functional head	One manager or supervisor	Potentially distributed leadership or coordination	One manager	Sponsor or change manager
Location	Colocated, dispersed, virtual	Dispersed	Dispersed	Often colocated	Colocated, dispersed, virtual
Purpose	Project achievement	BAU or Project	Change or development	Business as usual Change and development	Change and development
Authority	Dual accountability	Through the line or project manager	Depends	Through the line	Via project manager and project sponsor
Focus	Task	Task	Communication	Task and communication	Task and communication

types of team found in today's organizations (see Table 2.2).

Work team

Work teams or work groups are typically the type of team that most people within organizations will think of when we talk about teams. They are usually part of the normal hierarchical structure of an organization. This means that one person manages a group of individuals. That person is responsible for delivering a particular product or service either to the customer or to another part of the organization.

These teams tend to be relatively stable in terms of team objectives, processes and personnel. Their agenda is normally focused on maintenance and management of what is. This is a combination of existing processes and operational strategy. Any change agenda that they have is usually on top of their existing agenda of meeting the current operating plan.

Self-managed team

A sub-set of the work team is the self-managed team. The self-managed team has the attributes of the work team but without a direct manager or supervisor. This affects the way decisions are made and the way in which individual and team performance is managed. Generally this is through collective or distributed leadership.

Self-managed work teams are more prevalent in manufacturing industries rather than the service arena. Once again there is an emphasis on delivery of service or product rather than delivering change.

Parallel team

Parallel teams are different from work teams because they are not part of the traditional management hierarchy. They are run in tandem or parallel to this structure. Examples of parallel teams are:

- teams brought together to deliver quality improvement (for example, quality circles, continuous improvement groups);

- teams that have some problem-solving or decision-making input, other than the normal line management processes (for example, creativity and innovation groups);

- teams formed to involve and engage employees (for example, staff councils, diagonal slice groups);

- teams set up for a specific purpose such as a task force looking at an office move.

These teams have variable longevity, and are used for purposes that tend to be other than the normal 'business as usual' management. They are often of a consultative nature, carrying limited authority. Although not necessarily responsible or accountable for delivering changes, they often feed into a change management process.

Project team

Project teams are teams that are formed for the specific purpose of completing a project. They therefore are time limited, and we would expect to find clarity of objectives. The project might be focused on an external client or it might be an internal one-off, or cross-cutting project with an internal client group.

Depending on the scale of the project the team might comprise individuals on a full or part-time basis. Typically there is a project manager, selected for his or her specialist or managerial skills, and a project sponsor. Individuals report to the project manager for the duration of the project (although if they work part-time on the project they might also be reporting to a line manager). The project manager reports to the project sponsor, who typically is a senior manager.

We know the project team has been successful when it delivers the specific project on time, to quality and within budget. Brown and Eisenhardt (1995) noted that cross-functional teams, which are teams comprised of individuals from a range of organizational functions, were found to enhance project success.

Project teams are very much associated with implementing change. However, although change may be their very _raison d'être_ it does not necessarily mean that their members' ability to handle change is any different from the rest of us. Indeed built into their structure are potential dysfunctionalities:

- The importance of task achievement often reigns supreme, at the expense of investing time in meeting individual and team maintenance needs.

- The fact that individuals have increased uncertainty concerning their future can impact on motivation and performance.

- The dynamic at play between the project team and the organizational area into which the change will take place can be problematic.

Matrix team

Matrix teams generally occur in organizations that are run along project lines. The organization typically has to deliver a number of projects to achieve its objectives. Each project has a project manager, but the project team members are drawn from functional areas of the organization. Often projects are clustered together to form programmes, or indeed whole divisions or business units (for example, aerospace, defence or oil industry projects). Thus the team members have accountability both to the project manager and to their functional head. The balance of power between the projects and the functions varies from organization to organization, and the success of such structures often depends on the degree to which the project teams are enabled by the structure and the degree to which they are disabled.

Virtual team

Increasing globalization and developments in the use of new technologies mean that teams are not necessarily colocated any more. This has been true for many years for sales teams. Virtual teams either never meet or they meet only rarely. Townsend, DeMarie and Hendrickson (1998) defined virtual teams as 'groups of geographically and/or organizationally dispersed coworkers that are assembled using a combination of telecommunications and information technologies to accomplish an organizational task'. An advantage of virtual teams is that an organization can use the most appropriately skilled people for the task, wherever they are located. In larger companies the probability that the necessary and desired expertise for any sophisticated or complex task is in the same place geographically is low.

Disadvantages spring from the distance between team members. Virtual teams cross time zones, countries, continents and cultures. All these things create their own set of challenges. Current research suggests that synchronous working (being face to face or remote) is more effective in meeting more complex challenges. Team leadership for virtual teams also creates its own issues, with both day-to-day management tasks and developmental interventions being somewhat harder from a distance.

When it comes to change, virtual teams are somewhat paradoxical. Team members can perhaps be more responsive, balancing autonomy and interdependence, and more focused on their part of the team objective. However change creates an increased need for communication, clear goals, defined roles and responsibilities, and support and recognition processes. These things are more difficult to manage in the virtual world.

Networked team

National, international and global organizations can use networked teams in an attempt to add a greater cohesion to their organization, which would not otherwise be there. Additionally they may wish to capture learning in one part of the organization and spread it across the whole organization.

We might have grouped virtual and networked teams under the same category. However we could think of the networked team as being similar to a parallel team, in the sense that its primary purpose is not business as usual, but part of an attempt by the organization to increase sustainability and build capacity through increasing the reservoir of knowledge across the whole organization.

Networked teams are an important anchor for organizations in times of change. They can be seen as part of the glue that gives a sense of cohesion to people within the organization.

Management team

Management teams coordinate and provide direction to the sub-units under their jurisdiction, laterally integrating interdependent sub-units across key business processes.

(Mohrman, Cohen and Mohrman, 1995)

The management team is ultimately responsible for the overall performance of the business unit. In itself it may not deliver any product, service or project, but clearly its function is to enable that delivery. Management teams are pivotal in translating the organization's overarching goals into specific objectives for the various sub-units to do their share of the organization task.

Management teams are similar to work teams in terms of delivery of current operational plan, but are much more likely to be in a position of designing and delivering change as well. We expect a more senior management team to spend less time on business-as-usual matters and more time on the change agenda.

The senior management team in any organization is the team most likely to be held responsible for the organization's ultimate success or failure. It is in a pivotal position within the organization. On the one hand it is at the top of the organization, and therefore team members have a collective leadership responsibility. On the other hand it is accountable to the non-executive board and shareholders in limited companies, or to politicians in local and central government, or to trustees in not-for-profit organizations. Along with the change team (see below) the management team has a particular role to play within most change scenarios, for it is its members who initiate and manage the implementation of change.

Change team

Change teams are often formed within organizations when a planned or unplanned change of significant proportions is necessary. We have separated out this type of team because of its special significance. Sometimes the senior management team is called the change team, responsible for directing and sponsoring the changes. Sometimes the change team is a special project team set up to implement change. At other times the change team is a parallel team, set up to tap into the organization and be a conduit for feedback as to how the changes are being received.

Obviously different organizations have different terminologies, so what in one organization is called a project team delivering a change will be a change team delivering a project in another organization.

More and more organizations also realize that the management of change is more likely to succeed if attention is given to the people side of change. Hence a parallel team drawn from representatives of the whole workforce can be a useful adjunct in terms of assessing and responding to the impact of the changes on people.

We see the change team as an important starting point in the change process.

STOP AND THINK!

Q 2.4 Of the teams of which you are a member, which are more suitable to lead change and which more suitable to implement change? Justify your answer.

HOW TO IMPROVE TEAM EFFECTIVENESS

Rollin and Christine Glaser (1992) have identified five elements that contribute to the level of a team's effectiveness or ineffectiveness over time. They are:

- team mission, planning and goal setting;

- team roles;

- team operating processes;

- team interpersonal relationships; and

- inter-team relations.

If you can assess where a team is in terms of its ability to address these five elements, you will discover what the team needs to do to develop into a fully functioning team.

Team mission planning and goal setting

A number of studies have found that the most effective teams have a strong sense of their purpose, organize their work around that purpose, and plan and set goals in line with that purpose. Larson and LaFasto (1989) report, 'in every case, without exception, when an effectively functioning team was identified, it was described by the respondent as having a clear understanding of its objective'.

Clarity of objectives together with a common understanding and agreement of these was seen to be key. In addition Locke and Latham report that the very act of goal setting was a prime motivator for the team; the more your team sets clear goals the more likely it is to succeed. They also reported a 16 per cent average improvement in effectiveness for teams that use goal setting as an integral part of team activities.

Clear goals are even more important when teams are involved in change, partly because unless they know where they are going they are unlikely to get there, and partly because a strong sense of purpose can mitigate some of the more harmful effects of change. The downside occurs when a team rigidly adheres to its purpose when in fact the world has moved on and other objectives are more appropriate.

Team roles

The best way for a team to achieve its goals is for the team to be structured logically around those goals. Individual team members need to have clear roles and accountabilities. They need to have a clear understanding not only of what their individual role is, but also what the roles and accountabilities of other team members are.

When change happens – within, to or by the team – clarity around role has two useful functions. It provides a clear sense of purpose and it provides a supportive framework for task accomplishment. However, during change the situation becomes more fluid. Too much rigidity results in tasks falling down the gaps between roles, or overlaps going unnoticed. It might result in team members being less innovative or proactive or courageous.

Team operating processes

A team needs to have certain enabling processes in place for people to carry out their work together. Certain things need to be in place that will allow the task to be achieved in a way that is as efficient and as effective as possible. Glaser and Glaser (1992) comment, 'both participation in all of the processes of the work group and the development of a collaborative approach are at the heart of effective group work. Because of the tradition of autocratic leadership, neither participation nor collaboration are natural or automatic processes. Both require some learning and practice.'

Typical areas that a team need actively to address by discussing and agreeing include:

- frequency, timing and agenda of meetings;
- problem-solving and decision-making methodologies;
- groundrules;
- procedures for dealing with conflict when it occurs;
- reward mechanisms for individuals contributing to team goals;
- type and style of review process.

In the turbulence created by change all these areas will come under additional stress and strain, hence the need for processes to have been discussed and agreed at an earlier stage. During times of change when typically pressures and priorities can push people into silo mentality and away from the team, the team operating processes can act like a lubricant, enabling healthy team functioning to continue.

Team interpersonal relationships

The team members must actively communicate among themselves. To achieve clear understanding of goals and roles, the team needs to work together to agree and clarify them. Operating processes must also be discussed and agreed.

To achieve this level of communication, the interpersonal relationships within the team need to be in a relatively healthy state. Glaser and Glaser (1992) found that the literature on team effectiveness 'prescribes open communication that is assertive and task focused, as well as creating opportunities for giving and receiving feedback aimed at the development of a high trust climate'.

In times of change, individual stress levels rise and there is a tendency to focus more on the task than the people processes. High levels of trust within a team are the bedrock for coping with conflict.

Inter-team relations

Teams cannot work in isolation with any real hope of achieving their organizational objectives. The nature of organizations today – complex, sophisticated and with increasing loose and permeable boundaries – creates situations where a team's goals can rarely be achieved without input from and output to others.

However smart a team has been in addressing the previous four categories, the authors have found in consulting with numerous organizations that attention needs to be paid to inter-team relations now more than ever before. This is because of the rise of strategic partnerships and global organizations. Teams need to connect more. It is also because the environment is changing faster and is more complex, so keeping in touch with information outside of your own team is a basic survival strategy.

Table 2.3 Effective and ineffective teams

Element	Team mission, planning and goal setting	Team roles	Team operating processes	Team interpersonal relationships	Inter-team relations
Outcome					
Team more effective, adaptive and change oriented	Clarity of goals and clear direction lead to greater task accomplishment and increased motivation	Clear roles and responsibilities increase individual accountability and allow others to work at their tasks	Problem solving and decision making are smoother and faster. Processes enable task accomplishment without undue conflict	Open data flow and high levels of team working leading to task accomplishment in a supportive environment	Working across boundaries ensures that organizational goals are more likely to be achieved
Team less effective, less adaptive and change oriented	Lack of purpose and unclear goals result in dissipation of energy and effort	Unclear roles and responsibilities lead to increased conflict and reduced accountability	Unclear operating processes increase time and effort needed to progress task achievement	Dysfunctional team working causes tensions, conflict, stress and insufficient focus on task accomplishment	Teams working in isolation or against other teams reduce the likelihood of organizational goal achievement

STOP AND THINK!

Q 2.5 Using the five elements above, what is your current team effectiveness?

Q 2.6 What needs to change, and how would you go about it?

WHAT TEAM CHANGE LOOKS LIKE

All teams go through a change process when they are first formed, and when significant events occur such as a new member arriving, a key member leaving, a change of scope, increased pressure from outside, or a change in organizational climate.

Tuckman (1965) is one of the most widely quoted of researchers into the linear model of team development. His work is regularly used in team building within organizations. Most people will have heard of it as the 'forming, storming, norming, performing' model of team development. His basic premise is that any team will undergo distinct stages of development as it works or struggles towards effective

Table 2.4 Key attributes in the stages of team development

	Forming	Storming	Norming	Performing
Tuckman (1965)	**Forming** Attempt at establishing primary purpose, structure, roles, leader, task and process relationships, and boundaries of the team	**Storming** Arising and dealing of conflicts surrounding key questions from forming stage	**Norming** Settling down of team dynamic and stepping into team norms and agreed ways of working	**Performing** Team is now ready and enabled to focus primarily on its task while attending to individual and team maintenance needs
Schutz (1982)	**In or out** Members decide whether they are part of the team or not	**Top or bottom** Focus on who has power and authority within the team	**Near or far** Finding levels of commitment and engagement within their roles	
Modlin and Faris (1956)	**Structuralism** Attempt to recreate previous power within new team structures	**Unrest** Attempt to resolve power and interpersonal issues	**Change** Roles emerge based on task and people needs. Sense of team emerges	**Integration** Team purpose and structure emerge and accepted, action towards team goals
Whittaker (1970)	**Preaffiliation** Sense of unease, unsure of team engagement, which is superficial	**Power and control** Focus on who has power and authority within the team. Attempt to define roles	**Intimacy** Team begins to commit to task and engage with one another	**Differentiation** Ability to be clear about individual roles and interactions become workmanlike
Hill and Gruner (1973)	**Orientation** Structure sought	**Exploration** Exploration around team roles and relations		**Production** Clarity of team roles and team cohesion
Bion (1961)	**Dependency** Team members invest the leaders with all the power and authority	**Fight or flight** Team members challenge the leaders or other members. Team members withdraw	**Pairing** Team members form pairings in an attempt to resolve their anxieties	
Scott Peck (1990)	**Pseudocommunity** Members try to fake teamliness	**Chaos** Attempt to establish pecking order and team norms	**Emptiness** Giving up of expectations, assumptions and hope of achieving anything	**Community** Acceptance of each other and focus on the task

team functioning. Although we will describe Tuckman's model in some detail, we have selected a range of models to illustrate the team development process, as indicated in Table 2.4.

Tuckman's model of team change

Forming

Forming is the first stage. This involves the team asking a set of fundamental questions:

- What is our primary purpose?

- How do we structure ourselves as a team to achieve our purpose?

- What roles do we each have?

- Who is the leader?

- How will we work together?

- How will we relate together?

- What are the boundaries of the team?

If we were to take a logical rational view of the team we could imagine that this could all be accomplished relatively easily and relatively painlessly. And sometimes, on short projects with less than five team members, it is. However human beings are not completely logical rational creatures, and sometimes this process is difficult. We all have emotions, personalities, unique characteristics and personal motivations.

As we saw when we were exploring individual change, human beings react to change in different ways. And the formation of a new team is about individuals adjusting to change in their own individual ways.

Initially the questions may be answered in rather a superficial fashion. The primary task of the team might be that which was written down in a memo from the departmental head, along with the structure they first thought of. The leader might typically have been appointed beforehand and 'imposed' upon the team. Individuals' roles are agreed to in an initial and individual cursory meeting with the team leader.

The team may agree to relate via a set of groundrules using words that nobody could possibly object to, but nobody knows what they really mean in practice: 'be honest', 'team before self', 'have fun', and so on.

Storming

Tuckman's next stage is storming. This is a description of the dynamic that occurs when a team of individuals come together to work on a common task, and have passed through the phase of being nice to one another and not voicing their individual concerns. This dynamic occurs as the team strives or struggles to answer fully the questions postulated in the forming stage.

Statements articulated (or left unsaid) in some fashion or form might include ones such as:

- I don't think we should be aiming for that.

- This structure hasn't taken account of this.

- There are rather a lot of grey areas in our individual accountabilities.

- Why was he appointed as team leader when he hasn't done this before?

- I don't know whether I can work productively with these people.

- How can we achieve our goals without the support from others in the organization?

An alternative word to storming is 'testing'. Individuals and the team as a whole are testing out the assumptions that had been made when the team was originally formed. Obviously different teams will experience this stage with different degrees of intensity, but important points to note here are:

- It is a natural part of the process.

- It is a healthy part of the process.

- It is an important part of the process.

The storming phase – if successfully traversed – will achieve clarity around all the fundamental questions of the first phase, and enable common understanding of purpose and roles to be achieved. In turn it allows the authority of the team leader to be seen and acknowledged, and it allows everyone to take up their rightful place within the team. It also gives team members a sense of the way things will happen within the team. It becomes a template for future ways of acting, problem solving, decision making and relating.

Norming

The third stage of team development occurs when the team finally settles down into working towards achievement of its task without too much attention needed on the fundamental questions. As further challenges develop, or as individuals grow further into their roles, then further scrutiny of the fundamental questions may happen. They may be discussed, but if they instead remain hidden beneath the surface this can result in loss of attention on the primary task.

Tuckman suggests in his review of the research that this settling process can be relatively straightforward and sequential. The team moves through the storming phase into a way of working that establishes team norms. It can also be more sporadic and turbulent, with the team needing further storming before team norms are established. Indeed some readers might have experienced teams that permanently move back and forth between the norming and storming stages – a clear signal that some team issues are not being surfaced and dealt with.

Performing

The final stage of team development is performing. The team has successfully traversed the three previous stages and therefore has clarity around its purpose, its structure and its roles. It has engaged in a rigorous process of working out how it should work and relate together, and is comfortable with the team norms it has established. Not only has the team worked these things through, but it has embodied them as a way of working. It has developed a capacity to change and develop, and has learnt how to learn.

The team can quite fruitfully get on with the task in hand and attend to individual and team needs at the same time.

THE LEADERSHIP ISSUES IN TEAM CHANGE

FOOD FOR THOUGHT

Ralph Stacey, in his book _Strategic Management and Organisational Dynamics_ (1993), describes what happens when a group is brought together to study the experience of being in a group, without any further task and without an appointed leader. Known as a Group Relations Conference and run by the Tavistock Institute in London, this process involves a consultant who forms part of the group to offer views on the group process but otherwise takes no conscious part in the activity. This:

> *always provokes high levels of anxiety in the participants ... which ... find expression in all manner of strange behaviours. Group discussions take on a manic form with asinine comments and hysterical laughter ... the participants attack the visiting consultant ... becoming incredibly rude....*
>
> *Members try to replace the non-functioning consultant ... but they rarely seem to be successful in this endeavour. They begin to pick on an individual, usually some highly individualistic or minority member of the group, and then treat this person as some kind of scapegoat. They all become very concerned with remaining part of the group, greatly fearing exclusion. They show strong tendencies to conform to rapidly established group norms and suppress their individual differences, perhaps they are afraid of becoming the scapegoat ... the one thing they hardly do at all is to examine the behaviour they are indulging in, the task they have actually been given.*

The situation described in the box offers a way of exploring some of the unconscious group processes that are at work just below the surface. These are not always visible in more conventional team situations. The work of Bion (1961) and Scott Peck (1990) is useful to illuminate the phases that groups go through and highlight the challenges for leaders.

Moving through dependency

In any team formation the first thing people look for is someone to tell them what to do. This is a perfectly natural phenomenon, given that many people will want to get on with the task and many people will believe someone else knows what the task is and how it should be done.

In any unfamiliar situation or environment people can become dependent. Jon Stokes (in Obholzer and Roberts, 1994) describes what Bion observed in his experience with groups and called basic group assumptions:

> a group dominated by basic assumption of dependency behaves as if its primary task is solely to provide for the satisfaction of the needs and wishes of its members. The leader is expected to look after, protect and sustain the members of the group, to make them feel good, and not to face them with the demands of the group's real purpose.

The job of the leader, and indeed the group, is not only to establish leadership credibility and accountability but to establish its limits. This will imbue the rest of the team with sufficient power for them to accomplish their tasks. The leader can do this by modelling the taking of individual responsibility and empowering others to do the same, and by ensuring that people are oriented in the right direction and have a common understanding of team purpose and objectives.

Moving through conflict

Bion's second assumption is labelled fight or flight. Bion (1961) says:

> There is a danger or 'enemy', which should either be attacked or fled from ... members
> look to the leader to devise some appropriate action ... for instance, instead of consid-
> ering how best to organize its work, a team may spend most of the time worrying about
> rumours of organizational change. This provides a sense of togetherness, whilst also
> serving to avoid facing the difficulties of the work itself. Alternatively, such a group may
> spend its time protesting angrily, without actually planning any specific action to deal with
> the perceived threat.

The threat might not necessarily be coming from outside, but instead might be an
externalization – or projection – from the team. The real threat is from within, and
the potential for conflict is between the leader and the rest of the team, and between
team members themselves. Issues around power and authority and where people sit
in the 'pecking order' may surface at this stage.

The leadership task here is to surface any of these dynamics and work them
through, either by the building of trust and the frank, open and honest exchange of
views, or by seeking clarity and gaining agreement on roles and responsibilities.

Moving towards creativity

The third assumption that Bion explored was that of pairing. This is:

> based on the collective and unconscious belief that, whatever the actual problems and
> needs of the group, a future event will solve them. The group behaves as if pairing or
> coupling between two members within the group, or perhaps between the leaders of the
> group and some external person, will bring about salvation ... the group is in fact not
> interested in working practically towards this future, but only sustaining a vague sense of
> hope as a way out of its current difficulties ... members are inevitably left with a sense of
> disappointment and failure, which is quickly superseded by a hope that the next meeting
> will be better.

Once again there is a preoccupation. This time it is about creating something new,
but in a fantasized or unreal way, as a defence against doing anything practical or
actually performing. The antidote of course is for the leader to encourage the team
members to continue in their endeavours and to take personal responsibility for
moving things on. Collaborative working requires greater openness of communication and data flow.

Moving through cohesion and cosiness

Turquet (1974) has added a fourth assumption, labelled oneness. This is where the team seems to believe it has come together almost for a higher purpose, or with a higher force, so the members can lose themselves in a sense of complete unity.

There are parallels to the stage of performing, but somehow, once again, the team has fallen into an unconscious detraction from the primary task in hand. Attainment of a sense of oneness, cohesiveness or indeed cosiness is not the purpose the team set out to achieve. Good and close team working is often essential and can be individually satisfying, but it is not the purpose. Too much focus on team cohesion can lead to abdication from the task, and is only a stage on the way to full team working. The goal is interdependent working coexisting with collaborative problem solving. This requires the leader to set the scene and the pace, and team members to act with maturity.

See Chapter 4 for more ideas on leading change.

STOP AND THINK!

Q 2.7 Imagine that you are one of a team of 5 GPs working at a local practice. You want to initiate some changes in the way the team approaches non-traditional medical approaches such as counselling, homeopathy and osteopathy. The GPs meet monthly for one hour to discuss finances and review medical updates. They do not really know each other well or work together on patient care. There is no real team leader, although the Practice Manager takes the lead when the group discusses administration.

Using one of the models of team development described above, explain how you could lead the team towards a new way of working together. What obstacles to progress do you predict, and how might you deal with them?

HOW INDIVIDUALS AFFECT TEAM DYNAMICS

Here we use the Myers Briggs Type Indicator to see how individual personalities might influence and be influenced by the team. We also use Meredith Belbin's research into team types to indicate what types of individuals best make up an effective team.

MBTI and teams

'If it ain't broke, don't fix it'   'Let's think ahead'

'Let's just do it'   'Let's change it'

The Myers Briggs Type Indicator suggests that if you are a particular type you have particular preferences and are different from other people of different types (see table 1.5 for MBTI types). This means that when it comes to change, people with different preferences react differently to change, both when they initiate it and when they are on the receiving end of it. This is also true when you are a member of a team. Different people will bring their individual preferences to the table and behave in differing ways.

When undergoing team change, individual team members will typically react in one of four ways (see illustrations above):

● Some will want to ascertain the difference between what should be preserved and what could be changed. There will be things they want to keep.

- Some will think long and hard about the changes that will emerge internally from their visions of the future. They will be intent on thinking about the changes differently.

- Some will be keen to move things on by getting things to run more effectively and efficiently. They will be most interested in doing things now.

- Some will be particularly inventive and want to try something different or novel. They will be all for changing things.

The use of MBTI, or any other personality-profiling instrument, can have specific benefits when teams are experiencing or managing change. It can identify where individuals and the team itself might have strengths to be capitalized on, and where it might have weaknesses that need to be supported.

Behaviours exhibited by team members will run 'true to type', and thus knowing your preferences and those of the rest of the team will help aid understanding. It is also true that different team tasks might be suitable for different types – either because they are best matched or because it provides a development opportunity. Surfacing differences helps individuals see things from the other person's perspective, and adds to the effective use of diversity within the team.

Researching in the health care industry, Mary McCaulley (1975) made the point that similarity and difference within teams can have both advantages and disadvantages:

- The more similar the team members are, the sooner they will reach common understanding.

- The more disparate the team members, the longer it takes for understanding to occur.

- The more similar the team members, the quicker the decision will be made, but the greater the possibility of error through exclusion of some possibilities.

- The more disparate the team members, the longer the decision-making process will be, but the more views and opinions will be taken into account.

McCaulley also recognized that teams valuing different types can ultimately experience less conflict.

A particular case worth mentioning is the management team. Management teams both in the United States and the United Kingdom are skewed from the natural distribution of Myers Briggs types within the whole population. Typically they are composed of fewer people of the feeling types and fewer people of the perceiving types. This means that management teams, when making decisions around change, are more likely to put emphasis on the business case for change, and less likely to think or worry about the effect on people. You can see the result of this in most change programmes in most organizations. They are also more likely to want to close things down, having made a decision, rather than keep their options open – thus excluding the possibility of enhancing and improving on the changes or responding to feedback.

There are some simple reminders of the advantages and disadvantages of the preferences for teams making decisions about managing change within organizations, as listed in Table 2.5.

Table 2.5   Complementarity and conflict in teams

Extraversion	Where individuals draw their energy from	Introversion
Needed to raise energy, show enthusiasm, make contacts and take action. But they can appear superficial, intrusive and overwhelming.		Needed for thinking things through and depth of understanding. But can appear withdrawn, cold and aloof.
Sensing	What an individual pays attention to or how he/she receives data and information	**Intuition**
Needed to base ideas firmly in reality and be practical and pragmatic. Can appear rather mundane and pessimistic.		Needed to prepare for the future and generate innovative solutions. Can appear to have head in the clouds, impractical and implausible.
Thinking	How an individual makes decisions	**Feeling**
Needed to balance benefits against the costs and make tough decisions. Can appear rather critical and insensitive.		Needed to be in touch with emotional intelligence, to negotiate and to reconcile. Can appear irrational and too emotional.
Judging	What sort of lifestyle an individual enjoys	**Perceiving**
Needed for his/her organization and ability to complete things and see them through. Can appear overly rigid and immovable.		Needed for his/her flexibility, adaptability and information gathering. Can appear rather unorganized and somewhat irresponsible.

Belbin's team types

What people characteristics need to be present for a team to function effectively? Meredith Belbin (1981) has been researching this question for a number of years. The purpose of his research was to see whether high and low performing teams had certain characteristics. He looked at team members and found that in the higher performing teams, members played a role or number of roles. Any teams without members playing one of these roles would be more likely to perform at a lower level of effectiveness. Of course different situations require certain different emphasis.

He identified the following roles.

The Chairman: coordinates the working of the team towards its objectives, using his or her communication and people skills. Quite people focused.

The Shaper: focuses on task achievement. Attempts to bring shape and structure to the team's direction, using enthusiastic and proactive attitude.

The Plant: generates ideas for the team using imagination and intelligence, working at a high level rather than with the detail.

The *Monitor-Evaluator: has the ability to see how things are going. Takes in information, collates, interprets and evaluates data and progress.*

The *Company Worker:* is quite the pragmatist. Able to translate ideas into tangible actions. Aims for stability and agreed courses of action.

The *Resource Investigator:* has the ability to go out and ensure the necessary resources are obtained through his or her networking and interpersonal skills and positive attitude.

The *Team Worker:* focuses on the team's well being by being able to read the signals of the team dynamic and arbitrate, mediate and facilitate the team through difficult emotional terrain.

The Completer-Finisher: keeps working to meet deadlines. Very detail conscious and disciplined in his or her approach to task completion.

STOP AND THINK!

Q 2.8   What team role(s) are you likely to use?

Q 2.9   What are the advantages and disadvantages of each of the eight roles?

Belbin concluded that if teams were formed with individuals' preferences and working styles in mind, they would have a better chance of team cohesion and work-related goal achievement. Teams need to contain a good spread of Belbin team types.

Different teams might need different combinations of roles. Marketing and design teams probably need more plants, while project implementation teams need Company

Workers and Completer Finishers. Likewise, the lack of a particular team type can be an issue. A management team without a Chairman or Shaper would have problems. An implementation team without a Complete Finisher might also struggle.

HOW WELL TEAMS INITIATE AND ADAPT TO ORGANIZATIONAL CHANGE

Throughout the last decades of the 20th century many organizations repeated the mantra, 'people are our greatest assets', and many would then apologize profusely when they were forced into downsizing or 'rightsizing' the workforce. Similarly many organizations have sung the praises of teams and how essential they are within the modern organization. Many organizations have sets of competences or stated values that implicitly and explicitly pronounce that their employees need to work in the spirit of team work and partnership.

It was therefore interesting for the authors to discover that there was a real lack of any authoritative research on the interplay between organizational change and team working. We have seen in a previous chapter the effect that change has on individuals and groups of individuals; but what has not been studied is the effect of change on teams. And as a consequence there is very little research on strategies for managing and leading teams through organizational change.

Whelan-Berry and Gordon (2000), in their research into effective organizational change, conducted a multi-level analysis of the organizational change process. To quote them:

> they found no change process models at the group or team level of analysis in the organization studies and change literature. Literature exists which explores different aspects of team or group development, team or group effectiveness, implementation of specific interventions, and organizational and individual aspects of the change, but not a group/team change process model ... the lack of change process models for the team or group level change process in the context of organizational change leaves a major portion of the organizational change process unclear.

They continue:

> The primary focus of existing organizational change models is what to do as opposed to explaining or predicting the change process. Most of the models implicitly, and a few explicitly, acknowledge, the inherent (sub) processes of group level and individual level change, but do not include the details of these processes in the model. The question is how does the change process vary when considered across levels of analysis? For example, how does a vision get 'translated,' that is, take on meaning, in each location or

department? In addition, what happens at the point of implementation? We must 'double click' at the point of implementation in the organizational level change process; that is, we must look at the group and individual levels and their respective change processes to understand the translation and implementation of the organizational level change vision and desired change outcomes to group and subsequently to individual meanings, frameworks, and behaviours.

Table 2.6 examines each type of team previously identified, and looks at the way in which this type of team can impact or react to organizational change. We also look at the pros and cons of each team type when involved in an organizational change process.

Team development processes are disturbed in times of change. An external event can shift a performing team back into the storming stage. Only teams that are quite remote from the changes can simply incorporate a new scope or a new set of values and remain relatively untouched.

Table 2.6 Teams going through change

Team type	Group	Work	Parallel	Project	Matrix
Propensity to initiate change	Dependent on nature and composition of group	Limited	Limited in terms of organizational impact	Potentially high depending on integration into organization	Fair given propensity to address change
Propensity to adapt to change	Dependent on purpose and composition of group	Dependent on team members and team culture	Dependent on purpose and team members	Theoretically high. Good for limited changes in scope but not total	Dependent on degree of enabling or disabling structure
Advantages during change	Difficult to get alignment	Good at implementation once it is clear	Good for pilot schemes	Good focus for specific implementation goals	Flexible, so good for initiating ideas

Table 2.6 *continued*

Team type	Group	Work	Parallel	Project	Matrix
Disadvantages during change	Useful for coming up with out-of-the-box ideas	Does not like change too often	Can become alienated through failure, or through boasting about success	Not good for tackling complex topics such as values or leadership	Leadership sometimes not clear, so discussion can go on for ever
Advice for leaders	Good for initiating ideas and spreading the word	Need to involve the leaders or shapers of these teams early – especially if you need their commitment rather than compliance	Useful for starting things up and proving an idea. Do not let members become too isolated. Encourage them to link in with the outside world	Good for short-range tasks such as appointing consultants or researching techniques. Not good for the complex stuff. Do not be tempted to give complex issues like 'improve communication' to a project team	Good for initiating ideas and spreading the word

Team type	Virtual	Network	Management	Change
Propensity to initiate change	Limited unless project specific	Potentially large depending on nature and composition of group	Theoretically and practically high. Typically should be the team that initiates change	*Raison d'être*
Propensity to adapt to change	Dependent on purpose and team members	Dependent on purpose and team members	Theoretically and practically high. Sometimes will have difficulty adapting to others' change	Theoretically and practically high
Advantages during change	Brings disparate groups together if tightly focused	Wide reaching, so good for sharing sense of purpose and sense of urgency	Powerful, so makes an impact	Has increased energy and sense of purpose because it was set up to make change happen

Table 2.6 *continued*

Team type	Virtual	Network	Management	Change
Disadvantages during change	Lack of cohesion means purpose may be misunderstood and important issues are not raised	Not good for monitoring implementation because of lack of process and regularity	Often resistant to changing through lack of time or lack of teamwork, so role modelling of desired changes can be weak. Focus on events after the launch often poor due to packed agenda and belief that it will all happen smoothly	Not impactful if it lacks influence (presence of powerful people)
Advice for leaders	Involve the key virtual teams early – especially the leaders and shapers, but do not expect them to implement anything complicated	Good for initiating ideas and spreading the word	Do something surprising yourself if you want your management team to change the way it works. Insist on role modelling. Keep your eye on the ball because there *will* be problems	Recruit powerful people Work on alignment Ensure resources

SUMMARY AND CONCLUSIONS

- Groups and teams are different, with different characteristics and different reasons for existing.

- Teams are important in organizational life for accomplishing large or complex tasks.

- Team work is important for management teams when they work on risky issues that require them to share views and align.

- There are many different types of organizational team, each with significant benefits and downsides.

- Teams can become more effective by addressing five elements:
  - team mission, planning and goal setting;
  - team roles;

- team operating processes;
- team interpersonal relationships;
- inter-team relations.

- Teams develop over time. Tuckman's forming, storming, norming and performing model is useful for understanding this process.

- The team development process involves different leadership challenges at each stage.

- Bion's work highlights four possible pitfalls that need to be worked through:
  - dependency;
  - fight or flight;
  - pairing;
  - cosiness.

- The composition of a team is an important factor in determining how it can be successful. Belbin says that well-rounded teams are best. Deficiencies in a certain type can cause problems.

- The Myers Briggs profile allows mutual understanding of team member's preferences for initiating or adapting to change.

- Belbin's team types offer a way of analysing a team's fitness for purpose and encouraging team members to do something about any significant gaps.

- Leaders need to be aware of the types of team available during a change process, and how to manage these most effectively.

Below is a summary checklist of the key questions you need to be asking and answering before, during and after the change process:

- Where are the teams affected by the change process?

- What types of team are they and how might they respond to change?

- What do they need to be supported through the change process?

- How can we best use them throughout the change process?

- What additional types of team do we need for designing and implementing the changes?

- As all teams go through the transition, what resources shall we offer to ensure they achieve their objectives of managing business as usual and the changes?

- How do we ensure that teams that are dispersing, forming, integrating or realigning stay on task?

- What organizational process do we have for ensuring teams are clear about their:
    - mission, planning and goal setting;
    - roles and responsibilities
    - operating processes;
    - interpersonal relationships;
    - inter-team relations?

3

Organizational change

This chapter tackles the issue of organizational change. How does the process of organizational change happen? Must change be initiated and driven through by one strong individual? Or can it be planned collectively by a powerful group of people, and by sheer momentum, the change will happen? Perhaps there is a more intellectual approach that can be taken. Are there payoffs to understanding the whole system, determining how to change it, and predicting where resistance will occur? On the other hand, maybe change cannot be planned at all. Something unpredictable could spark a change, which then spreads in a natural way.

This chapter addresses the topic of organizational change in three sections:

- how organizations really work;

- models and approaches to organizational change;

- summary and conclusions.

In the first section we look at assumptions about how organizations work in terms of the metaphors that are most regularly used to describe them. This is an important starting point for those who are serious about organizational change. Once you become aware of the range of assumptions that shape people's attitudes to and understanding of organizations, you can take advantage of the possibilities of other ways of looking at things, and you can begin to understand how other people in your organization may view the world. You can also begin to see the limitations of each mindset and the disadvantages of taking a one-dimensional approach to organizational change.

In the second section, we set out a range of useful models and ideas developed by some of the most significant writers on organizational change. This section aims to illustrate the variety of ways in which you can view the process of organizational change. We also make sense of the different models and approaches by identifying the assumptions underpinning each one. When you understand the assumptions behind a model, you can start to see its benefits and limitations.

In the third section, we come to some conclusions about organizational change, and stress the importance of being aware of underlying assumptions and having the flexibility to employ a range of different approaches.

HOW ORGANIZATIONS REALLY WORK

We all have our own assumptions about how organizations work, developed through a combination of experience and education. The use of metaphor is an important way in which we express these assumptions. Some people talk about organizations as if they were machines. This metaphor leads to talk of organizational structures, job design and process reengineering. Others describe organizations as political systems. They describe the organization as a seething web of political intrigue where coalitions are formed and power rules supreme. They talk about hidden agendas, opposing factions and political manoeuvring.

Gareth Morgan's (1986) work on organizational metaphors is a good starting point for understanding the different beliefs and assumptions about change that exist. He says:

> Metaphor gives us the opportunity to stretch our thinking and deepen our understanding, thereby allowing us to see things in new ways and act in new ways… Metaphor always creates distortions too… We have to accept that any theory or perspective that we bring to the study of organization and management, while capable of creating valuable insights, is also incomplete, biased, and potentially misleading.

Morgan identifies eight organizational metaphors:

- machines;

- organisms;

- brains;

- cultures;

- political systems;

- psychic prisons;

- flux and transformation.

We have selected four of Morgan's organizational metaphors to explore the range of assumptions that exists about how organizational change works. These are the four that we see in use most often by managers, writers and consultants, and that appear to us to provide the most useful insights into the process of organizational change. These are:

- organizations as machines;

- organizations as political systems;

- organizations as organisms;

- organizations as flux and transformation.

Descriptions of these different organizational metaphors appear below. See also Table 3.1 which sets out how change might be approached using the four different metaphors. In reality most organizations use combinations of approaches to tackle organizational change, but it is useful to pull the metaphors apart to see the difference in the activities resulting from different ways of thinking.

MACHINE METAPHOR?

The new organizational structure represents an injection of fresh skills into the Marketing Function. Fred Smart will now head up the implementation of the Marketing Plan which details specific investment in marketing skills training and IT systems. We intend to fill the identified skills gaps and to upgrade our customer databases and market intelligence databank. A focus on following correct marketing procedures will ensure consistent delivery of well targeted brochures and advertising campaigns.

MD, Engineering Company

Organizations as machines

The machine metaphor is a well-used metaphor which is worth revisiting to examine its implications for organizational change. Gareth Morgan says, 'When we think of organizations as machines, we begin to see them as rational enterprises designed and  structured to achieve predetermined ends.' This picture of an organization implies routine operations, well-defined structure and job roles, and efficient working inside and between the working parts of the machine (the functional areas). Procedures and standards are clearly defined, and are expected to be adhered to.

Many of the principles behind this mode of organizing are deeply ingrained in our assumptions about how organizations should work. This links closely into behaviourist views of change and learning (see description of behavioural approach to change in Chapter 1).

The key beliefs are:

- Each employee should have only one line manager.

- Labour should be divided into specific roles.

- Each individual should be managed by objectives.

- Teams represent no more than the summation of individual efforts.

- Management should control and there should be employee discipline.

This leads to the following assumptions about organizational change:

- The organization can be changed to an agreed end state by those in positions of authority.

- There will be resistance, and this needs to be managed.

- Change can be executed well if it is well planned and well controlled.

What are the limitations of this metaphor? The mechanistic view leads managers to design and run the organization as if it were a machine. This approach works well in stable situations, but when the need for a significant change arises, this will be seen and experienced by employees as a major overhaul which is usually highly disruptive and therefore encounters resistance. Change when approached with these assumptions is therefore hard work. It will necessitate strong management action, inspirational vision, and control from the top down.

See the works of Frederick Taylor and Henri Fayol if you wish to examine further some of the original thinking behind this metaphor.

Organizations as political systems

When we see organizations as political systems we are drawing clear parallels between how organizations are run and systems of political rule. We may refer to 'democracies', 'autocracy' or even 'anarchy' to describe what is going on in a particular organization. Here we are describing the style of power rule employed in that organization.

The political metaphor is useful because it recognizes the important role that power play, competing interests and conflict have in organizational life. Gareth Morgan comments, 'Many people hold the belief that business and politics should be kept apart... But the person advocating the case of employee rights or industrial democracy is not introducing a political issue so much as arguing for a different approach to a situation that is already political.'

The key beliefs are:

- You can't stay out of organizational politics. You're already in it.

- Building support for your approach is essential if you want to make anything happen.

- You need to know who is powerful, and who they are close to.

- There is an important political map which overrides the published organizational structure.

- Coalitions between individuals are more important than work teams.

- The most important decisions in an organization concern the allocation of scarce resources, that is, who gets what, and these are reached through bargaining, negotiating and vying for position.

This leads to the following assumptions about organizational change:

- The change will not work unless it's supported by a powerful person.

- The wider the support for this change the better.

- It is important to understand the political map, and to understand who will be winners and losers as a result of this change.

- Positive strategies include creating new coalitions and renegotiating issues.

What are the limitations of this metaphor? The disadvantage of using this metaphor to the exclusion of others is that it can lead to the potentially unnecessary development of complex Machiavellian strategies, with an assumption that in any organizational endeavour, there are always winners and losers. This can turn organizational life into a political war zone.

See Pfeiffer's book, *Managing with Power: Politics and influence in organizations* (1992) to explore this metaphor further.

Organizations as organisms

This metaphor of organizational life sees the organization as a living, adaptive system. Gareth Morgan says, 'The metaphor suggests that different environments favour different species of organisations based on different methods of organising ... congruence with the environment is the key to success.' For instance, in stable environments a more rigid bureaucratic organization would prosper. In more fluid, changing environments a looser, less structured type of organization would be more likely to survive.

This metaphor represents the organization as an 'open system'. Organizations are seen as sets of interrelated subsystems designed to balance the requirements of the environment with internal needs of groups and individuals. This approach implies that when designing organizations, we should always do this with the environment in mind. Emphasis is placed on scanning the environment, and developing a healthy adaptation to the outside world. Individual, group and organizational health and happiness are essential ingredients of this metaphor. The assumption is that if the social needs of individuals and groups in the organization are met, and the organization is well designed to meet the needs of the environment, there is more likelihood of healthy adaptive functioning of the whole system (socio-technical systems).

The key beliefs are:

- There is no 'one best way' to design or manage an organization.

- The flow of information between different parts of the systems and its environment is key to the organization's success.

- It is important to maximize the fit between individual, team and organizational needs.

This leads to the following assumptions about organizational change:

- Changes are made only in response to changes in the external environment (rather than using an internal focus).

- Individuals and groups need to be psychologically aware of the need for change in order to adapt.

- The response to a change in the environment can be designed and worked towards.

- Participation and psychological support are necessary strategies for success.

What are the limitations of this metaphor? The idea of the organization as an adaptive system is flawed. The organization is not really just an adaptive unit, at the mercy of its environment. It can in reality shape the environment by collaborating with communities or with other organizations, or by initiating a new product or service that may change the environment in a significant way. In addition the idealized view of coherence and flow between functions and departments is often unrealistic. Sometimes different parts of the organization run independently, and do so for good reason. For example the research department might run in a very different way and entirely separately from the production department.

The other significant limitation of this view is noted by Morgan, and concerns the danger that this metaphor becomes an ideology. The resulting ideology says that individuals should be fully integrated with the organization. This means that work should be designed so that people can fulfil their personal needs through the organization. This can then become a philosophical bone of contention between 'believers' (often, but not always the HR Department) and 'non-believers' (often, but not always, the business directors). See Burns and Stalker's book *The Management of Innovation* (1961) for the original thinking behind this metaphor.

Organizations as flux and transformation

Viewing organizations as flux and transformation takes us into areas such as complexity, chaos and paradox. This view of organizational life sees the organization as part of the environment, rather than as distinct from it. So instead of viewing the organization as a separate system that adapts to the environment, this metaphor allows us to look at organizations as simply part of the ebb and flow of the whole environment, with a capacity to self-organize, change and self-renew in line with a desire to have a certain identity.

This metaphor is the only one that begins to shed some light on how change happens in a turbulent world. This view implies that managers can nudge and shape progress, but cannot ever be in control of change. Gareth Morgan says, 'In complex systems no one is ever in a position to control or design system operations in a comprehensive way. Form emerges. It cannot be imposed.'

The key beliefs are:

- Order naturally emerges out of chaos.

- Organizations have a natural capacity to self-renew.

- Organizational life is not governed by the rules of cause and effect.

- Key tensions are important in the emergence of new ways of doing things.

- The formal organizational structure (teams, hierarchies) only represents one of many dimensions of organizational life.

This leads to the following assumptions about organizational change:

- Change cannot be managed. It emerges.

- Managers are not outside the systems they manage. They are part of the whole environment.

- Tensions and conflicts are an important feature of emerging change.

- Managers act as enablers. They enable people to exchange views and focus on significant differences.

What are the limitations of this metaphor? This metaphor is disturbing for both managers and consultants. It does not lead to an action plan, or a process flow diagram or an agenda to follow. Other metaphors of change allow you to predict the process of change before it happens. With the flux and transformation metaphor, order emerges as you go along, and can only be made sense of after the event. This can lead to a sense of powerlessness that is disconcerting, but probably realistic!

See Shaw (2002) and Stacey (2001) for further reading on this metaphor.

Table 3.1 Four different approaches to the change process

Metaphor	How change is tackled	Who is responsible	Guiding principles
Machine	Senior managers define targets and timescale. Consultants advise on techniques. Change programme is rolled out from the top down. Training is given to bridge behaviour gap.	Senior management	Change must be driven. Resistance can be managed. Targets set at the start of the process define the direction.
Political system	A powerful group of individuals builds a new coalition with new guiding principles. There are debates, manoeuverings and negotiations which eventually leads to the new coalition either winning or losing. Change then ensues as new people are in power with new views and new ways of allocating scarce resources. Those around them position themselves to be winners rather than losers.	Those with power	There will be winners and losers. Change requires new coalitions and new negotiations.
Organisms	There is first a research phase where data is gathered on the relevant issue (customer feedback, employee survey etc). Next the data is presented to those responsible for making changes. There is discussion about what the data means, and then what needs to be done. A solution is collaboratively designed and moved towards, with maximum participation. Training and support are given to those who need to make significant changes.	Business improvement/HR/OD managers	There must be participation and involvement, and an awareness of the need for change. The change is collaboratively designed as a response to changes in the environment. People need to be supported through change.

Table 3.1   *continued*

Metaphor	How change is tackled	Who is responsible	Guiding principles
Flux and transformation	The initial spark of change is an emerging topic. This is a topic that is starting to appear on everyone's agenda, or is being talked about over coffee. Someone with authority takes the initiative to create a discussion forum. The discussion is initially fairly unstructured, but well facilitated. Questions asked might be 'Why have you come?', 'What is the real issue?', 'How would we like things to be?' The discussion involves anyone who has the energy to be interested. A plan for how to handle the issue emerges from a series of discussions. More people are brought into the net.	Someone with authority to act	Change cannot be managed; it emerges. Conflict and tension give rise to change. Managers are part of the process. Their job is to highlight gaps and contradictions.

Gareth Morgan's metaphors used with permission of Sage Publications Inc.

STOP AND THINK!

Q 3.1   Which view of organizational life is most prevalent in your organization?

What are the implications of this for the organization's ability to change?

Q 3.2   Which view are you most drawn to personally?

What are the implications for you as a leader of change?

Q 3.3   Which views are being espoused here? (See A, B, C, D.)

A   *All staff memo from management team*

The whole organization is encountering a range of difficult environmental issues, such as increased demand from our customers for faster delivery and higher quality, more legislation in key areas of our work, and rapidly developing competition in significant areas.

Please examine the attached information regarding the above (customer satisfaction data, benchmarking data vs competitors, details of new legislation) and start working in your teams on what this means for you, and how you might respond to these pressures.

The whole company will gather together in October of this year to begin to move forward with our ideas, and to strive for some alignment between different parts of the organization. We will present the management's vision and decide on some concrete first steps.

B E-mail from CEO

A number of people have spoken to me recently about their discomfort with the way we are tackling our biggest account. This seems to be an important issue for a lot of people. If you are interested in tackling this one, please come to an open discussion session in the Atrium on Tuesday between 10.00 and 12.00 where we will start to explore this area of discomfort. Let Sarah know if you intend to come.

C E-mail from one manager to another

John seems to be in cahoots with Sarah on this issue. If we want their support for our plans we need to reshape our agenda to include their need for extra resource in the operations team. I will have a one to one with Sarah to check out her viewpoint. Perhaps you can speak to John.

Our next step should be to talk this through with the key players on the Executive Board and negotiate the necessary investment.

D Announcement from MD

As you may know, consultants have been working with us to design our new objective setting process which is now complete. This will be rolled out starting 1 May 2003 starting with senior managers and cascading to team members.

The instructions for objective setting are very clear. Answers to frequently asked questions will appear on the company Web site next week.

This should all be working smoothly by end of May 2003.

MODELS OF AND APPROACHES TO ORGANIZATIONAL CHANGE

Now we have set the backdrop to organizational behaviour and our assumptions about how things really work, let us now examine ways of looking at organizational change as represented by the range of models and approaches developed by the key authors in this field. Table 3.2 links Gareth Morgan's organizational metaphors with the models of and approaches to change discussed below.

Table 3.2 Models of change and their associated metaphors

Model or approach	Machine	Political system	Organism	Flux and transformation
		Metaphor		
Lewin, three-step model	✓		✓	
Bullock and Batten, planned change	✓			
Kotter, eight steps	✓	✓	✓	
Beckhard and Harris, change formula			✓	
Nadler and Tushman, congruence model		✓	✓	
William Bridges, managing the transition	✓		✓	✓
Carnall, change management model		✓	✓	
Senge, systemic model		✓	✓	✓
Stacey and Shaw, complex responsive processes		✓		✓

Lewin, three-step model: *organism, machine*

Kurt Lewin (1951) developed his ideas about organizational change from the perspective of the organism metaphor. His model of organizational change is well known and much quoted by managers today. Lewin is responsible for introducing force field analysis, which examines the driving and resisting forces in any change situation (see Figure 3.1). The underlying principle is that driving forces must outweigh resisting forces in any situation if change is to happen.

Using the example illustrated in Figure 3.1, if the desire of a manager is to speed up the executive reporting process, then either the driving forces need to be augmented or the resisting forces decreased. Or even better, both of these must happen. This means for example ensuring that those responsible for making the changes to the executive reporting process are aware of how much time it will free

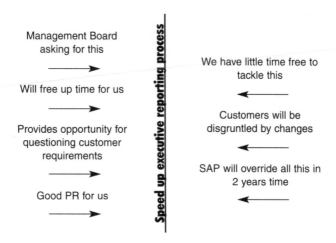

Figure 3.1 Lewin's force field analysis
Source: Lewin (1951)

up if they are successful, and what benefits this will have for them (augmenting driving force). It might also mean spending some time and effort managing customer expectations and supporting them in coping with the new process (reducing resisting force).

Lewin suggested a way of looking at the overall process of making changes. He proposed that organizational changes have three steps. The first step involves unfreezing the current state of affairs. This means defining the current state, surfacing the driving and resisting forces and picturing a desired end-state. The second is about moving to a new state through participation and involvement. The third focuses on refreezing and stabilizing the new state of affairs by setting policy, rewarding success and establishing new standards. See Figure 3.2 for the key steps in this process.

Lewin's three-step model uses the organism metaphor of organizations, which includes the notion of *homeostasis* (see box). This is the tendency of an organization to maintain its equilibrium in response to disrupting changes. This means that any organization has a natural tendency to adjust itself back to its original steady state. Lewin argued that a new state of equilibrium has to be intentionally moved towards, and then strongly established, so that a change will 'stick'.

Lewin's model was designed to enable a process consultant to take a group of people through the unfreeze, move and refreeze stages. For example, if a team of people began to see the need to radically alter their recruitment process, the consultant would work with the team to surface the issues, move to the desired new state and reinforce that new state.

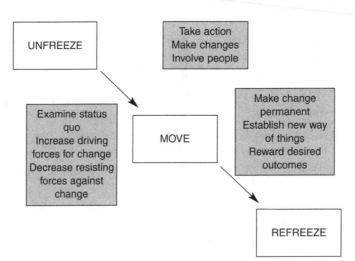

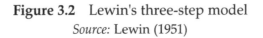

Figure 3.2 Lewin's three-step model
Source: Lewin (1951)

HOMEOSTASIS IN ACTION

In the 1990s many organizations embarked on TQM (total quality management) initiatives which involved focusing on customer satisfaction (both internally and externally) and process improvement in all areas of the organization. An Economic Intelligence Unit report indicated that two-thirds of these initiatives started well, but failed to keep the momentum going after 18 months. Focus groups were very active to start with, and suggestions from the front line came rolling in. After a while the focus groups stopped meeting and the suggestions dried up. Specific issues had been solved, but a new way or working had not emerged. Things reverted to the original state of affairs.

Our view

Lewin's ideas provide a useful tool for those considering organizational change. The force field analysis is an excellent way of enabling for instance a management team to discuss and agree on the driving and resisting forces that currently exist in any change situation. When this analysis is used in combination with a collaborative definition of the current state versus the desired end state, a team can quickly move to defining the next steps in the change process. These next steps are usually combinations of:

* communicating the gap between the current state and the end state to the key players in the change process;

- working to minimize the resisting forces;

- working to maximize or make the most of driving forces;

- agreeing a change plan and a timeline for achieving the end state.

We have observed that this model is sometimes used by managers as a planning tool, rather than as an organizational development process. The unfreeze becomes a planning session. The move translates to implementation. The refreeze is a post-implementation review. This approach ignores the fundamental assumption of the organism metaphor that groups of people will change only if there is a felt need to do so. The  change process can then turn into an ill-thought-out plan that does not tackle resistance and fails to harness the energy of the key players. This is rather like the process of blowing up a balloon and forgetting to tie a knot in the end!

Bullock and Batten, planned change: _machine_

Bullock and Batten's (1985) phases of planned change draw on the disciplines of project management. There are many similar 'steps to changing your organization' models to choose from. We have chosen Bullock and Batten's:

- exploration;

- planning;

- action;

- integration.

Exploration involves verifying the need for change, and acquiring any specific resources (such as expertise) necessary for the change to go ahead. Planning is an activity involving key decision makers and technical experts. A diagnosis is completed and actions are sequenced in a change plan. The plan is signed off by management before moving into the action phase. Actions are completed according to plan, with feedback mechanisms which allow some replanning if things go off track. The final integration phase is started once the change plan has been fully actioned. Integration involves aligning the change with other areas in the organization, and formalizing them in some way via established mechanisms such as policies, rewards and company updates.

This particular approach implies the use of the machine metaphor of organizations. The model assumes that change can be defined and moved towards in a planned way. A project management approach simplifies the change process by isolating one part of the organizational machinery in order to make necessary changes, for example developing leadership skills in middle management, or reorganizing the sales team to give more engine power to key sales accounts.

Our view

This approach implies that the organizational change is a technical problem that can be solved with a definable technical solution. We have observed that this approach works well with isolated issues, but works less well when organizations are facing complex, unknowable change which may require those involved to discuss the current situation and possible futures at greater length before deciding on one approach.

For example we worked with one organization recently that, on receiving a directive from the CEO to 'go global', immediately set up four tightly defined projects to address the issue of becoming a global organization. These were labelled global communication, global values, global leadership and global balanced scorecard. While on the surface, this seems a sensible and structured approach, there was no upfront opportunity for people to build any awareness of current issues, or to talk and think more widely about what needed to change to support this directive. Predictably, the projects ran aground around the 'action' stage due to confusion about goals, and dwindling motivation within the project teams.

Kotter, eight-steps: *machine, political, organism*

Kotter's (1995) 'eight steps to transforming your organisation' goes a little further than the basic machine metaphor. Kotter's eight-step model derives from analysis of his consulting practice with 100 different organizations going through change. His research highlighted eight key lessons, and he converted these into a useful eight-step model. The model addresses some of the power issues around making change happen, highlights the importance of a 'felt need' for change in the organization, and emphasizes the need to communicate the vision and keep communication levels extremely high throughout the process (see box).

KOTTER'S EIGHT-STEP MODEL

1. **Establish a sense of urgency.** Discussing today's competitive realities, looking at potential future scenarios. Increasing the 'felt-need' for change.

2. **Form a powerful guiding coalition.** Assembling a powerful group of people who can work well together.

3. **Create a vision.** Building a vision to guide the change effort together with strategies for achieving this.

4. **Communicate the vision.** Kotter emphasizes the need to communicate at least 10 times the amount you expect to have to communicate. The vision and accompanying strategies and new behaviours needs to be communicated in a variety of different ways.

   The guiding coalition should be the first to role model new behaviours.

5. **Empower others to act on the vision.** This step includes getting rid of obstacles to change such as unhelpful structures or systems. Allow people to experiment.

6. **Plan for and create short-term wins.** Look for and advertise short-term visible improvements. Plan these in and reward people publicly for improvements.

7. **Consolidate improvements and produce still more change.** Promote and reward those able to promote and work towards the vision. Energize the process of change with new projects, resources, change agents.

8. **Institutionalize new approaches.** Ensure that everyone understands that the new behaviours lead to corporate success.

Source: Kotter (1995)

Our view

This eight-step model is one that appeals to many managers with whom we have worked. However, what it appears to encourage is an early burst of energy, followed by delegation and distance. The eight steps do not really emphasize the need for managers to follow through with as much energy on Step 7 and Step 8 as was necessary at the start. Kotter peaks early, using forceful concepts such as 'urgency' and 'power' and 'vision'. Then after Step 5, words like 'plan', 'consolidate' and 'institutionalize' seem to imply a rather straightforward process that can be managed by others lower down the hierarchy. In our experience the change process is challenging and exciting and difficult all the way through.

When we work as change consultants, we use our own model of organizational change (see Figure 3.3), which is based on our experiences of change, but has close parallels with Kotter's eight steps. We prefer to model the change process as a continuous cycle rather than as a linear progression, and in our consultancy work we emphasize the importance of management attention through all phases of the process.

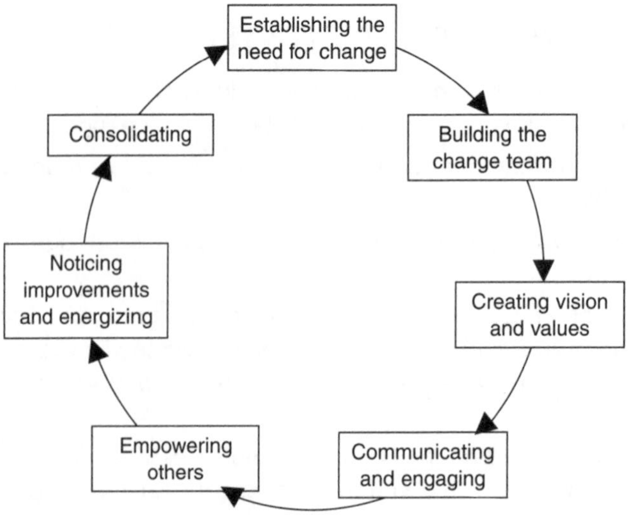

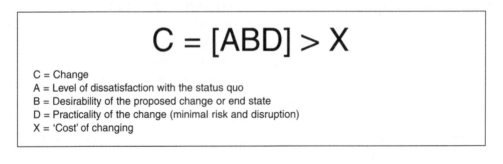

Figure 3.3   Cycle of change
Source: Cameron Change Consultancy Ltd

STOP AND THINK!

Q 3.4   Reflect on an organizational change in which you were involved. How much planning was done at the start? What contribution did this make to the success or otherwise of the change?

Beckhard and Harris, change formula: *organism*

Beckhard and Harris (1987) developed their change formula from some original work by Gelicher. The change formula is a concise way of capturing the process of change, and identifying the factors that need to be strongly in place for change to happen.

$$C = [ABD] > X$$

C = Change
A = Level of dissatisfaction with the status quo
B = Desirability of the proposed change or end state
D = Practicality of the change (minimal risk and disruption)
X = 'Cost' of changing

Figure 3.4   Beckhard's formula

Beckhard and Harris say:

> Factors A, B, and D must outweigh the perceived costs [X] for the change to occur. If any person or group whose commitment is needed is not sufficiently dissatisfied with the present state of affairs [A], eager to achieve the proposed end state [B] and convinced of the feasibility of the change [D], then the cost [X] of changing is too high, and that person will resist the change.
>
> ... resistance is normal and to be expected in any change effort. Resistance to change takes many forms; change managers need to analyze the type of resistance in order to work with it, reduce it, and secure the need for commitment from the resistant party.

The formula is sometimes written $(A \times B \times D) > X$. This adds something useful to the original formula. The multiplication implies that if any one factor is zero or near zero, the product will also be zero or near zero and the resistance to change will not be overcome. This means that if the vision is not clear, or dissatisfaction with the current state is not felt, or the plan is obscure, the likelihood of change is severely reduced. These factors (A, B, D) do not compensate for each other if one is low. All factors need to have weight.

This model comes from the organism metaphor of organizations, although it has been adopted by those working with a planned change approach to target management effort. Beckhard and Harris emphasized the need to design interventions that allow these three factors to surface in the organization.

Our view

This change formula is deceptively simple but extremely useful. It can be brought into play at any point in a change process to analyse how things are going. When the formula is shared with all parties involved in the change, it helps to illuminate what various parties need to do to make progress. This can highlight several of the following problem areas:

- Staff are not experiencing dissatisfaction with the status quo.

- The proposed end state has not been clearly communicated to key people.

- The proposed end state is not desirable to the change implementers.

- The tasks being given to those implementing the change are too complicated, or ill-defined.

We have noticed that depending on the metaphor in use, distinct differences in approach result from using this formula as a starting point. For instance, one public sector organization successfully used this formula to inform a highly consultative approach to organizational change. The vision was built and shared at a large-scale event involving hundreds of people. Dissatisfaction was captured using an employee survey that was fed back to everyone in the organization, and discussed at team meetings. Teams were asked to work locally on using the employee feedback and commonly created vision to define their own first steps.

In contrast, a FTSE 100 company based in the UK, used the formula as a basis for boosting its change management capability via a highly rated change management programme. Gaps in skills were defined and training workshops were run for the key managers in every significant project team around the company. Three areas of improvement were targeted:

- **Vision:** project managers were encouraged to build and communicate clearer, more compelling project goals.

- **Dissatisfaction:** this was translated into two elements, clear rationale and a felt sense of urgency. Project managers were encouraged to improve their ability to communicate a clear rationale for making changes. They were also advised to set clear deadlines and stick to them, and to visibly resource important initiatives, to increase the felt need for change.

- **Practical first steps:** project managers were advised to define their plans for change early in the process and to communicate these in a variety of ways, to improve the level of buy-in from implementers and stakeholders.

Nadler and Tushman, congruence model: *political, organism*

Nadler and Tushman's congruence model takes a different approach to looking at the factors influencing the success of the change process (Nadler and Tushman, 1997). This model aims to help us understand the dynamics of what happens in an organization when we try to change it.

This model is based on the belief that organizations can be viewed as sets of inter-acting sub-systems that scan and sense changes in the external environment. This model sits firmly in the open systems school of thought, which uses the organism metaphor to understand organizational behaviour. However, the political backdrop is not ignored; it appears as one of the sub-systems (informal organization – see below).

This model views the organization as a system that draws inputs from both internal and external sources (strategy, resources, environment) and transforms them into outputs (activities, behaviour and performance of the system at three levels: individual, group and total). The heart of the model is the opportunity it offers to analyse the transformation process in a way that does not give prescriptive answers, but instead stimulates thoughts on what needs to happen in a specific organizational context. David Nadler writes, 'it's important to view the congruence model as a tool for organizing your thinking ... rather than as a rigid template to dissect, classify and compartmentalize what you observe. It's a way of making sense out of a constantly changing kaleidoscope of information and impressions.'

The model draws on the sociotechnical view of organizations that looks at managerial, strategic, technical and social aspects of organizations, emphasizing the assumption that everything relies on everything else. This means that the different elements of the total system have to be aligned to achieve high performance as a whole system. Therefore the higher the congruence the higher the performance.

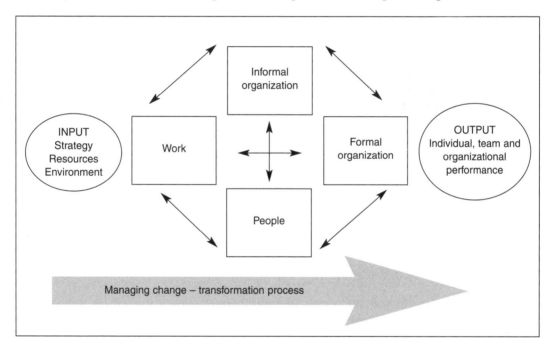

Figure 3.5 Nadler and Tushman's congruence model
Source: Nadler and Tushman (1997). Copyright © Oxford University Press.
Use by permission of Oxford University Press, Inc.

In this model of the transformation process, the organization is composed of four components, or sub-systems, which are all dependent on each other. These are:

- **The work.** This is the actual day-to-day activities carried out by individuals. Process design, pressures on the individual and available rewards must all be considered under this element.

- **The people.** This is about the skills and characteristics of the people who work in an organization. What are their expectations, what are their backgrounds?

- **The formal organization.** This refers to the structure, systems and policies in place. How are things formally organized?

- **The informal organization.** This consists of all the unplanned, unwritten activities that emerge over time such as power, influence, values and norms.

This model proposes that effective management of change means attending to all four components, not just one or two components. Imagine tugging only one part of

a child's mobile. The whole mobile wobbles and oscillates for a bit, but eventually all the different components settle down to where they were originally. So it is with organizations. They easily revert to the original mode of operation unless you attend to all four components.

For example, if you change one component, such as the type of work done in an organization, you need to attend to the other three components too. The following questions pinpoint the other three components that may need to be aligned:

- How does the work now align with individual skills? (The people.)

- How does a change in the task line up with the way work is organized right now? (The formal organization.)

- What informal activities and areas of influence could be affected by this change in the task? (The informal organization.)

If alignment work is not done, then organizational 'homeostasis' (see above) will result in a return to the old equilibrium and change will fizzle out. The fizzling out results from forces that arise in the system as a direct result of lack of congruence. When a lack of congruence occurs, energy builds in the system in the form of resistance, control and power:

- Resistance comes from a fear of the unknown or a need for things to remain stable. A change imposed from the outside can be unsettling for individuals. It decreases their sense of independence. Resistance can be reduced through participation in future plans, and by increasing the anxiety about doing nothing (increasing the felt need for change).

- Control issues result from normal structures and processes being in flux. The change process may therefore need to be managed in a different way by for instance employing a transition manager.

- Power problems arise when there is a threat that power might be taken away from any currently powerful group or individual. This effect can be reduced through building a powerful coalition to take the change forward (see Kotter above).

Our view

The Nadler and Tushman model is useful because it provides a memorable checklist for those involved in making change happen. We have also noticed that this model is particularly good for pointing out in retrospect why changes did not work, which although psychologically satisfying is not always a productive exercise. It is important to note that this model is problem-focused rather than solution-focused, and lacks any reference to the powerful effects of a guiding vision, or to the need for setting and achieving goals.

We have found that the McKinsey seven 'S' model is a more rounded starting point for those facing organizational change. This model of organizations uses the same metaphor, representing the organization as a set of interconnected and inter-dependent sub-systems. Again, this model acts as a good checklist for those setting out to make organizational change, laying out which parts of the system need to adapt, and the knock-on effects of these changes in other parts of the system.

The seven 'S' categories are:

- Staff: important categories of people.

- Skills: distinctive capabilities of key people.

- Systems: routine processes.

- Style: management style and culture.

- Shared values: guiding principles.

- Strategy: organizational goals and plan, use of resources.

- Structure: the organization chart.

See _Managing on the Edge_ by Richard Pascale (1990) for full definitions of the seven S framework.

William Bridges, managing the transition: *machine, organism, flux and transformation*

Bridges (1991) makes a clear distinction between planned change and transition. He labels transition as the more complex of the two, and focuses on enhancing our understanding of what goes on during transition and of how we can manage this process more effectively. In this way, he manages to separate the mechanistic functional changes from the natural human process of becoming emotionally aware of change and adapting to the new way of things.

Bridges says:

> Transition is about letting go of the past and taking up new behaviours or ways of thinking. Planned change is about physically moving office, or installing new equipment, or restructuring. Transition lags behind planned change because it is more complex and harder to achieve. Change is situational and can be planned, whereas transition is psychological and less easy to manage.

Bridges' ideas on transition lead to a deeper understanding of what is going on when an organizational change takes place. While focusing on the importance of understanding what is going on emotionally at each stage in the change process, Bridges also provides a list of useful activities to be attended to during each phase (see Chapter 4 on Leading change).

Transition consists of three phases: ending, neutral zone and new beginning.

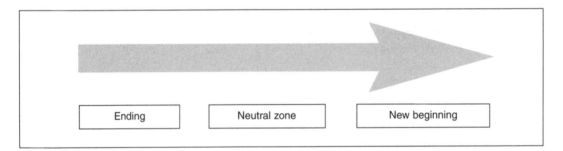

Figure 3.6 Bridges: endings and beginnings

Ending

Before you can begin something new, you have to end what used to be. You need to identify who is losing what, expect a reaction and acknowledge the losses openly. Repeat information about what is changing – it will take time to sink in. Mark the endings.

Neutral zone

In the neutral zone, people feel disoriented. Motivation falls and anxiety rises. Consensus may break down as attitudes become polarized. It can also be quite a creative time. The manager's job is to ensure that people recognize the neutral zone and treat it as part of the process. Temporary structures may be needed – possibly task forces and smaller teams. The manager needs to find a way of taking the pulse of the organization on a regular basis.

William Bridges suggested that we could learn from Moses and his time in the wilderness to really gain an understanding of how to manage people during the neutral zone.

MOSES AND THE NEUTRAL ZONE

- **Magnify the plagues.** Increase the felt need for change.
- **Mark the ending.** Make sure people are not hanging on to too much of the past.
- **Deal with the murmuring.** Don't ignore people when they complain. It might be significant.
- **Give people access to the decision makers.** Two-way communication with the top is vital.
- **Capitalize on the creative opportunity provided by the wilderness.** The neutral zone provides a difference that allows for creative thinking and acting.
- **Resist the urge to rush ahead.** You can slow things down a little.
- **Understand the neutral zone leadership is special.** This is not a normal time. Normal rules do not apply.

Source: Bridges and Mitchell (2002)

New beginning

Beginnings should be nurtured carefully. They cannot be planned and predicted, but they can be encouraged, supported and reinforced. Bridges suggests that people need four key elements to help them make a new beginning:

- the _purpose_ behind the change;
- a _picture_ of how this new organization will look and feel;
- a step by step _plan_ to get there;
- a _part to play_ in the outcome.

The beginning is reached when people feel they can make the emotional commitment to doing something in a new way. Bridges makes the point that the neutral zone is longer and the endings are more protracted for those further down the management hierarchy. This can lead to impatience from managers who have emotionally stepped into a new beginning, while their people seem to lag behind, seemingly stuck in an ending (see box).

IMPATIENT FOR ENDINGS?

As part of the management team, I knew about the merger very early, so by the time we announced it to the rest of the company, we were ready to fly with the task ahead.

What was surprising, and annoying, was the slow speed with which everyone else caught up. My direct reports were asking detailed questions about their job specifications and exactly how it was all going to work when we had fully merged. Of course I couldn't answer any of these questions. I was really irritated by this.

The CEO had to have a long, intensive heart to heart with the whole team explaining what was going on and how much we knew about the future state of the organization before we could really get moving.

Our view

This phased model is particularly useful when organizations are faced with inevitable changes such as closure of a site, redundancy, acquisition or merger. The endings and new beginnings are real tangible events in these situations, and the neutral zone important, though uncomfortable. It is more difficult to use the model for anticipatory change or home-grown change where the endings and beginning are more fluid, and therefore harder to discern.

We use this model when working with organizations embarking on mergers, acquisitions and significant partnership agreements. In particular, the model encourages everyone involved to get a sense of where they are in the process of transition. The image of the trapeze artist is often appreciated as it creates the feeling of leaping into the unknown, and trusting in a future that cannot be grasped fully. This is a scary process.

The other important message which Bridges communicates well is that those close to the changes (managers and team leaders) may experience a difficulty when they have reached a new beginning and their people are still working on an ending. This is one of the great frustrations of this type of change process, and we counsel managers to:

● recognize what is happening;

- assertively tell staff what will happen while acknowledging their feelings;

- be prepared to answer questions about the future again and again and again;

- say you don't know, if you don't know;

- expect the neutral zone to last a while and give it a positive name such as 'setting our sights' or 'moving in' or 'getting to know you'.

Carnall, change management model: _political, organism_

Colin Carnall (1990) has produced a useful model that brings together a number of perspectives on change. He says that the effective management of change depends on the level of management skill in the following areas:

- managing transitions effectively;

- dealing with organizational cultures;

- managing organizational politics.

A manager who is skilled in _managing transitions_ is able to help people to learn as they change, and create an atmosphere of openness and risk-taking.

A manager who _deals with organizational cultures_ examines the current organizational culture and starts to develop what Carnall calls 'a more adaptable culture'. This means for example developing better information flow, more openness, and greater local autonomy.

A manager who is able to _manage organizational politics_ can understand and recognize different factions and different agendas. He or she develops skills in utilizing and recognizing various political tactics such as building coalitions, using outside experts and controlling the agenda.

Carnall (see Figure 3.7) makes the point that 'only by synthesising the management of transition, dealing with organisational cultures and handling organisational politics constructively, can we create the environment in which creativity, risk-taking and the rebuilding of self-esteem and performance can be achieved'.

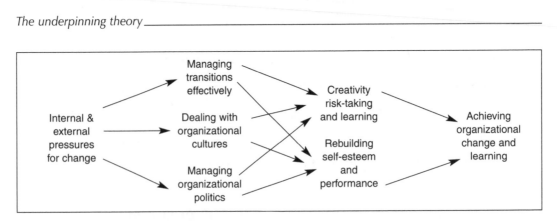

Figure 3.7 Carnall: managing transitions

Source: Carnall (1990). Printed with permission of Pearson Education Ltd.

Our view

Carnall's model obviously focuses on the role of the manager during a change process, rather than illuminating the process of change. It provides a useful checklist for management attention, and has strong parallels with William Bridges' ideas of endings, transitions and beginnings.

STOP AND THINK!

Q 3.5 Compare the Nadler and Tushman congruence model with William Bridges' ideas on managing transitions. How are these ideas the same? How are they different?

Senge *et al*: systemic model: *political, organism, flux and transformation*

If you are interested in sustainable change, then the ideas and concepts in Senge *et al* (1999) will be of interest to you. This excellent book, *The Dance of Change*, seeks to help 'those who care deeply about building new types of organisations' to understand the challenges ahead.

Senge *et al* observe that many change initiatives fail to achieve hoped for results. They reflect on why this might be so, commenting, 'To understand why sustaining significant change is so elusive, we need to think less like managers and more like biologists.' Senge *et al* talk about the myriad of 'balancing processes' or forces of homeostasis which act to preserve the status quo in any organization.

HOMEOSTASIS IN ACTION

We wanted to move to a matrix structure for managing projects. There was significant investment of time and effort in this initiative as we anticipated payoff in terms of utilization of staff and ability to meet project deadlines. This approach would allow staff to be freed up when they were not fully utilized, so that they could work on a variety of projects.

Consultants worked with us to design the new structure. Job specs were rewritten. People understood their new roles. For a couple for months, it seemed to be working. But after four months, we discovered that the project managers were just carrying on working in the old way, as if they still owned the technical staff. They would even lie about utilization, just to stop other project managers from getting hold of their people.

I don't think we have moved on very much at all.

Business Unit Manager, Research Projects Department

Senge *et al* say:

> Most serious change initiatives eventually come up against issues embedded in our prevailing system of management. These include managers' commitment to change as long as it doesn't affect them; 'undiscussable' topics that feel risky to talk about; and the ingrained habit of attacking symptoms and ignoring deeper systemic causes of problems.

Their guidelines are:

- Start small.
- Grow steadily.
- Don't plan the whole thing.
- Expect challenges – it will not go smoothly!

Senge *et al* use the principles of environmental systems to illustrate how organizations operate and to enhance our understanding of what forces are at play. Senge says in his book, *The Fifth Discipline* (Senge 1993):

> Business and other human endeavours are also systems. They too are bound by invisible fabrics of interrelated actions, which often take years to fully play out their effects on each other. Since we are part of that lacework ourselves, it's doubly hard to see the whole patterns of change. Instead we tend to focus on snapshots of isolated parts of the systems, and wonder why our deepest problems never seem to get solved.

The approach taken by Senge *et al* is noticeably different from much of the other work on change, which focuses on the early stages such as creating a vision, planning, finding energy to move forward and deciding on first steps. They look at the longer-term issues of sustaining and renewing organizational change. They examine the challenges of first initiating, second sustaining and third redesigning and rethinking change. The book does not give formulaic solutions, or 'how to' approaches, but rather gives ideas and suggestions for dealing with the balancing forces of equilibrium in organizational systems (resistance).

What are the balancing forces that those involved in change need to look out for? Senge *et al* say that the key challenges of initiating change are the balancing forces that arise when any group of people starts to do things differently:

- 'We don't have time for this stuff!' People working on change initiatives will need extra time outside of the day to day to devote to change efforts, otherwise there will be push back.

- 'We have no help!' There will be new skills and mindsets to develop. People will need coaching and support to develop new capabilities.

- 'This stuff isn't relevant!' Unless people are convinced of the need for effort to be invested, it will not happen.

- 'They're not walking the talk!' People look for reinforcement of the new values or new behaviours from management. If this is not in place, there will be resistance to progress.

They go on to say that the challenges of sustaining change come to the fore when the pilot group (those who start the change) becomes successful and the change begins to touch the rest of the organization:

- 'This stuff is ____!' This challenge concerns the discomfort felt by individuals when they feel exposed or fearful about changes. This may be expressed in a number of different ways such as ,'This stuff is taking our eye off the ball', or 'This stuff is more trouble that it's worth.'

- 'This stuff isn't working!' People outside the pilot group, and some of those within the pilot group, may be impatient for positive results. Traditional ways of measuring success do not always apply, and may end up giving a skewed view of progress.

- 'We have the right way!'/'They don't understand us!' The pilot group members become evangelists for the change, setting up a reaction from the 'outsiders'.

The challenges of redesigning and rethinking change appear when the change achieves some visible measure of success and starts to impact on ingrained organizational habits:

- 'Who's in charge of this stuff?' This challenge is about the conflicts that can arise between successful pilot groups, who start to want to do more, and those who see themselves as the governing body of the organization.

- 'We keep reinventing the wheel!' The challenge of spreading knowledge of new ideas and processes around the organization is a tough one. People who are distant from the changes may not receive good quality information about what is going on.

- 'Where are we going and what are we here for?' Senge says, 'engaging people around deep questions of purpose and strategy is fraught with challenges because it opens the door to a traditionally closed inner sanctum of top management'.

Our view

We like the ideas of Senge _et al_ very much. They are thought-provoking and highly perceptive. If we can persuade clients to read the book, we will. However, in the current climate of time pressure and the need for fast results, these ideas are often a bitter pill for managers struggling to make change happen despite massive odds.

Whenever possible we encourage clients to be realistic in their quest for change, and to notice and protect areas where examples of the right sort of behaviours already exist. The messages we carry with us resulting from Senge _et al_'s thoughts are:

- Consider running a pilot for any large-scale organizational change.

- Keep your change process goals realistic, especially when it comes to timescales and securing resources.

- Understand your role in staying close to change efforts beyond the kick-off.

- Recognize and reward activities that are already going the right way.

- Be as open as you can about the purpose and mission of your enterprise.

There are no standard 'one size fits all' answers in the book, but plenty of thought-provoking ideas and suggestions, and a thoroughly inspirational reframing of traditional ways of looking at change. However, those interested in rapid large-scale organizational change are unlikely to find any reassurance or support in Senge _et al_'s book. The advice is, start small.

STOP AND THINK!

Q 3.6 Reflect on an organizational change in which you were involved that failed to achieve hoped-for results. What were the balancing forces that acted against the change? Use Senge *et al*'s ideas to prompt your thinking.

Stacey and Shaw, complex responsive processes: *political, flux and transformation*

There is yet another school of thought represented by people such as Ralph Stacey (2001) and Patricia Shaw (2002). These writers use the metaphor of flux and transformation to view organizations. The implications of this mode of thinking for those interested in managing and enabling change are significant:

- Change, or a new order of things, will emerge naturally from clean communication, conflict and tension (not too much).

- As a manager, you are not outside of the system, controlling it, or planning to alter it, you are part of the whole environment.

In Patricia Shaw's book *Changing Conversations in Organizations*, rather than address the traditional questions of 'How do we manage change?' she addresses the question, 'How do we participate in the ways things change over time?' This writing deals bravely with the paradox that 'our interaction, no matter how considered or passionate, is always evolving in ways that we cannot control or predict in the longer term, no matter how sophisticated our planning tools'.

Our view

This is disturbing stuff, and a paradox that sets up some anxiety in managers and consultants who are disquieted by the suggestion that our intellectual strivings to collectively diagnose problems and design futures may be missing the point. Shaw says, 'I want to help us appreciate ourselves as fellow improvisers in ensemble work, constantly constructing the future and our part in it'. Stacey says of traditional views of organizations as systems, 'This is not to say that systems thinking has no use at all. It clearly does if one is trying to understand, and even more, trying to design interactions of a repetitive kind to achieve kinds of performance that are known in advance'.

Ralph Stacey and Patricia Shaw have both written about complexity and change. Managers, and particularly consultants, often find this difficult reading because on first viewing it appears to take away the rational powers we have traditionally endowed upon our managers, change agents and consultants. Patricia Shaw says of the traditional view of the process consultant:

> I would say that [the] ideal of the reflective practitioner [who can surface subconscious needs so that groups of people can consciously create a directed form of change] is the one that mostly continues to grip our imaginations and shape our aspirations to be effective and competent individual practitioners engaged in lifelong learning. Instead, I have been asking what happens when spontaneity, unpredictability and our capacity to be surprised by ourselves are not explained away but kept at the very heart [of our work].

In contrast, those working in hugely complex environments such as the health sector or government have told us that they find the ideas in this area to be a tremendous relief. The notion that change cannot be managed reflects their own experiences of trying to manage change; the overwhelming feeling they have of constantly trying to push heavy weights uphill.

But how can managers and consultants use these ideas in real situations? We have distilled some groundrules for those working with complex change processes, although the literature we have researched studiously avoids any type of prescription for action.

In complex change, the leader's role is to:

- Decide what business the organization is in, and stretch people's thinking on how to get there.

- Ensure that there is a high level of connectivity between different parts of the organization, encouraging feedback, optimizing information flow, enabling learning.

- Focus people's attention on important differences: between current and desired performance, between style of working, between past and present results.

SUMMARY AND CONCLUSIONS

- It is useful to understand our own assumptions about managing change, in order to challenge them and examine the possibilities offered by different assumptions. It is useful to compare our own assumptions with the assumptions of others with whom we work. This increased understanding can often reduce frustration.

- Gareth's Morgan's work on organizational metaphors provides a useful way of looking at the range of assumptions that exist about how organizations work.

- The four most commonly used organizational metaphors are:
  - the machine metaphor;
  - the political metaphor;
  - the organism metaphor;
  - the flux and transformation metaphor.

- The machine metaphor is deeply ingrained in our ideas about how organizations run, so tends to inform many of the well-known approaches to organizational change, particularly project management, and planning oriented approaches.

- Models of organizations as open, interconnected, interdependent sub-systems sit within the organism metaphor. This model is very prevalent in the human resource world, as it underpins much of the thinking that drove the creation of the HR function in organizations. The organism metaphor views change as a process of adapting to changes in the environment. The focus is on designing interventions to decrease resistance to change, and increase the forces for change.

- The political map of organizational life is recognized by many of the key writers on organizational change as highly significant.

- The metaphor of flux and transformation appears to model the true complexity of how change really happens. If we use this lens to view organizational life it does not lead to neat formulae, or concise how-to approaches. There is less certainty to inform our actions. This can be on the one hand a great relief, and on the other hand quite frustrating.

- There are many approaches to managing and understanding change to choose from, none of which appears to tell the whole story, most of which are convincing up to a point. See Table 3.3 for a summary of our conclusions for each model.

- To be an effective manager or consultant we need to be able flexibly to select appropriate models and approaches for particular situations. See the illustrations of different approaches in Part Two.

Table 3.3 Our conclusions about each model of change

Model	Conclusions
Lewin, three-step model	Lewin's ideas are valuable when analysing the change process at the start of an initiative. His force-field analysis and current state/end state discussions are extremely useful tools. However, the model loses its worth when it is confused with the mechanistic approach, and the three steps become 'plan, implement, review'.
Bullock and Batten, planned change	The planned change approach is good for tackling isolated, less complex issues. It is not good when used to over-simplify organizational changes, as it ignores resistance and overlooks interdependencies between business units or sub-systems.
Kotter, eight steps	Kotter's eight steps are an excellent starting point for those interested in making large or small-scale organizational change. The model places most emphasis on getting the early steps right: building coalition and setting the vision rather than later steps of empowerment and consolidation. Change is seen as linear rather than cyclical, which implies that a pre-designed aim can be reached rather than iterated towards.
Beckhard and Harris, change formula	The change formula is simple but highly effective. It can be used at any point in the change process to analyse what is going on. It is useful for sharing with the whole team to illuminate barriers to change.
Nadler and Tushman, congruence model	The congruence model provides a memorable checklist for the change process, although we think the seven S model gives a more rounded approach to the same problem of examining interdependent organizational sub-systems. Both are also useful for doing a post-change analysis of what went wrong! Both encourage a problem focus rather than enabling a vision-setting process.
William Bridges, managing the transition	Bridge's model of endings, neutral zone and beginnings is good for tackling inevitable changes such as redundancy, merger or acquisition. It is less good for understanding change grown from within, where endings and beginnings are less distinct.
Carnall, change management model	Carnall's model combines a number of key elements of organizational change together in a neat process. Useful checklist.

Table 3.3   *continued*

Model	Conclusions
Senge, systemic model	Senge challenges the notion of top-down, large-scale organizational change. He provides a hefty dose of realism for those facing organizational change: start small, grow steadily, don't plan the whole thing. However, this advice is hard to follow in today's climate of fast pace, quick results and maximum effectiveness.
Stacey and Shaw, complex responsive processes	The complex responsive process school of thought is new, exciting and challenging; however it is not for the faint-hearted. There are no easy solutions (if any at all), the leader's role is hard to distinguish and the literature on the subject tends to be almost completely non-prescriptive.

STOP AND THINK!

Q 3.7   Which model of organizational change would help you to move forward with each of the following changes:

- Combining two well-respected universities to form one excellent seat of learning.

- Turning Boston Philharmonic Orchestra into Boston Improvisational Jazz Band.

- Evolving a group of mature MBA students into a networked organization of management consultants.

Q 3.8   A fast food organization introduced a set of values recently which were well communicated and enthusiastically welcomed. The senior management team publicly endorsed the values and said, 'This is where we want to be in 12 months' time so that we are ready for industry consolidation. You will all be measured on achieving these values in your day to day work.'

   The values were put together by a consultancy, which put a great deal of effort into interviewing a broad range of people in the organization. People at all levels like the look of the values, but the situation three months later is that activity and conversations around the values are diminishing. A lot of people are saying 'We are doing this already.' There is still some enthusiasm, but people are now getting scared that they will fall short of the values somehow, and are starting to resent them.

   What needs to happen now?

Q 3.9   If Stacey and Shaw have 'got it right' with their ideas about how change emerges naturally, does that make books such as this one redundant? Answers on a postcard!

4

Leading change

INTRODUCTION

In this chapter we look at the leader's role in the change process. The objectives of the chapter are to:

- enable leaders of change to explore the different roles they, and their colleagues need to play in a change process;
- identify how leaders of change can adapt their style and focus to the different phases of the change process;
- emphasize the importance of self-knowledge and inner resources in any leadership role.

The chapter is divided into six sections:

- visionary leadership;
- roles that leaders play;
- leadership styles and skills;
- different leadership for different phases of change;
- the importance of self-knowledge and inner resources;
- summary and conclusions.

It is important to first make the point that good leadership is well-rounded leadership. We believe that all four metaphors of organizations give rise to useful notions of leadership. Leaders go wrong when they become stuck in one metaphor, or in one way of doing things, and therefore appear one-dimensional in their range of styles and approaches.

To begin, we link leadership to the ideas presented in Chapter 3 on organizational change, by looking at the type of leadership that follows from approaching organizational change using each of the four key metaphors (see Table 4.1):

- the machine metaphor;

- the political system metaphor;

- the organism metaphor;

- The flux and transformation metaphor.

Table 4.1 illustrates that the use of each metaphor brings both advantages and disadvantages for those wishing to be successful leaders of change.

Table 4.1   Leadership linked to organizational metaphors

Metaphor	Nature of change	Leader's role	Type of leadership required	Typical pitfalls for the leader
Machine	The designed end state can be worked towards. Resistance must be managed. Change needs to be planned and controlled.	Chief designer and implementer of the changes	Project management. Goal setting. Monitoring and controlling.	Micro-management by leader means activity focuses on measuring, rather than experimenting or taking risks
Political system	Changes must be supported by a powerful person. Change needs a powerful coalition behind it. Winners and losers are important.	Politician – powerful speaker and behind the scenes negotiator	Visionary. Building a powerful coalition. Connecting agendas.	Change leaders are seen as Machiavellian manipulators. Leaders cannot be trusted, so people comply rather than commit. People do the minimum. Leaders begin to follow their own agenda (cover their backs), rather than some higher purpose.

Organism	Change is adaptive. Individuals and groups need to be psychologically aware of the 'felt need' for change. End state can be defined and worked towards.	Coach, counsellor and consultant, holding up the mirror	Coaching and supporting	The metaphor becomes an ideology. The change process becomes self-serving and achieves very little. There is a focus on reacting rather than initiating. Change happens, but too little too late.
Flux and trans-formation	Change cannot be managed, it emerges. Managers are part of the system, not outside the system. Conflict is useful. Managers enable good connections between people.	Facilitator of emergent change	Getting the governing principles right. Enabling connectivity. Amplifying issues.	Leaders and others involved become confused and frustrated. The change effort becomes vague and directionless. There is no sense of progress to motivate future effort.

The machine metaphor draws attention to clear goals and the need for structure, but overuse of this metaphor results in micromanagement of outcomes and too little risk taking. The political system metaphor adds the harsh reality of organizational life, and reminds us of the necessity for involving influential people when change is desired, but overuse can be seen as manipulation. The organism metaphor highlights the need for people to be involved, and to feel the need for change, but runs the risk of moving too slowly and too late. Finally the flux and transformation model is useful as a reminder that organizations and their people cannot be wholly controlled unless we rule by fear! Leaders must encourage discussion of conflicts and tensions to enable change to emerge, while avoiding the trap of being too vague and lacking direction.

We believe that successful change leadership is achieved by combining aspects of all four metaphors. This is evidenced by the models and approaches introduced in Chapter 3, which combine different metaphors to some degree (see Table 3.2).

COMBINING THE METAPHORS: REFLECTIVE COACHING SESSION

Once I realized that my boss was using a completely different organizational metaphor from myself, I began to see how we were clashing in our discussions about how to run projects and how to improve processes.

I prefer the machine metaphor. I like things to be pretty clear. In my area we have a well-defined structure with clear roles and objectives set for each person. The team runs like a well-oiled machine, with me in the engine room pulling levers and thinking about plans and processes.

On the other hand, my boss prefers a more fluid style of working. Objectives are flexible and revised daily, and the hierarchy means very little to him. If someone shows initiative and promise, he will go directly to that person and have a quite intense conversation to convey the importance of a particular initiative. It used to drive me crazy. I couldn't keep control.

One day we had a chat about this using metaphor to discuss our differences. It was most illuminating, and we started to see the pros and cons of each approach. As a result I agreed to incorporate more flexibility in certain projects, and he agreed to stick with the plan rather than review and change other, more stable processes. We still clash from time to time, but it doesn't cause quite so much irritation!

Global Services Manager, Oil Company – on use of metaphor to enhance understanding
of other people's viewpoints

Table 4.1 is also useful because it reveals a wide range of styles and skills required of leaders, depending on the metaphor in use:

- goal setting;

- monitoring and controlling;

- coaching and supporting;

- building vision;

- communicating vision;

- building coalitions;

- networking;

- negotiating;

- facilitating;

- dealing with conflict.

The difficulty with a list of skills this long is that is seems unattainable. In this chapter we try to help leaders to find a way through the various requirements of a leader to pinpoint the most important roles, skills, styles and areas of focus needed to make change happen.

VISIONARY LEADERSHIP

The first basic ingredient of leadership is a guiding vision. The leader has a clear idea of what he wants to do – professionally and personally – and the strength to persist in the face of setbacks, even failures. Unless you know where you are going, and why, you cannot possibly get there.

Warren Bennis (1994)

Visionary leadership has become something of a holy grail. It seems to be a rare commodity which is greatly sought after. Our recent research (see box) indicates that today's business leaders place considerable value on visionary leadership as a tool for organizational change. But is visionary leadership really the answer?

In our change leadership sessions with private sector senior and middle managers in the UK we ask people to name significant leaders of change. The top four names mentioned over the period 1997–2002 were:

- Winston Churchill.
- Margaret Thatcher.
- Nelson Mandela.
- Adolf Hitler.

The top five characteristics that emerged through a typical discussion of these significant leaders were:

- Clear vision.
- Determination.
- Great speaker, great presence.
- Tough when needed.
- Able to stand alone.

Cameron Change Consultancy data 2002

125

Here we explore the views of the supporters of visionary leadership, and those who make the case against it.

Bennis on the characteristics of visionary leaders

Warren Bennis identified three basic ingredients of leadership:

- a guiding vision;

- passion;

- integrity.

He also developed a useful comparison of the differences between management and leadership (see Table 4.2) which unpacks some of the different qualities of a visionary leader.

Table 4.2 Managers and leaders

A manager	A leader
Administers	Innovates
Is a copy	Is an original
Maintains	Develops
Focuses on systems and structure	Focuses on people
Relies on control	Inspires trust
Has a short-range view	Has a long-range perspective
Asks how and when	Asks why
Has his eye on the bottom line	Has his eye on the horizon
Imitates	Originates
Accepts the status quo	Challenges the status quo
Classic good soldier	His own person
Does things right	Does the right thing

Source: Bennis (1994)

This comparison exercise separates management from leadership in a very clear way. This is useful for those wishing to take on more of a leadership role, although it is sometimes interpreted as slightly downplaying the important role of a good manager in organizational life. Most managers have to do both roles.

Kotter on what leaders really do

Kotter (1996) echoes the ideas of Bennis. He says, 'we have raised a generation of very talented people to be managers, not leader/managers, and vision is not a component of effective management. The management equivalent to vision creation is planning.' He says that leaders are different from managers. 'They don't make plans; they don't solve problems; they don't even organise people. What leaders really do is prepare organizations for change and help them cope as they struggle through it.' He identifies three areas of focus for leaders and contrasts these with the typical focus of a manager:

- setting direction versus planning and budgeting;

- aligning people versus organizing and staffing;

- motivating people versus controlling and problem solving.

VISIONARY LEADERSHIP

We go to liberate, not to conquer.
We will not fly our flags in their country.
We are entering Iraq to free a people and the only flag which will be flown in that ancient land is their own.
Show respect for them.

There are some who are alive at this moment who will not be alive shortly.
Those who do not wish to go on that journey, we will not send.
As for the others, I expect you to rock their world.
Wipe them out if that is what they choose.
But if you are ferocious in battle remember to be magnanimous in victory.
Iraq is steeped in history.
It is the site of the Garden of Eden, of the Great Flood and the birthplace of Abraham.
Tread lightly there.

You will see things that no man could pay to see
– and you will have to go a long way to find a more decent, generous and upright people than the Iraqis.
You will be embarrassed by their hospitality even though they have nothing.

Don't treat them as refugees for they are in their own country.
Their children will be poor, in years to come they will know that the light of liberation in their lives was brought by you.

Extract from speech widely hailed in the UK press as visionary. It was given by Lieutenant Colonel Tim Collins to around 800 men of the battlegroup of the 1st Battalion of the Royal Irish Regiment, at their Fort Blair Mayne camp in the Kuwaiti desert about 20 miles from the Iraqi border on Wednesday 19 March 2003. His intention was to prepare the men for the battle that lay ahead. Many of the men were young and the support from people back in the UK was patchy.

I HAVE A DREAM

I have a dream that one day this nation will rise up and live out the true meaning of its creed: 'We hold these truths to be self-evident: that all men are created equal.' I have a dream that one day on the red hills of Georgia the sons of former slaves and the sons of former slave owners will be able to sit down together at the table of brotherhood.

I have a dream that one day even the state of Mississippi, a state sweltering with the heat of injustice, sweltering with the heat of oppression, will be transformed into an oasis of freedom and justice.

I have a dream that my four little children will one day live in a nation where they will not be judged by the color of their skin but by the content of their character.

I have a dream today.

I have a dream that one day, down in Alabama, with its vicious racists, with its governor having his lips dripping with the words of interposition and nullification; one day right there in Alabama, little black boys and black girls will be able to join hands with little white boys and white girls as sisters and brothers.

I have a dream today.

I have a dream that one day every valley shall be exalted, every hill and mountain shall be made low, the rough places will be made plain, and the crooked places will be made straight, and the glory of the Lord shall be revealed, and all flesh shall see it together. This is our hope. This is the faith that I go back to the South with. With this faith we will be able to hew out of the mountain of despair a stone of hope. With this faith we will be able to transform the jangling discords of our nation into a beautiful symphony of brotherhood. With this faith we will be able to work together, to pray together, to struggle together, to go to jail together, to stand up for freedom together, knowing that we will be free one day.

Extract from speech by Martin Luther King, Jr. He was a driving force in the non-violent push for racial equality in the 1950s and the 1960s. This speech was given on 28 August 1963, on the steps of the Lincoln memorial. It mobilized supporters and acted as the catalyst for the 1964 Civil Rights Act.

Bass: proof that visionary leadership works!

Bass (in Bryman, 1992) developed the notion of transformation leadership, which many managers find meaningful and helpful. He distinguished between transactional leadership and transformational leadership (see box), and identified through extensive research that charismatic and inspirational leadership were the components most likely to be associated with leadership success.

TRANSFORMATIONAL LEADERSHIP

Transformational leadership involves the leader raising the followers' sense of purpose and levels of motivation. The aims of the leader and the followers combine into one purpose, and the leader raises the followers' confidence and expectations of themselves. Transformational leadership comprises:

- charisma;
- inspiration;
- intellectual stimulation;
- individualized consideration.

Transactional leadership is simply an exchange in which the leaders hands over rewards when followers meet expectations.

- contingent reward;
- management by exception.

Source: Bryman (1992)

Gardner: the need for leaders to embody a story

Howard Gardner's (1996) influential research into the nature of successful leaders gave rise to some interesting lessons about visionary leadership. He chose eleven 20th century leaders who have really made a difference, and researched their lives and their work by reading their biographies and tracking down any speeches, letters, audiotapes and videotapes that were available.

He chose a mixture of different types of leader, combining business leaders, political leaders and those who influenced our thinking and behaviours without being in a position to lead directly. The list included among others Alfred Sloan, head of General Motors, Pope John XXIII, one of the most influential and popular popes of modern times, Martin Luther King, the advocate of African Americans, and Margaret Mead, a cultural anthropologist who deeply influenced our ideas about childhood, family life and society. (There have been attempts made to discredit her research, but she is still supported by many as being highly innovative and influential.)

Gardner's findings indicated that those leaders who had really made a difference to the way others thought, felt and acted all appeared to have a central story or message.

Stories not only provide background, but help the followers to picture the future. The story must connect with the audience's needs and be embodied in the leader him or herself. Gardner makes the point that phonies are never in short supply, and the individual who does not embody or act out his or her messages will eventually be found out.

LEADERS' STORIES

Margaret Thatcher

'Britain has lost its way in defeatism and socialism. We must reclaim the leadership from 'them' (socialists, union trouble makers and the 'wets') and restore earlier grandeur.'

Margaret Mead

'As human beings we can make wise decisions about our own lives by studying options that many other cultures pursue.'

Mahatma Gandhi

'We in India are equal in status and worth to all other human beings. We should work cooperatively with our antagonists if possible, but be prepared to be confrontational if necessary.'

Leadership stories from Gardner (1996)

Heifetz and Laurie: vision is not the answer

Heifetz and Laurie (1997) say that vision is not the answer. They say that the senior executive needs to alter his or her approach to match the needs of 21st century organizations. They say that what is needed is adaptive leadership. This is about challenging people, taking them out of their comfort zones, letting people feel external pressure and exposing conflict.

'Followers want comfort and stability, and solutions from their leaders. But that's babysitting. Real leaders ask hard questions and knock people out of their comfort zones. Then they manage the resulting distress.' They believe the call for vision and inspiration is counter-productive and encourages dependency from employees.

There is a difference between the type of leadership needed to solve a routine technical problem and the type of leadership needed to enable complex organizational change. Leaders of change should concentrate on scanning the environment, and drawing people's attention to the complex adaptive challenges that the organization needs to address, such as culture changes, or changes in core processes. This means not solving the problems for people, but giving the work back to them. It also means not protecting people from bad news and difficulty, but allowing them to feel the distress of things not working well. These ideas are quite a long way from the concept of transformational leadership mentioned above, which indicates that successful leaders are charismatic, visionary and inspirational.

Jean Lipman-Blumen: leaders need to make connections rather than build one vision

Jean Lipman-Blumen (2002) says that vision is no longer the answer. She encourages leaders to search for meaning and make connections, rather than build one vision. She notes that there is a growing sense that old forms of leadership are untenable in an increasingly global environment. She says that the sea change in the conditions of leadership imposed by the new global environment require new ways of thinking and working, which confront and deal constructively with both interdependence (overlapping visions, common problems) and diversity (distinctive character of individuals, groups and organizations).

Lipman-Blumen talks about connective leaders (see box) who perceive connections among diverse people, ideas and institutions even when the parties themselves do not. In the new 'connective era', she says that leaders will need to reach out and collaborate even with old adversaries. Mikhail Gorbachev is a good example of this in the political arena. Nelson Mandela is another.

Again, this approach is different from the suggestion that leaders need to develop and communicate clear vision in an inspiring way. Jean Lipman-Blumen encourages leaders to help others to make good connections, and to develop a sense of common purpose across boundaries, thus building commitment across a wide domain.

SIX IMPORTANT STRENGTHS FOR CONNECTIVE LEADERS

- **Ethical political savvy.** A combination of political know-how with strong ethics. Adroit and transparent use of others and themselves to achieve goals.

- **Authenticity and accountability.** Authenticity is achieved by dedicating yourself to the purpose of the group. Accountability is achieved by being willing to have every choice scrutinized.

- **A politics of commonalities.** Searching for commonalities and common ground, and building communities.

- **Thinking long-term, acting short-term.** Coaching and encouraging successors, and building for a long-term future despite the current demands of the day to day.

- **Leadership through expectation.** Scrupulously avoiding micro-managing. Setting high expectations and trusting people.

- **A quest for meaning.** Calling supporters to change the world for the better.

Source: Lipman-Blumen (2002)

Leadership for the 21st century: less vision, more connection?

The world is changing. Organizations are more dispersed and less hierarchical. More information is more freely available. People want more from their jobs than they used to. Does this then change the role of the leader of change?

As we write this book, the US and UK governments are trying to persuade the rest of the world that war on Iraq was the only way to ensure a peaceful future. However, opinion polls within Europe and the United States indicate that increasing numbers of people are against armed conflict and no longer believe that this is a good way of resolving international issues. Perhaps things are different now. The increasingly globalized economy and access to news and information are perhaps encouraging people to form cooperative relationships with a measure of independence. Are people's needs for strong leadership starting to shift? Perhaps clear, visionary, authoritative leadership is no longer working?

When we look inside organizations, the territory is also changing. John Kotter (1996) draws our attention to changes in organizational structures, systems and cultures (see Table 4.3). What does this mean for leading change? We think this means a shift from expectations of one visionary leader to the need for increased connectivity and overlapping agendas between different groups.

Table 4.3 20th century organizations and 21st century organizations

	Structure	Systems	Culture	Leadership of change
20th century organizations	• bureaucratic; • multileveled; • organized with the expectation that senior management will manage; • characterized by policies and procedures that create many complicated internal interdependencies.	• depend on fewer performance information systems; • distribute performance information to executives only; • offer management training and support systems to senior people only.	• inwardly focused; • centralized; • slow to make decisions; • political; • risk averse.	*Our thoughts:* • directive; • visionary; • charismatic; • participative at top levels only.

| **21st century organizations** | • nonbureaucratic, with fewer rules and employees;
• limited to fewer levels;
• organized with the expectation that management will lead, lower-level employees will manage;
• characterized by policies and procedures that produce the minimal internal interdependence needed to serve customers. | • depend on many performance information systems, providing data on customers especially;
• distribute performance information widely;
• offer management training and support systems to many people. | • externally oriented;
• empowering;
• quick to make decisions;
• open and candid;
• more risk tolerant. | *Our thoughts:*
• scanning and interpreting environmental changes;
• encouraging connectedness;
• giving meaning and purpose. |

Source: adapted from Kotter (1996)

STOP AND THINK!

Q 4.1   Name your top five contemporary leaders and say why you chose each one. Reflect on how important visionary leadership is to you.

Q 4.2   What are the most significant changes that have happened in the world since your childhood? Who was responsible for leading these? Did visionary leadership play a key role?

Q 4.3   Draw up a table identifying the pros and cons of:

- visionary leadership;

- adaptive leadership;

- connective leadership.

Q 4.4   Re-read Kotter's (1996) comparison of 20th and 21st century organizational structures, systems and cultures. Then fill in your own ideas about leadership of change.

ROLES THAT LEADERS PLAY

There are various views about the role a leader should play in the change process (see Table 4.1):

- The machine metaphor implies that the leader sits at the top of the organization, setting goals and driving them through to completion.

- The political system metaphor implies that the leader needs to become the figure-head of a powerful coalition which attracts followers by communicating a compelling and attractive vision, and through negotiation and bargaining.

- The organism metaphor says the leader's primary role is that of coach, counsellor and consultant.

- The flux and transformation metaphor says the leader is a facilitator of emergent change.

How does the leader of a change process ensure that all the necessary roles are carried out? Should the leader try to perform all these roles personally, or select a specific role for him or herself and distribute supporting roles amongst his or her colleagues?

Senge: dispersed leadership

Senge (Senge *et al*, 1999) has some fairly challenging ideas about this. He says that successful leadership of change does not have to come from the top of an organization. It comes from within the organization. He remarks that senior executives do not have as much power to change things as they would like to think.

He asks why we are struggling so much with changing our organizations, and he attacks our dependence on the 'hero leader'. He claims it results in a vicious circle. The circle begins with a crisis, which leads to the search for a new CEO in whom all hopes are invested. The new CEO acts proactively and aggressively, and makes some dramatic short-term improvements such as cutting costs and improving productivity. Everyone then falls in line to please the new CEO, who does not suffer fools gladly. Employees comply rather than work hard to challenge the status quo, and a new crisis inevitably occurs. This vicious circle does not result in new thinking or organizational learning or renewal, or even growth, and in turn feeds our desire to find new hero-leaders. See Figure 4.1.

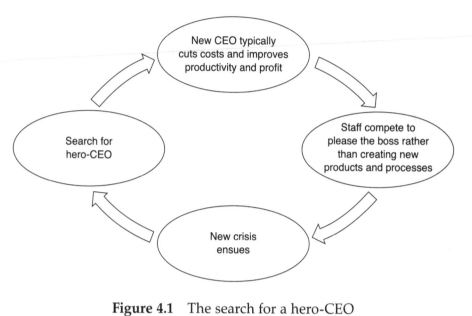

Figure 4.1   The search for a hero-CEO
Source: Senge *et al* (1999)

Senge offers some stark truths about organization change, which counteract the reliance on top-level vision set out by Bennis and Kotter.

- Little significant change can occur if it is driven from the top.

- CEO programmes rolled out from the top are a great way to foster cynicism and distract everyone from real efforts to change.

- Top management buy-in is a poor substitute for genuine commitment and learning capabilities at all levels in an organization.

You can see Senge's point. How could one or two brave people at the top of an organization really be responsible for envisaging and tackling the enormous range of challenges that present themselves when fundamental change is attempted? He claims that we need to think about developing communities of interdependent leaders across organizations. Different types of leaders have different types of role. He identifies three important, interconnected types of leader: local line leaders, executive leaders and network leaders.

Local line leaders

These are the front-line managers who design the products and services and make the core processes work. Without the commitment of these people, no significant change will happen. These people are usually very focused on their own teams and customers. They rely on network leaders to link them with other parts of the organization, and on executive leaders to create the right infrastructure for good ideas to emerge and take root.

Executive leaders

These are management board members. Senge does not believe that all change starts here. Rather, he states that these leaders are responsible for three key things: designing the right innovation environment and the right infrastructure for assessment and reward, teaching and mentoring local line leaders, and serving as role models to demonstrate their commitment to values and purpose.

Network leaders

Senge makes the point that the really significant organizational challenges occur at the interfaces between project groups, functions and teams. Network leaders are people who work at these interfaces. They are guides, advisors, active helpers and accessors (helping groups of people to get resource from elsewhere), working in partnership with line leaders. They often have the insight to help local line leaders to move forward and make changes happen across the organization.

The interconnections are hard to achieve in reality. We have observed the following obstacles to achieving smooth interconnection between the different roles:

- Executive leaders are busy, hard-to-get-hold-of people who can become quite disconnected from their local line leaders.

- Executive leaders and local line leaders rarely meet face to face and communicate by e-mail, if at all.

- Network leaders, such as internal consultants or process facilitators, are often diverted from their leadership roles by requests either to perform expert tasks or to implement HR-led initiatives.

- Network leaders may be busy and effective, but are usually undervalued as leaders of change. They often have to battle to get recognized as important players in the organization.

Senge's model recognizes the need for all three types of leader, and the need for connectivity between different parts of the organization if change is desired.

O'Neill: four key roles for successful change

Mary Beth O'Neill (2000) agrees with Senge's idea of communities of leaders, and identifies four specific leadership roles necessary for successful and sustained change efforts in organizations. She uses Daryl Conner's work on family therapy as her model for the change process, and identifies the important roles as sponsor, implementer, advocate and agent. See Table 4.4.

Table 4.4   Roles in a change process

Role	Description	Hint
Sponsor	Has the authority to make the change happen. Has control of resources.	Needs to have a clear vision for the change. Identify goals and measurable outcomes.
Sustaining sponsor	Sponsors change in own area, although top-level responsibility lies further up the hierarchy.	Must be careful not to transmit cynicism
Implementer	Implements the change. Reports to sponsor. Responsible for giving live feedback to the sponsor on change progress.	Needs to listen, enquire and clarify questions with the sponsor at the start of an initiative
Change agent	Facilitator of change. Helps sponsor and implementers stay aligned. Keeps sponsor on board. No direct authority over implementers.	Acts as data gatherer, educator, advisor, meeting facilitator, coach
Advocate	Has an idea. Needs a sponsor to make it happen. Usually highly motivated.	Must make idea appealing to sponsor

Source: adapted from O'Neill (2000)

Sponsor

The sponsor has the authority to make the change happen. He or she legitimizes and sanctions the change, and has line authority over the people who will implement the change and control of resources – such as time, money and people. There are also sustaining sponsors who are responsible for sponsoring change in their own area.

Good sponsors have a clear vision for the change. They identify goals and measurable outcomes for the initiative. Sustaining sponsors must be careful not to telegraph cynicism about the change to the team of implementers.

Implementer

Implementers are the people who must actually implement the change. They have direct line responsibilities to the sponsor. Their job is to provide the sponsor with live feedback from the change initiative. They can save the sponsor from tunnel vision, or from being surprised by obstacles that those closest to the change sometimes notice first.

Implementers are most effective when they listen, inquire and clarify their questions and concerns with the sponsor at the beginning of an initiative. This means they can commit to an effort rather than falsely complying early on and sabotaging later.

Change agent

A change agent is the facilitator of the change. He or she helps the sponsor and the implementers stay aligned with each other. The effectiveness of this role depends on the sponsor not abandoning the change agent to the implementers. The sponsor must not 'drop the ball'. When this happens the change agent can over-function, making the system ineffective and unbalanced, and the change temporary.

The change agent acts as data gatherer, educator, advisor, meeting facilitator and coach. Most often he or she has no direct line authority over the implementers, and is therefore in a naturally occurring triangle among sponsor–implementer–agent.

Advocate

An advocate has an idea about how a change can happen but needs a sponsor for his or her idea. All change needs to be sponsored.

Advocates are often passionate and highly motivated to make the change happen. They must remember the key factor, which is to get a sponsor. Without this, advocates become frustrated and demoralized. Shrewd advocates promote ideas by showing their compatibility with issues near and dear to sponsors' change projects and goals.

We have included Mary Beth O'Neill's definitions of these roles because they provide a clear framework for those approaching organizational change, and illustrate the range of leadership roles necessary for change to occur. Our experience is that people at all levels in organizations find this framework useful for kicking off and sustaining change, and for judging how well the community of leaders is supporting the change process. This model seems to provide the necessary amount of clarity in today's organizations, where hierarchy is unclear and jobs and projects overlap. There is often a need for a simple but flexible way of defining who does what in any process of change.

STOP AND THINK!

Q 4.5   Use Mary Beth O'Neill's four roles to analyse a change process in your organization. Who performed which role? How well were the roles performed? What contribution did the performance of these roles make to the level of success of the changes?

LEADERSHIP STYLES AND SKILLS

Much has been written about leadership skills and leadership style. We have chosen the work of Goleman because we find it illuminating and useful when working with leaders at any stage in a change process. His work on leadership styles identifies a set of six styles for the leader to choose from in any situation and at any point in a change process. Leaders we have worked with find this very useful (see boxed examples).

This set of six styles is underpinned by Goleman's work on emotional intelligence, which sets out the underlying competencies associated with successful leadership. This acts as a convenient checklist for those assessing their skills.

Goleman: leadership that gets results

In his quest to discover the links between emotional intelligence and business results, Daniel Goleman (2000) developed a set of six distinct leadership styles through studying the performance of over 3,800 executives worldwide. These six leadership styles, arising from various different components of emotional intelligence, are used

interchangeably by the best leaders. He encourages leaders to view the styles as six golf clubs, with each one being used in a different situation. Goleman also found that each style taken individually has a unique effect on organizational climate over time, some positive and some negative. This in turn has a major influence on business results.

Goleman links the competence of leaders directly to business results, but also identifies the situations in which each style is effective:

- **Coercive style.** Only to be used sparingly if a crisis arises. This is a useful style to employ if urgent changes are required now, but must be combined with other styles for positive results long term. Negative effects such as stress and mistrust result if this style is overused.

- **Authoritative style.** Useful when a turnaround is required and the leader is credible and enthusiastic. This is the 'visionary' leadership style. Goleman indicates that this style will only work if the leader is well respected by his or her people, and is genuinely enthusiastic about the change required. He does acknowledge the strongly positive effect of this approach, given the right prevailing conditions.

- **Affiliative style.** This style helps to repair broken relationships and establish trust. It can be useful when the going gets tough in a change process and people are struggling. However, it must be used with other styles to be effective in setting direction and creating progress.

- **Democratic.** This is an effective style to use when the team knows more about the situation than the leader does. They will be able to come up with ideas and create plans with the leader operating as facilitator. However it is not useful for inexperienced team members as they will go round in circles and fail to deliver.

- **Pacesetting.** This style can be used effectively with a highly motivated, competent team, but does not lead to positive results long term if used in isolation. Overuse of this style alone results in exhausted staff who feel directionless and unrewarded. The leader needs to switch out of this style to move into a change process rather than simply drive for more of the same.

- **Coaching.** This is an appropriate style to use if individuals need to acquire new skills or knowledge as part of changes being made.

THE COERCIVE-AFFILIATIVE MANAGER

I realize on reflection that I have been using just two leadership styles all my working life. I am 54, and this has been something of a revelation. I have been using the coercive style together with the affiliative style. It never occurred to me to do it any other way. I would tell the staff how things would be, give them a dressing down, and make up afterwards by talking about the football or asking about the family.

No one would make suggestions or use their initiative, and no one ever seemed to learn anything new. I was completely in charge of an efficient but stagnant site.

It wasn't easy incorporating other styles, but once I had cracked the coaching style, things began to change. The staff began to see me as more accessible. Now my people trust me more, and they are prepared to take responsibility and to suggest things and to make changes. I use less energy to carry out my role, and can think more clearly about how best to lead.

General manager of a manufacturing plant

THE PACESETTING MANAGER

At first glance I thought I was using all six styles in the right measure. Then when I began to talk to my team about it, I realized that I was using the pacesetting style 85 per cent of the time. Even my attempts at being friendly (or affiliative) turned out to be pacesetting approaches. People described how a casual chat with me would end up feeling like an interrogation. People on the shop floor actively avoided me after a while. Or they spent ages preparing for an encounter with me.

Of course, all my star performers loved this style. They found it thrilling and stimulating. The others fell by the wayside as I had no time for coaching at all. My style became a self-fulfilling prophecy. The competent people did well, and those who needed to learn didn't get the airtime from me that they needed, so they failed.

I'm not saying that this has completely changed. But now I do recognize when I need to coach and when I need to paceset. My actions are more aligned to my intentions, rather than being simply a question of habit.

Head teacher

See Table 4.5 for our summary of the six different styles and their uses.

Table 4.5 Our summary of Goleman's six leadership styles

	Coercive	Authoritative	Affiliative	Democratic	Pace-setting	Coaching
Short definition	Telling people what to do when	Persuading and attracting people with an engaging vision	Building relationships with people through use of positive feedback	Asking the team what they think, and listening to this	Raising the bar and asking for a bit more. Increasing the pace.	Encouraging and supporting people to try new things. Developing their skills.
When to use this style	When there is a crisis	When step change is required. When manager is both credible and enthusiastic.	When relationships are broken	When the team members have something to contribute	When team members are highly motivated and highly competent	When there is a skills gap
Disadvantages of this style	Encourages dependence. People stop thinking.	Has a negative effect if manager is not credible	Not productive if it is the only style used	May lead nowhere if team is inexperienced	Exhausting if used too much. Not appropriate when team members need help.	If manager is not a good coach, or if individual is not motivated, this style will not work

Goleman: the importance of emotional intelligence for successful leaders

Underpinning Goleman's six leadership style is his work on emotional intelligence (see Goleman, 1998). This is worth examining as it sets out all the competencies required to be a successful leader.

Goleman's research into the necessity for emotional intelligence is convincing. First, his investigation into 181 different management competence models drawn from 121 organizations worldwide indicated that 67 per cent of the abilities deemed essential for management competence were emotional competencies. Further research carried out by Hay/McBer looked at data from 40 different corporations to determine the difference in terms of competencies between star performers and average performers. Again emotional competencies were found to be twice as important as skill-based or intellectual competencies.

EMOTIONAL COMPETENCIES FOR LEADERS

Self-awareness

Knowing one's internal states, preferences, resources, and intuitions:

- Emotional awareness: recognizing one's emotions and their effects.
- Accurate self-assessment: knowing one's strengths and limits.
- Self-confidence: a strong sense of one's self-worth and capabilities.

Self-management

Managing one's internal states, impulses, and resources:

- Self-control: keeping disruptive emotions and impulses in check.
- Trustworthiness: maintaining standards of honesty and integrity.
- Conscientiousness: taking responsibility for personal performance.
- Adaptability: flexibility in handling change.
- Achievement orientation: striving to improve or meeting a standard of excellence.
- Initiative: readiness to act on opportunities.

Social awareness

Awareness of others' feelings, needs, and concerns:

- Empathy: sensing others' feelings and perspectives, and taking an active interest in their concerns.
- Organizational awareness: reading a group's emotional currents and power relationships.
- Service orientation: anticipating, recognizing, and meeting customers' needs.

Social skills

Adeptness at inducing desirable responses in others:

- Developing others: sensing others' development needs and bolstering their abilities.
- Leadership: inspiring and guiding individuals and groups.
- Influence: wielding effective tactics for persuasion.
- Communication: listening openly and sending convincing messages.
- Change catalyst: initiating or managing change.
- Conflict management: negotiating and resolving disagreements.
- Building bonds: nurturing instrumental relationships.
- Teamwork and collaboration: working with others toward shared goals. Creating group synergy in pursuing collective goals.

   Source: Goleman (1998), reproduced with permission of Bloomsbury, London

Goleman defined a comprehensive set of emotional competencies for leaders (see box). He grouped these competencies into four categories:

- self-awareness;
- self-management;
- social awareness;
- social skills.

Self-awareness, he says, is at the heart of emotional intelligence. To back this up, Goleman's research shows that if self-awareness is not present in a leader, the chance of that person being competent in the other three categories is much reduced.

THE IMPORTANCE OF SELF-MANAGEMENT

The managers that we work with often have high drive levels and are also very intelligent. When this combination of characteristics is present in an individual, that individual often experiences a lot of frustration. Other people are either too slow, or too relaxed, or simply 'not getting it'.

This was crystallized by a very dynamic and successful IT manager whom I worked with recently. When I went through her emotional intelligence feedback with her using HayGroup's Emotional Competence Inventory, her self-management scores were low, especially in the area of self-control. I asked her how often she felt frustrated in her work. She paused for a moment and then with a sudden realization she said, 'All the time.' Up until that point, she had not realized that there was an issue. This had just become a way of life. Others were experiencing her as bad tempered, moody and occasionally bullying. Then we started to talk about strategies for dealing with this.

Esther Cameron, 2003

A brief scan of the competence set will confirm that self-awareness, self-management and social awareness are all competencies that are not necessarily observable. We call this _inner leadership_. Only the social skills category contains obvious observable behaviours. We call this _outer leadership_.

In our experience those involved in leading change have to develop especially strong inner leadership because of the emotions arising from their own drive to achieve, coupled with potential resistance from many levels, and the discomfort involved with letting go of old habits. It is a very emotional landscape!

Daniel Goleman says that it is vital that leaders develop emotional competencies. He says:

> In the new stripped-down, every-job-counts business climate, these human realities will matter more than ever. Massive change is constant; technical innovations, global competition, and the pressures of institutional investors are ever-escalating forces for flux. As organizations shrink through waves of downsizing, those people who remain are more accountable – and more visible.

Whereas a bully, or a hypersensitive manager, might have gone unnoticed deep in many organizations 10 years ago, he or she is much more visible now.

STOP AND THINK!

Q 4.6 Draw a pie chart that represents your own use of Goleman's six leadership styles. Are you using them in the right proportion? If not, what do you plan to do differently and why? Try this exercise again, but this time use the framework to help someone else to focus on his or her leadership style. Write up the conversation, indicating what insights the exercise provoked.

DIFFERENT LEADERSHIP FOR DIFFERENT PHASES OF CHANGE

In this section we examine the different phases of the change process, to identify the need for a leader to perform different skills or activities during each phase. We do this by using three different but complimentary models of the change process.

Cameron and Green: inner and outer leadership

In our own experience of working with leaders on change processes, it is important to establish phases of change so that plans can be made and achievements recognized. This phasing also enables a leader to see the need for flexibility in leadership style, as the change moves from one phase into another phase. We have identified both the outer leadership and inner leadership requirements of a leader of change for each phase. See Table 4.6.

Table 4.6 Leadership of change phase by phase, comparing inner and outer leadership requirements

Phase of change	Outer leadership – observable actions of the leader	Inner leadership – what goes on inside the leader
1. Establishing the need for change The leader illuminates a problem area through discussion	Influencing, understanding, researching, presenting, listening	Managing emotions, maintaining integrity, being courageous, being patient, knowing yourself, judging whether you really have the energy to do this
2. Building the change team The leader brings the right people together and establishes momentum through teamwork.	Chairing meetings, connecting agendas, facilitating discussion, building relationships, building teams, cutting through the politics	Social and organizational awareness, self-awareness, managing emotions, adaptability, taking initiative, having the drive to achieve, maintaining energy despite knock-backs
3. Creating vision and values The leader works with the group to build a picture of success.	Initiating ideas, brainstorming, encouraging divergent and creative thinking, challenging others constructively, envisaging the future, facilitating agreement	Strategic thinking, taking time to reflect, social awareness, drive to achieve, managing emotions
4. Communicating and engaging The leader plays his or her role in communicating direction, giving it meaning, being clear about timescale and letting people know what part they will be playing.	Persuading and engaging, presenting with passion, listening, being assertive, being creative with ways of communicating	Patience, analysis of how to present to different audiences, managing emotions with regard to other people's resistance, social awareness, adaptability, empathy
5. Empowering others The leader entrusts those who have been involved in the creation of the new vision with key tasks.	Clear target setting, good delegation, managing without micromanaging or abdicating, coaching	Integrity, trust, patience, drive to achieve, steadiness of purpose, empathy

6. Noticing improvements and energizing The leader stays interested in the process. This involves the ability to juggle lots of different projects and initiatives	Playing the sponsorship role well, walking the talk, rewarding and sharing success, building on new ideas	Steadiness of purpose, organizational and social awareness, empathy, managing emotions, drive to achieve
7. Consolidating The leader encourages people to take stock of where they are, and reflect on how much has been achieved	Reviewing objectively, celebrating success, giving positive feedback before moving on to what's next	Social awareness, empathy, drive to achieve, taking time to reflect, steadiness of purpose

Kotter: the importance of getting the early steps right

Kotter's eight steps to transforming your organization (see Chapter 3) form a comprehensive guide to tackling the process of change. Kotter says that good leaders must get all eight steps right. However, he predicts that the process will be a great deal easier if groundwork is done well.

In _Leading Change_ (1996), Kotter describes some of the actions a leader needs to take during all eight steps. In Table 4.7 we give some of Kotter's suggestions for the first four steps, as they seem to necessitate the most direct action from the leader.

Table 4.7 Kotter's recommended actions for the first four change steps

Kotter's step	Recommended actions
1. Establishing a sense of urgency	Push up the urgency level. Create a crisis by exposing issues rather than protecting people from them. Send more data to people about customer satisfaction, especially where weaknesses are demonstrated. Encourage more honest discussion of these issues.
2. Creating the guiding coalition	Include enough main line managers, enough relevant expertise, enough people with good credibility and reputation in the organization and enough ability to lead. Avoid big egos and snakes (who engender distrust). Talk a lot together, build trust and build a common goal.
3. Developing a vision and strategy	Vision building is a messy, difficult and sometimes emotionally charged exercise. Take time to do the process properly and expect it to take months. It is never achieved in a single meeting.
4. Communicating the change vision	Keep the communication simple and use metaphor and analogy. Creativity is necessary to ensure that many different forms of communication are used to repeat the message, including leading by example. Use two-way discussions and listen to the feedback.

Rosabeth Moss Kanter: learning how to persevere

Rosabeth Moss Kanter (2002) highlights the need for keeping going in the change process, even when it gets tough. She says that too often executives announce a plan, launch a task force and then simply hope that people find the answers. Kanter's emphasis is different from Kotter's. She says the difficulties will come after the change is begun.

Kanter says that leaders need to employ the following strategies to ensure that a change process is sustained beyond the first flourish:

1. **Tune into the environment.** Create a network of listening posts to listen and learn from customers.

2. **Challenge the prevailing organizational wisdom.** Promote kaleidoscopic thinking. Send people far afield, rotate jobs and create interdisciplinary project teams to get people to question their assumptions.

3. **Communicate a compelling aspiration.** This is not just about communicating a picture of what could be, it is an appeal to better ourselves and become something more. The aspiration needs to be compelling as there are so many sources of resistance to overcome.

4. **Build coalitions.** Kanter says that the coalition-building step, though obvious, is one of the most neglected steps in the change process. She says that change leaders need the involvement of people who have the resources, the knowledge and the political clout to make things happen.

5. **Transfer ownership to a working team.** Once a coalition is formed, others should be brought on board to focus on implementation. Leaders need to stay involved to guarantee time and resources for implementers. The implementation team can then build its own identity and concentrate on the task.

6. **Learn to persevere.** Kanter says that everything can look like a failure in the middle. If you stick with the process through the difficult times (see box), good things may emerge. The beginning is exciting and the end satisfying. It is the hard work in the middle that necessitates the leader's perseverance.

7. **Make everyone a hero.** Leaders need to remember to reward and recognize achievements. This skill is often underused in organizations, and it is often free! This part of the cycle is important to motivate people to give them the energy to tackle the next change process.

STICKY MOMENTS IN THE MIDDLE OF CHANGE AND HOW TO GET UNSTUCK:

- **Forecasts fall short.** Change leaders must be prepared to accept serious departures from plans, especially when they are doing something new and different.
- **Roads curve.** Expect the unexpected. Do not panic when the path of change takes a twist or a turn.
- **Momentum slows.** When the going gets tough it is important to review what has been achieved and what remains – and to revisit the mission.
- **Critics emerge.** Critics will emerge in the middle when they begin to realize the impact of proposed changes. Change leaders should respond to this, remove obstacles and move forward.

Source: Kanter (2002)

Bridges: leading people through transition

William Bridges (1991) has very clear ideas about what leaders need to do to make change work. Bridges says that what often stops people from making new beginnings in a change process is that they have not yet let go of the past. He sees the leader as the person who helps to manage that transition. We see this as a particularly useful frame of thinking when an inevitable change such as a merger, acquisition, reorganization or site closure is underway.

In Chapter 3 we referred to his three phases of transition:

- ending;
- neutral zone;
- new beginning.

Leadership for the ending

Here is Bridges' advice for how to manage the ending phase (or how to get them to let go):

- Study the change carefully and identify who is likely to lose what.
- Acknowledge these losses openly – it is not stirring up trouble. Sweeping losses under the carpet stirs up trouble.
- Allow people to grieve and publicly express your own sense of loss.

- Compensate people for their losses. This does not mean handouts! Compensate losses of status with a new type of status. Compensate loss of core competence with training in new areas.

- Give people accurate information again and again.

- Define what is over and what is not.

- Find ways to 'mark the ending' (see box).

- Honour rather than denigrate the past.

MARKING THE END

When a large public owned utility company in the UK split up into a myriad of small privatized units, there was a great sense of loss. Old teams and old friendships were breaking up. It was the end of an era. The organization held a wake, at which everyone moaned and complained and generally got things off their chest. There was much talk late into the night. The transition moved more smoothly after that event as people began to accept the reality and inevitability of the ending.

Leadership for the neutral zone

The neutral zone is an uncomfortable place to be. This is the time when for instance, the reorganization has been announced, but the new organization is not in place, or understood, or working. Anxiety levels go up and motivation goes down, and discord amongst the team can rise. This phase needs to be managed well, or it can lead to chaos. A selection of Bridges' tips for this phase are listed below (he itemizes 21 in his book):

- Explain the neutral zone as an uncomfortable time which with careful attention can be turned to everyone's advantage.

- Choose a new and more affirmative metaphor with which to describe it.

- Reinforce the metaphor with training programmes, policy changes and financial rewards for people to keep doing their jobs during the neutral zone.

- Create temporary policies, procedures, roles and reporting relationships to get you through the neutral zone.

- Set short-range goals and checkpoints.

- Set up a transition monitoring team to keep realistic feedback flowing upward during the time in the neutral zone.

- Encourage experimentation and risk taking. Be careful not to punish all failures.

- Encourage people to brainstorm many answers to the old problems – the ones that people say you just have to live with. Do this for your own problems too.

Leadership for the new beginning

Here are some of Bridges' ideas for this phase:

- Distinguish in your own mind the difference between the start, which can happen on a planned schedule, and the beginning, which will not.

- Communicate the purpose of the change.

- Create an effective picture of the change and communicate it effectively.

- Create a plan for bringing people through the three phases of transition, and distinguish it from the change management plan.

- Help people to discover the part they will play in the new system.

- Build some occasions for quick success.

- Celebrate the new beginning and the conclusion of the time of transition.

STOP AND THINK!

Q 4.7 Reflect on an organizational change in which you were involved. Did the 'sticky moments' suggested by Rosabeth Moss Kanter arise, and how were they dealt with? What could have been done differently by those leading the change?

Q 4.8 Imagine that the organization you work for as a line manager is about to be taken over by one of your key competitors. You have been told that everyone in your area will still have a job, but you will have to learn about the other organization's way of doing business and drop many of the products and services you deliver now. Use the William Bridges' tips to list some of the things you would need to start doing to enable the transition.

THE IMPORTANCE OF SELF-KNOWLEDGE AND INNER RESOURCES

Much is expected of a leader throughout a change process. It takes courage, a sense of purpose, the ability to manage your emotions, high integrity and a wide range of skills to lead change well. A great deal has been written about skills development, but what about self-knowledge and inner resources? How great a part does the inner life of the leader play in his or her ability to lead change, and how can this capacity be developed or improved?

We believe that this is the key to successful leadership; so does Daniel Goleman. See above to read about his research into leadership success which indicates that self-awareness forms the bedrock of the emotionally intelligent leader.

Bennis: the role of self-knowledge

Warren Bennis (1994) emphasizes the need to know yourself in order to become a good leader. He says that leaders must have self-knowledge if they want to be freed up sufficiently to think in new ways. Bennis claims that you make your life your own by understanding it, and become your own designer, rather than being designed by your own experience. He itemizes four lessons of self-knowledge. These are:

- **One: be your own teacher.** Leaders assume responsibility for their own learning, and treat it as a route to self-knowledge and self-expression. No one can teach them the lessons they need to learn. Stumbling blocks can be denial and blame.

- **Two: accept responsibility and blame no one.** Do not expect other people to take charge, or do things for you.

- **Three: you can learn anything you want to learn.** Leadership involves a kind of fearlessness, an optimism and a confidence.

- **Four: true understanding comes from reflecting on your experience.** Leaders make reflection part of their daily life. An honest look at the past prepares you for the future.

Bennis also notes the potential benefits of leaders recalling their childhoods honestly, reflecting on them, understanding them, and thereby overcoming the influence that childhood has on them. He quotes Erikson, the famed psychoanalyst, who says that there are eight stages of life each with an accompanying crisis (see Table 4.8). Erikson claims that the way in which we resolve the eight crises determines who we will be.

He also notes that we may get stuck at a particular stage if we do not manage to solve the crisis satisfactorily. For instance many of us never overcome the inner struggle between initiative and guilt, and so we lack purpose.

As a leader you may need to overcome some of the habits you developed at an early age, which will be challenging but rewarding. Usually this process is accomplished via coaching, counseling or therapy depending on how deep you want or need to go.

Table 4.8 Development stages and their challenges

Stage	Crisis	Resolution	Conditions for optimal development
Infancy (0–18 months)	Trust vs mistrust	Hope or withdrawal	Mirroring Acceptance
Early childhood (18 months–3 years)	Autonomy vs shame and doubt	Will or compulsion	Security (routines and rituals)
Play age (3–5 years)	Initiative vs guilt	Purpose or inhibition	Clear boundaries Vision setting
School age (8–12 years)	Industry vs inferiority	Competence or inertia	Spectators Discipline
Adolesence (12–28 years)	Identity vs identity confusion	Fidelity or repudiation	Sampling Modelling
Young adulthood (28–40 years)	Intimacy vs isolation	Love or exclusivity	Maturity Identity
Adulthood (40–55 years)	Generativity vs stagnation	Care or rejectivity	Balance Mastery
Maturity (55+)	Integrity vs despair	Wisdom or disdain	Support Forgiveness

Source: adapted from Erik Erikson in Bennis (1994)

Covey: the need for principle-centred leadership

Steve Covey is a writer and teacher who has had a tremendous effect on the psyche of UK and US managers. His book _Principle-Centred Leadership_ (1992) was a _New York Times_ bestseller for 220 weeks. His characteristics of principle-centred leaders (see box) and his seven habits (see below) are much quoted in management and leadership training courses. Again, his focus is on inner leadership, that is, on how to *be* rather than on what to *do*.

EIGHT CHARACTERISTICS OF PRINCIPLE-CENTERED LEADERS

- They are continually learning.
- They are service oriented.
- They radiate positive energy.
- They believe in other people.
- They lead balanced lives.
- They see life as an adventure.
- They are synergistic.
- They exercise for renewal on all four dimensions of human personality – physical, mental, emotional and spiritual.

Source: Covey (1992)

Covey's organization runs workshops and programmes underpinned by a humanistic self-development approach. Unlike Bennis, he does not advocate revisiting your childhood to overcome difficulties, but encourages us to focus on visualizing a positive outcome and working with energy and enthusiasm towards it.

Covey's seven habits (Covey, 1989) connect the leader's outer habits with the inner capability, which he labels endowments:

- **Habit 1: Be proactive.** Know what needs to be done, and decide to do it. Do not be driven by circumstances. (Needs self-awareness and self-knowledge.)

- **Habit 2: Begin with the end in mind.** Have a clear sense of what you are trying to achieve in each year, month, day, moment. (Needs imagination and conscience.)

- **Habit 3: Put first things first.** This is about organizing how you spend your time in line with Habit 2. He talks about looking at level of urgency and level of importance of activities, and comments that we spend too much time responding to urgent issues. (Needs willpower.)

- **Habit 4: Think win–win.** Manage all interactions with the assumption that mutually beneficial solutions are possible. (Needs an abundance mentality.)

- **Habit 5: Seek first to understand, then to be understood.** Be prepared to clarify what other people are getting at before you put your point across. (Needs courage balanced with consideration.)

- **Habit 6: Synergize.** Value differences in people and work with others to create a sum that is greater than the parts. (Needs creativity.)

- **Habit 7: Sharpen the saw.** Avoid the futility of endless 'busyness'. Make time to renew. Covey says, 'Without this discipline, the body becomes weak, the mind mechanical, the emotions raw, the spirit insensitive, and the person selfish.' (Needs continuous improvement or self-renewal.)

STOP AND THINK!

Q 4.9 Identify the top five inner leadership strengths that you believe the headmaster or headmistress of an underperforming school needs to have. Use the ideas of Bennis and Covey in the section above, and consider also Goleman's emotional competencies. Justify your choices. How could these areas be developed if they were lacking?

Q 4.10 Reflect on your own leadership using Covey's seven habits. What are your strengths and weak areas?

Q 4.11 Imagine you have just been asked to lead a cultural change programme in a 10,000 strong organization based throughout Europe and the United States. The organization is a microelectronics company which has grown through acquisition and now wants to strengthen its unique culture as one organization emphasizing commercial applications, customer service and innovation. Using the ideas presented in this chapter, describe the approach you would take to leading this initiative and explain why.

SUMMARY AND CONCLUSIONS

- Different metaphors of change lead to different assumptions about what good leaders do. We believe that the most effective ideas about change combine a number of metaphors, bringing the maximum benefits and avoiding the pitfalls of blinkered thinking.

- A popular notion of leadership is of the hero-leader who leads from the front with determination, great vision and independence of mind.
  - Bennis places visionary leadership high on the agenda, and makes a point of distinguishing leadership from management. Kotter echoes this view.
  - Studies that compared the effects of 'transformational leadership' with those of 'transactional leadership' at the end of the 20th century indicated that charismatic and inspirational leadership were the elements that led most reliably to team success.
  - Howard Gardner's research into the minds of significant 20th century leaders indicated that leaders who had great influence embodied stories and took care to connect well with their audiences.
  - Heifetz and Laurie and Jean Lipman-Blumen all argue against the need for visionary leadership. Heifetz and Laurie advocate adaptive leadership which is about taking people out of their comfort zones, letting people feel external pressure and exposing conflict. Jean Lipman-Blumen instead emphasizes the need for leaders to ensure connectivity. She says leaders need to be able to perceive connections among diverse people, ideas and institutions even when the parties themselves do not.

- 21st-century organizations are different, and the pace of change is even faster. This has given rise to new ideas about where leaders need to put their energies. Perhaps this means less vision and more connectivity.

- Different metaphors of the change process imply different leadership roles. Senge advocates dispersed leadership, identifying three key types of leader in an organizational system. If these three roles are in place and are well connected, then change will happen naturally. Mary Beth O'Neill names four key leadership roles in any change process.

- Inner leadership is about what goes on inside the leader. Outer leadership is about what the leader does. Outer and inner leadership are both important for achieving organizational change.

- Daniel Goleman defines six leadership styles. A leader can select the right style for the right situation, taking into account the necessary conditions for success and long-term consequences. Goleman's checklist of emotional intelligence competencies is useful for any leader wishing to be successful. These competencies include both inner and outer leadership elements.

- Kotter says that the hard work must be put in early in the change process, while Rosabeth Moss Kanter says the hardest part comes in the middle and that perseverance is key. Bridges identifies specific leadership tasks during endings, the neutral zone and beginnings.

- Bennis and Covey both place high value on the inner life of leaders. Bennis emphasizes the need for self-knowledge, whereas Covey lists a set of principles and guidelines to help leaders to develop positive thinking patterns.

Leadership is a fascinating subject. We all have different experiences and different views about what makes a good leader, and many of these views are ones we hold quite strongly. There are many apparent contradictions here. It is always intriguing to see how leaders with very different styles can both be equally successful. This observation can appear baffling to those wishing to make a rational assessment of what works in leadership and what does not work.

So how do we get to the truth about leaders? Do our heroes give us useful clues? The hero-leader is an enduring theme in discussions of leadership. Even the process of asking people to name their 'top leaders' encourages an individualist perspective, and automatically results in the naming of heroes. Perhaps this type of information is flawed, as it depends so much on the profile-raising skills of the leader, and his or her own personal brand. The facts concerning how these leaders demonstrated good leadership get lost in the general impression of success.

Leaders who offer a vision, or have a strong story, tend to be the most memorable. Their stories, or new ways of thinking, if taken on, may outlive the leader. Is this a sign of great leadership: when the story begins to live outside of the leader? There is also a strong sense that today's followers need more than just a good story. They need a credible story that stands up to scrutiny.

On the other hand, those who doubt the viability of the role of visionary leadership suggest that leaders need to focus instead on connecting agendas and highlighting painful challenges. Our view is that all these things are necessary to create change, including the articulation of an attractive vision. Just read the words of Martin Luther-King again to feel the power of a well-articulated vision. Other things need to be in place too: the timing has to be right, and the vision has to be accepted by followers.

The leader of change has to be courageous and self-aware. He or she has to choose the right action at the right time, and to keep a steady eye on the ball. However, the leader cannot make change happen alone. A team needs to be in place, with well-thought-out roles, and committed people who are in for the duration, not just for the kick-off.

One thing is certain: the going will not be smooth.

Part Two

The applications

INTRODUCTION: STRATEGIC CHANGE OPTIONS

Strategy is the pattern or plan that integrates an organization's major goals, policies and action sequences into a cohesive whole.

James Quinn (1980)

In Part One we looked at change and the management of change from three different perspectives: the individual, the team and the organization. We also examined the roles, styles and skills needed to become a successful leader of change.

In Part Two we apply this learning to specific types of change. We have identified four generic change scenarios, and we look at the particular management challenges involved in initiating and implementing each type of change. These change scenarios are:

- structural change;
- mergers and acquisitions;
- cultural change;
- IT-based process change.

We look at what differentiates these changes, and for each scenario we identify which approach to managing organizational change is the most relevant, and look at the implications for individuals and teams. We also give tips and resources for managers in these situations.

In this introduction we briefly review the strategic change process, identifying the elements that make a strategic change process successful.

STRATEGIC CHANGE PROCESS

When we look at Figure II.1 we can see that typically the whole process begins with an internal or external trigger for change. In a way we compartmentalize the universe in order to make sense of it. This whole book is an attempt to make order out of the chaos we sometimes feel around change. It is very rare that anyone could say for sure that this change began on that particular day or at that particular meeting. But in our ideal universe these triggers for change make us take a long hard look at the market or industry we are in, examine our customer and stakeholder relationships, and scrutinize our organizational capability. And as a result we review where we want to be, how we want to get there and what we need to do to get there. We develop our new vision, mission and values.

Now all sorts of changes may need to happen as a result of this exercise, but typically we will need to adjust one or all of the following:

- the organizational structure;
- the commercial approach;
- the organizational culture;
- the relevant processes.

OVERVIEW OF STRUCTURE

We tackle all four types of change identified above. In Chapter 5 we tackle structural changes head on. This is because we observe how many strategic changes result in structural changes, and we wanted to write something helpful about how to make this approach work well. Chapter 6 tackles mergers and acquisitions, and deals with change situations when competitors or suppliers (and indeed customers) are brought into the organization. Although it is not specifically addressed, many of the issues raised are pertinent to partnering as well. Chapter 7 focuses on cultural change, and

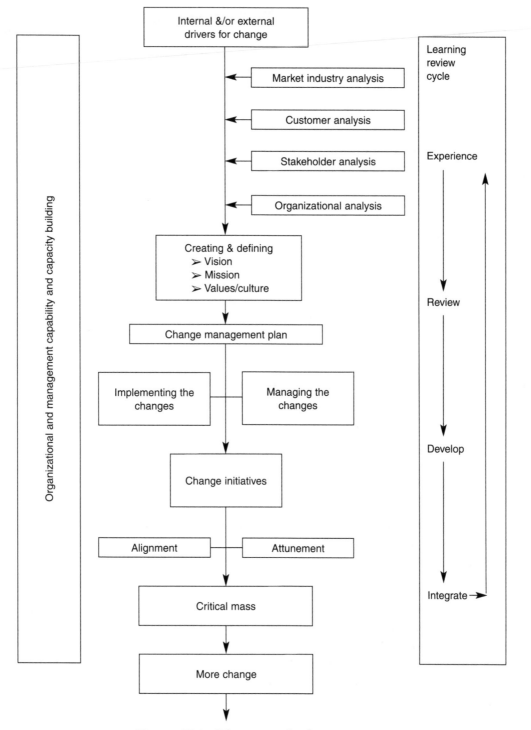

Figure II.1   The strategic change process

specifically deals with three areas: aligning the organization to a market and customer focus, aligning the organization to its overarching objectives, and developing an employee brand. All three areas have something important to say about how to tackle cultural change. Finally Chapter 8 is focused on IT-enabled process change, as so many of us have undergone change as a direct result of developments in technology or the re-engineering of processes.

Other important aspects of the change process

There are five other essential characteristics of successful strategic change initiatives:

- **Alignment** is an important feature of a successful change initiative. This is about ensuring that all the components of the change plan are an integrated whole. This means that they have an internal integrity but are also linked into the whole organizational system and beyond, if necessary.

- **Attunement** is important too. This is about mirroring the preferred organizational culture, and ensuring that all aspects of the change are carried out in line with organizational values and with sufficient attention to the human side of change.

- **Critical mass** is vital. The aim of a change management plan is to develop momentum and build sustainability. This occurs when a sufficiently critical mass of people are aligned and in tune with senior management.

- **Building organizational capability.** Change management capacity and capability within organizations vary dramatically. Even organizations that seem to go through constant change do not necessarily have this as a key competency within their people. Our contention is that the more the senior management recognizes the need to develop this capability within itself and a significant proportion of its managers, the sooner change can become a way of life and not something to be feared, shunned and avoided.

- **Encouraging individual learning.** Change managers should be well supported with training and coaching if they are to be successful. Some succeed without this, but they are the exception. Usually the demands of implementing change, together with a need to keep the day-to-day requirements of the job going, mean that everything gets done in a rush, without pausing to review, develop or integrate. The habit is then set: managers hop from experience to experience without learning very much.

As you go through the following chapters, it may help to refer back to Figure II.1 as you think through how each type of change can be achieved successfully as part of an organization-wide strategic change.

5

Restructuring

We trained hard. But is seemed that every time we were beginning to form into teams, we would be reorganised. I was to learn later in life that we tend to meet any new situation by reorganising. And what a wonderful method it can be for creating the illusion of progress while producing confusion, inefficiency, and demoralisation.
Gaius Petronius Arbiter, *The Satyricon*,
1st century AD

These words spoken two millennia ago might be very familiar to some of you. They certainly are to us, and we believe they are as insightful now as they were then. However, even though these words have been much quoted, organizations do not necessarily take any notice of them!

Although some managers are now getting this process right, most people's experience of restructuring is negative. People often roll their eyes and say 'Not again', 'It failed', 'Why didn't they manage it better?', and 'Why can't they leave us to just get on with the job?'

Restructuring as a theme for change might seem a little strange because restructuring as a key strategic objective is not particularly meaningful. Surely we should be looking at the reasons behind the change. There are a number of important points here:

- It seems that restructuring becomes the solution to a variety of organizational issues, and in that sense we need to look at the restructuring process itself as it impacts on so many people's lives.

- Given that managers and staff are restructured so often, it is important to understand the dynamics of restructuring, what typically goes wrong and what a good process looks like.

- In our view restructuring should be the last option considered by management rather than the first option. It is often a method for not addressing the organizational issues that it seeks to resolve.

This chapter looks at:

- the reasons for restructuring;
- the restructuring processes:
    - strategic review and reasons for change;
    - critical success factors, design options and risk assessment;
    - learnings from previous projects and best practice;
    - project planning and project implementation;
    - monitoring and review;
- restructuring from an individual change perspective – the special case of redundancy;
- enabling teams to address organizational change.

In the UK the Chartered Institute of Personnel and Development (CIPD) is running an ongoing research project 'Organising for Success in the 21st century' (www.cipd.org.uk) looking at current and future themes of restructuring in organizations today. It stresses the importance to companies of this process:

> [W]hen DuPont announced its reorganisation in February 2002, its stock price rose 12%, putting a valuation on the new organisation design of $7 billion (£4.5 billion). Less fortunate was the reception of Proctor and Gamble's ... launched in 1999 by the company's new chief executive, Durk Jager, this reorganisation had a $1.9 billion (£1.2 billion) budget over six years. Within 18 months, the perceived difficulties ... had cost Jager his job.

On a macro level, the survey found that during the 1990s the top 50 UK companies moved from having on average one major reorganization every five years to having one every three years. On a micro level, individual managers had personally experienced seven reorganizations within their organizations. Not all of the seven were major organization-wide change, some were more local. Nonetheless managers encountered various challenges as a result: managing the changes within themselves, managing the changes within their staff, ensuring that both large-scale and minor changes were aligned to the wider organizational strategies, and last but by no means least, delivering on business as usual and ensuring staff were motivated to deliver on business as usual.

REASONS FOR RESTRUCTURING

We are concerned in this chapter with the dynamics of change and restructuring, less so with why the organization or part thereof is being restructured. Restructuring can occur for numerous reasons:

- downsizing or rightsizing (market conditions or competitiveness);

- rationalization or cost-cutting (market conditions or competitiveness);

- efficiency or effectiveness (drive towards internal improvement);

- decentralization or centralization (drive towards internal improvement);

- flattening of the hierarchy (drive towards internal improvement);

- change in strategy (strategy implementation);

- merger or acquisition (strategy implementation);

- new product or service (strategy implementation);

- cultural change (strategy implementation);

- internal market re-alignment (strategy implementation);

- change of senior manager (leadership decision);

- internal or external crisis (unforeseen/unplanned change).

We believe that restructuring should only take place as a result of a change in strategy. It should have a clear rationale and should be done in conjunction with other parallel changes such as process change and culture change. Of course this is not always the case. Sometimes other events kick off restructuring processes, such as a new boss arriving, a process or product failure, an argument, a dissatisfied client or an underperforming person or department. In these cases it is sometimes difficult for employees to curb their cynicism when changes in structure seem to be a knee-jerk reaction, which lacks direction, appears cosmetic and fails to lead to any real improvement.

We look at specific cases of restructuring such as mergers and acquisitions, cultural change, rebranding and IT-based change in the other application chapters.

THE RESTRUCTURING PROCESS

Whereas some of the other change scenarios we discuss in this book are more problematic (for instance, culture change and merger/acquisition), on the surface a restructuring of the organization should be a relatively straightforward affair. If we recollect the organizational change metaphors, the restructure could be quite neatly placed into the machine metaphor.

> The key beliefs of the machine metaphor are:
> - Each employee should have only one line manager.
> - Labour should be divided into specific roles.
> - Each individual should be managed by objectives.
> - Teams represent no more than the summation of individual efforts.
> - Management should control and there should be employee discipline.
>
> This leads to the following assumptions about organizational change:
> - The organization can be changed to an agreed end state by those in positions of authority.
> - There will be resistance, and this needs to be managed.
>
> Change can be executed well if it is well planned and well controlled.

Within this metaphor we could perhaps draw on Kurt Lewin's three-step process of organizational change. You will remember that Lewin proposed that organizational change has three steps. The first step involves unfreezing the current state of affairs. This means defining the current state, surfacing the driving and resisting forces and picturing a desired end state. The second step is about moving to a new state through participation and involvement. The third step focuses on refreezing and stabilizing the new state of affairs by setting policy, rewarding success and establishing new standards. Clearly an organizational restructuring process could follow this model. There is a current state that needs unfreezing and a perceived end state that is required. The main focus therefore is the need to ensure that movement between the former to the latter state is as smooth and quick as necessary.

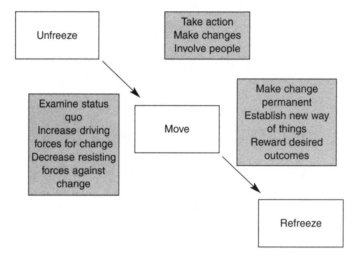

Figure 5.1   Lewin's three-step model
Source: Lewin (1951)

However, our experience when facilitating organizational change is that a restructuring process will not be successful if it is focused solely on generating organizational structure charts and project plans. It is disappointing to note that the CIPD research (CIPD, 2003) suggests that organizations typically devote much more time during restructuring to areas other than human resources. The finance and systems functions accounted for double the time and attention that HR issues received. Anyone managing or experiencing restructuring knows that there are many other factors to consider. The politics of the situation and the psychological needs of managers and staff play a key role. It is also important to ensure that the restructuring process is positioned as a framework to enable the organization to do something it has not done before, rather than simply as a tool for changing the structure around.

It is therefore useful to remind ourselves of Nadler and Tushman's congruence model, which derives from the political and organism metaphors. One of the key aspects of the congruence model is that if you change something in one part of the organizational system, the whole system and other component parts are affected. If you do not factor this into your change equation you may well face unintended consequences. For example, restructuring in one part of the organization means that people in other areas may well have to develop a whole new set of relationships. Very often little is done to communicate the changes, let alone actively work to foster new working relationships.

The authors have witnessed numerous restructures in a variety of public and private sector organizations, and have concluded that perhaps the best way to approach the restructuring process is as a mixture of the machine and organism metaphors. Beckhard and Harris' change formula is useful here:

$$C = [ABD] > X$$

C = Change
A = Level of dissatisfaction with the status quo
B = Desirability of the proposed change or end state
D = Practicality of the change (minimal risk and disruption)
X = 'Cost' of changing.

According to this formula, important factors in any restructuring are threefold. First, the reasons, timing and rationale for the restructure must be made very clear. Second, the end goal or vision must be communicated in an appealing way. Third, the whole exercise must appear doable by being well planned and well implemented. For the majority of individuals the overwhelming experience is one of upheaval. The cost of changing is high. It is therefore imperative that the benefits are accentuated and then planned for in the most authentic and genuine way as possible.

In Figure 5.2 we outline our generic approach to restructuring, which can be tailored to individual circumstances. We highlight areas of potential problems and also suggest ways of making it a more effective process.

Strategic review and reasons for change

Any attempt to restructure needs to have a clear communicable rationale. This will typically come from a review of strategy that highlights the need to address a specific issue relating to the internal or external business environment. In the CIPD research cited above, restructuring was often done to improve customer responsiveness, gain market share or improve organizational efficiency. Key drivers in the private sector were 'typically performance declines, mergers and acquisitions and a change of chief executive. In the public sector, key drivers are the need for new collaborations and legislative and regulatory change, though chief executive changes are again important.'

Critical success factors

Planning a structure requires the generation of critical success factors, design options and a risk assessment. The purpose of a restructure is to align the organization to

Figure 5.2   A generic approach to restructuring

better achieve its strategy. Critical success factors are important to define, because if they are met, they will ensure success for the new structure and by implication the strategy. Although identification of these key factors is an important prerequisite to any restructuring, this task is not necessarily clear-cut. The factors themselves will depend on the organizational strategy, its culture, its market, its infrastructure and its internal processes.

We give an example from a local government authority that needed to reorientate itself to have a much greater customer and citizen focus. One of the explicit strategies was to restructure the organization in a way that would dissolve the traditional departmental boundaries and their associated destructive tensions and unhelpful silo mentality.

CRITICAL SUCCESS FACTORS FOR A LOCAL AUTHORITY

Public service users (and relevant stakeholders) not providers are the focus

Will this structure result in clear, measurable deliverables to the customers and citizens?
   To what extent have we consulted with our customers?

New working relationships are accommodated such as community leadership, neighbourhood working and political management arrangements

Does the structure reflect and support key changes in the political arrangements and thinking?

A realistic interaction is demonstrated between policy planning in all its forms, business development and financial planning at every level

Does the structure enable clear links between the different types of plans and the relevant timescales?

Better prioritization of objectives and decision making on workloads and resourcing can take place

Does the structure enable clarity around the authority's strategic objectives?
   Are there linkages across the organization?
   Is there clarity as to who is accountable for what?
   Are there supporting processes that manage potentially conflicting priorities?

Individuals are clear about their responsibilities and accountabilities and can act in an empowered way

Does the structure enable better application of the performance management system?
Are individual and team development needs identified and resourced to meet business outcomes?

A performance and feedback culture is developed across the organization, internally and externally

Does the structure help strengthen the performance and feedback culture?

Design options

Once it has been decided what factors it is important for the restructure to meet, it is important to demonstrate that these are better achieved through this structure rather than any other one.

Design options are the different ways in which the particular organization can be structured. It is not within the scope of this book to discuss in depth the different types of organizational structure – readers are encouraged to read an overview in *Organization Theory* edited by D S Pugh (1990). However we are interested not only in the general impact of restructuring but also in any specifics relating to a move from one type of structure to another. Miles and Snow (1984) detailed the evolution of organizational structure and its relationship to business strategy:

- An entrepreneurial structure when there is a single product or service, or local/regional markets.

- A functional structure when there is a limited, standardized product or service line, or regional/national markets.

- A divisional structure when there is a diversified, changing product or service line, or national/international markets.

- A matrix structure when there are standard and innovative products or services, or stable and changing markets.

- A dynamic network when there is the need for product or service design or global changing markets.

The majority of organizations are structured according to an entrepreneurial, functional, divisional or matrix structure. All have their advantages and their limitations, as outlined in Table 5.1.

Risk assessment

As you can detect from the limitations described for each of the organizational structures, there are risks attached to the restructuring process. Those identified here are obviously generic risks; however each organization will need to identify the specific risks associated with moving from one structure to another. The management therefore needs to understand fully the nature of these risks. As a concrete example we have included in the box excerpts from a risk assessment generated for a medium-sized company that had decided to move from a function-oriented organization to a divisionalized structure incorporating five product-based business units together with a centralized 'shared services' and financial control unit.

RISKS OF NEW STRUCTURE

Structure and interdependencies

Business unit structures will require some level of consistency (shape, size, roles and responsibilities, reporting lines, etc) amongst themselves to ensure that they can be adequately serviced from the centre.

Being very clear about the boundaries of the businesses we are in. That is, boundaries of the markets and boundaries between the business units.

There needs to be clarity of role and responsibility between the central services, shared services and business units.

Shared services/central service effectiveness

Shared services and, to a slightly lesser degree, central services need to be closely aligned culturally and process-wise with the business units that they interact with, to encourage efficient and effective management across the boundary.

How support services are devolved, shared and centralized requires careful planning to ensure cost-effective, efficient and productive functions.

Corporate identity

The corporate identity will be dissipated and may not be replaced.

In some areas staff's 'affinity' will be significantly diminished – how can this be managed?

Synergies

Synergies may be harder to exploit (eg deploying e-commerce solutions across business units).

Cost

Costs are likely to increase if we move to devolved support functions – what are the specific proposals that will increase income?

Cost inefficiency is a risk – the structure will inevitably lead to some duplication of costs across the business units. The structure is not ideal from a cost point of view.

Root cause

We may not address some true causes of problems that we have by thinking that we are dealing with them by restructuring.

The task for the management team was to generate an honest list, assess the degree of risk (probability x impact) and agree actions to minimize the risks. In addition, and as an example of good practice, a risk assessment was also completed for the process of managing the change as well as the changes themselves, as listed in the box.

Table 5.1 Advantages and limitations of different types of organization structure

Structure	Entrepreneurial	Functional	Divisional by product, geography or both	Matrix
Main features	Organized around one central figure. Totally centralized; no division of responsibility	Organized around tasks to be carried out. Centralized.	Divisions likely to be profit centres and may be seen as strategic business units for planning and control purposes. Divisions/business units headed by general managers who have responsibility for their own resources. Decentralized.	Double definition of profit centres. Permanent and full dual control of operating units – though one will be generally more powerful than the other. Authority and accountability defined in terms of particular decisions.
Situations where appropriate	Simple companies in early stages of their development	Small companies, few plants, limited product or service diversity. Relatively stable situations.	Growing in size and complexity. Appropriate divisional/business splits exist. Organizations growing through mergers and acquisition. Turbulent environments. When producing a number of different products or services. Geographic splits with cultural distinctions in company's markets.	Large multi-product, multinational companies with significant interrelationships and interdependencies. Small sophisticated service companies.

Advantages	Enables the founder, who has a logical or intuitive grasp of the business, to control its early growth and development	Controlled by strategic leaders/chief executive. Relatively low overheads. Efficient. Clearly delineated external relationships. Specialist managers develop expertise. Relatively simple lines of control. Can promote competitive advantage through the functions.	Spreads profit responsibility. Enables evaluation of contributions of various activities. Motivates managers and facilitates development of both specialists and generalists. Enables adaptive change. CEO concentrates on corporate strategy. Growth through acquisition easier. Can be entrepreneurial. Divestment can be managed more easily.	Decisions can be taken locally, decentralized within a large corporation, which might otherwise be bureaucratic. Optimum use of skills and resources – and high-quality informed decisions, reconciling conflicts within the organization. Enables control of growth and increasing complexity. Opportunities for management development.
Limitations	Founder may have insufficient knowledge in certain areas. Only appropriate up to a certain size.	Succession problems – specialists not generalists are created. Unlikely to be entrepreneurial or adaptive. Profit responsibility exclusively with CEO. Becomes stretched by growth and product diversification. Functional managers may concentrate on short-term routine activities at the expense of longer-term strategic developments. Problems of ensuring coordination between functions – rivalry may develop. Functional experts may seek to build mini-empires.	Conflict between divisions for resources. Possible confusion over locus of responsibility (local or head office). Duplication of efforts and resources. Divisions may think short-term and concentrate on profits. Divisions may be of different sizes and some may grow very large. Evaluation of relative performances may be difficult. Coordination of interdependent divisions and establishing transfer pricing may be difficult.	Difficult to implement. Dual responsibilities can cause confusion. Accounting and control difficulties. Potential conflict between the two wings, with one generally more powerful. High overhead costs. Decision making can be slow.

Source: summarized from Thompson (2001)

RISKS INHERENT IN MANAGING CHANGE

Management of change

The organization will spend another six months to a year with the 'eye off the ball'.

There is a lack of change/implementation expertise and skills.

The executive management team tends to get 'bored with the detail' quickly and therefore may lose interest and impetus and let both the transition and the transformation peter out.

Communications

Staff may see this as 'yet another restructure' not tackling the real problems, and therefore become demotivated.

People

We need to ensure the best people possible for each job. We need to ensure that we keep the people we want to keep.

Management of synergies

Loss of knowledge – we need to capture and transfer knowledge of, for example, strategy formulation and implementation.

We need to ensure best practice in one part of the company is transferred across the company.

Roles, responsibilities and interdependencies

Risk of business units declaring 'UDI' and not fully engaging with central services and company-wide issues.

We need to ensure those in the centre are motivated and their performance measured. We need to establish levers other than the policeman role and the threat of regulators etc.

Learning from previous projects and best practice

Clearly you do not have to reinvent the wheel when it comes to restructuring. Given the propensity for restructuring that most organizations have, you and your colleagues will have a reservoir of knowledge as to what has worked before. You will also know quite a lot about what has not worked! Now is the time to check back to see what the learnings are from previous change projects. If your organization has not formally retained this knowledge, a requisite variety of managers and staff can quite easily generate such a list. We include an example list (see box). The headings are the central themes that emerged during the session. These were the most relevant issues for the organization under review. Yours might well be different.

In terms of best practice there are many resources: this book for example, a wide range of literature, professional bodies and consultancy firms. It is important to get the right balance between what has worked elsewhere and what will work in your organization. And there is no guaranteed formula for that.

LEARNINGS FROM PREVIOUS CHANGE PROJECTS

Change management/project management

Preparation
Utilize previous learning from projects.
Check for false assumptions.
Always, always do a potential problem analysis.
Look for design faults at an early stage and throughout.
Significant top-level commitment.

Communication
Induction for all in the change.
Ensure earliest possible involvement of stakeholders.
Take the board with you.
Ensure cohesion across organization.
Harness energy and enthusiasm across organization.

Objectives
Lack of focus produces failures.
Link the hard and soft interventions and measures.
Have clear objectives.
Differentiate between the what and the how.
Specific behaviour objectives help.

Implementation
It helps to have people who have been through similar projects before.
Network of people and resources.
Dedicated project management.
Multidisciplinary approach.
Build the change management team.

Monitoring
Build in a process of automatic review.
Always evaluate, financially and otherwise.
To ensure sustainability have follow-through.

Leadership and strategy

Vision, mission and values need to be overt, obvious, communicated and followed.
Ensure alignment to strategy.

People

Don't let line managers duck the issues – build responsibilities and accountabilities into the process.

Requires involvement of people – as part of buy in, and they can actually help!

Requires communication with people.

Be honest with people.

All the new teams need to be motivated and built.

Get the right people in the right jobs.

Profitability

Always cost the initiative.

Be clear where the value is added.

Separate infrastructure investment from return on investment.

Check for false assumptions.

Project planning and project implementation

Leadership

The restructuring process can create considerable turbulence within an organization, its managers and its staff. In the box is a copy of a note to a chief executive shortly after a restructuring process had begun. It clearly identifies the state of confusion that people throughout the organization were experiencing.

MEMO TO CEO DESCRIBING THE EFFECT OF CHANGE ON STAFF

People were still very much in the throes of the changes – many clearly still affected on an emotional level by the restructuring process and all highlighting areas that need clarifying going forward.

People thought that there was a tremendous energy surrounding the changes – seeing lots of activity and lots of change being managed at a rapid pace. The downside to this was the sense that it was too fast and out of control, certainly outside of their control.

The majority of people felt positive at the ideas introduced at a high level by the strategy. Some saw it as new and exciting, others as providing one clear direction and having a certain theoretical clarity. However the overwhelming feeling was a sense that whilst the Vision was fine, there was a real lack of clarity around how it would be translated into a living workable strategy. They needed something not only motivating to aim for but also something quite specific.

Coupled with people's sense of the pace of change, many reported that not only was the direction somewhat hazy, but they saw different managers going off in different directions.

There was a certain resignation to the fact that the organization was going round and round – a 'here we go again' attitude – a sense that they had been here before and wondering whether this time would be any different.

They recognized that the direction might be clearer from the top; perhaps they were not in the right place to be seeing the bigger picture. Some people complained of having too little information, whilst others complained of having too much information. Although one could say that staff going through change may never be satisfied – or that management will always get it wrong (damned if you do, damned if you don't) – the key question is 'How do we deliver the right message, at the right time, to the right people, through the right medium?'

Coupled with this theme of communication was the perceived need to provide answers to the many questions people have when they are experiencing (psychologically) the chaos of change. Often people were left with no one to ask, or asking questions of managers who either didn't know or were themselves preoccupied with their own reactions to changes they were going through.

In summary, and from an emotional perspective, the effect of combining the various themes described above is quite a heady one. People have reported feelings of being lost and confused, anxious and worried, degrees of uncertainty and puzzlement, an inability to piece the jigsaw together and, to some, the tremendous strain of having to wait whilst the changes were revealed. Points to note here include the feeling of having no control over their destiny and also watching as others (often their managers) were suffering the traumatic effects of the changes which they themselves might have to suffer at some stage.

This is often at the very time that 'business as usual' efforts need to be redoubled. The tasks of those leading the restructure are to ensure that business as usual continues; that people are readied for operating within the new structure; and that the transition from the one structure to the new structure is smooth and timely.

Attention to both the task and people sides of the process is imperative. Depending on people's predisposition, normally one will take precedence over the other. There is a need to ensure that plans are in place for all the necessary processes that are part of the change:

- Communication plans: what, to whom, when and how.

- Selection/recruitment plans: clear guidelines for both those undergoing selection, their managers and interested onlookers. These should include criteria for selection, information about the process, timescales and rationale behind the process.

- Contingency plans: necessary if key people are unavailable at critical times or if timescales look like slipping.

Future direction and strategy

For many people the strategy and future direction behind a restructure is hazy. This is very often a case of too much vision and not enough pragmatism, but sometimes a case of too much pragmatism and not enough vision! A balance is needed.

In any restructure it is imperative to describe a positive future as well as to explain fully the rationale behind it, how it links to the strategy, how it will work in practice, how it differs from what went before, how it is better than what went before and what the benefits will be from it.

Communication

Communication in any change is absolutely essential. However communications are often variable. There is sometimes too much communication, but more often too little too late. An added problem is communication by e-mail. This is such a useful mechanism when managers need large numbers of people to receive the same information at the same time, but it is so impersonal and so heartless when delivering messages of an emotional and potentially threatening nature.

A more tailored or personalized approach is better. The greater the access to people who know the answers to the important questions, the better. FAQs (frequently asked questions) are useful to compile and communicate, but do not expect this to be the end of the story. Just because you think you have told someone something it does not mean to say he or she has heard it or assimilated it or believed. People do strange things under stress, like not listen. And they need to see the whites of your eyes when you respond!

Key questions in people's minds will be:

- What is the purpose of the restructure?

- How will it operate in practice?

- Who will be affected and how?

- What are the steps along the way, including milestones and timescales?

- How will new posts be filled and people selected?

- What happens to the others?

- Where do you go to get help and how do you get involved?

- What is the new structure and what are the new roles?

- What new behaviours be required?

- Will training and development be provided?

Communication needs to be well planned, and these plans need to be clear about how to get the right information to the right people at the right time through the right medium (for the recipient). This includes well-presented briefing notes for managers if they are to be the channel for further communication. It is also worth checking for understanding before these messengers are required to communicate the message.

Change in any form can trigger a number of emotional responses. If the messages can be personalized the recipient is more likely to receive them in a positive frame of mind. Personalized messages such as face-to-face and one-to-one communications are especially relevant when an individual may be adversely affected by the change.

Different communities of interest have different needs when it comes to communications. Some people will need to be involved, some consulted and some told. It is important that the right people get the appropriate level of communication. It is important for them and it is important for those around them. If your manager is seen to be ignored, what does it say about the value of your work section?

Thought needs to be given to the recipients of the communication. Those responsible for communicating need to ask:

- What are their needs for information?

- What is their preferred form of communication?

- When is the best time for them to be communicated with?

For example, people in a contact centre just may not have the time to read endlessly long e-mails informing them of changes in other parts of the business. However, they would probably like to be told face to face of events that will involve changes to their management structure, or the introduction of a new way of working.

To prevent the rumour mill growing it is important that communication is timely, and reaches each of the chosen communities at the agreed time. Start–stop–start again communications do not help either. A continuing flow of communication will engender more confidence in the change process.

Implementation process

The complexity of the restructuring task is often underestimated. Timescales are often not met. Staff directly affected by the change and potentially facing redundancy are subjected to undue stress because the whole process takes too long to complete.

Managing people's expectations is key. If you announce a plan, it needs to be adhered to, or changes to plan clearly communicated.

Supporting mechanisms

In order to make the restructuring as smooth as possible and ensure that the new structure gets up and running quickly, a number of support mechanisms need to be in place.

Visible managerial support

A key response of people going through the process is that their management was often ineffectual at managing change during this period. This is not necessarily the manager's fault. Many experience having to go through a selection process for themselves, many do not seem to get adequately briefed as to the nature of the changes, and some either lose their jobs or get appointed new into new positions and so do not or cannot provide the necessary support through change.

Management styles across an organization can also be variable. Often there is a reduced management visibility at these times rather than an increased visibility.

People can see a restructure as just that – a change in structure, rather than an internal realignment that would help them and the business focus on, for example, their customers and with a different way of doing things. It is the role of the manager to translate the purpose of the restructure into an understandable and viable way of doing things differently.

Continued communication of the purpose

There needs to be an ongoing planned and 'personalized' communication programme to ensure the right people get the right information at the right time in the right format for them. People need to be told and involved in how the organization will be operating differently in the future. In these two-way communications staff and managers' perspectives need to be listened to, and where valid, need to be addressed.

Clear selection process

During any selection process certain things need to be in place: first, a selection process plan that is agreed, is sensible, has an inner integrity, is consistent, equitable and scheduled; and second, clear guidelines for those undergoing selection, their managers and interested onlookers. These should include criteria for selection, information about the process, timescales, and rationale behind the process.

Senior management attention

In most instances where senior management are involved their presence is generally appreciated, even if the restructure is perceived as a negative change. The more people see the commitment of senior management the better, be it attending meetings, visiting departments, branches or contact centres to explain rationale, and face the staff.

Constructive consultation

Different organizations will have different ways of involving staff in changes. We believe that if middle managers and staff have a say in the planning of change, some of the inconsistencies and incongruities emerging from the change are picked up and addressed at a much earlier stage. If there is more input and involvement at an earlier stage from those managers who have a responsibility to manage the changes, this too has an impact on the success of the change.

Monitoring and review

Monitoring and review is not something just to be done at the end of the process and written up for the next time. If you have adopted the machine approach to restructuring, perhaps you might think that once the plan is in place, all it needs is a robotic implementation. Of course organizations are not entirely mechanistic, and individuals and groups going through change can react in all sorts of ways. The restructuring plan needs to be monitored constantly to see how both the task and people aspects of the plan are progressing. Feedback loops need to be built into the plan so that senior managers and those responsible for implementation have their fingers on the pulse of the organization.

In our discussion of individual change (see Chapter 1) we remarked that a certain amount of resistance to proposed changes is to be expected. Just because people resist change does not mean to say that you are doing it wrong! It is a naturally healthy human reaction for individuals and groups to express both positive and negative emotions around change. Managers can help this process along by encouraging straight talk.

Also, just because people resist change it does not mean to say that they have got it wrong! They might well see gaps and overlaps, or things that just are not going to work. Listening to the people who will have to make the new structure work is not only a nice thing to do, it is a useful thing to do and constitutes effective use of management time.

The process of monitoring and review should begin at the planning stage and be an important part of the whole process, right through to the point where you evaluate the effectiveness of the new structure in the months and years after implementation.

RESTRUCTURING FROM AN INDIVIDUAL CHANGE PERSPECTIVE: THE SPECIAL CASE OF REDUNDANCY

This section looks at redundancy, and how it affects those made redundant and those who survive. David Noer spent many years working with individuals in organizations and supporting them through change. He has captured much of this experience in his book *Healing the Wounds: Overcoming the trauma of layoffs and revitalizing downsized organizations* (copyright © David Noer, 1993. Sections reprinted by permission of John Wiley & Sons, Inc). Although, as the title suggests, the book is primarily focused on redundancy, there is much of benefit to anyone who wants to tackle organizational change and change management.

Noer's research is useful for illuminating the short, medium and long-term impact of change. He also suggests how a manager can intervene on a number of levels to help smoothen and perhaps quicken the change process.

Table 5.2 The individual and organizational short to long-term impact of redundancy

	Individual impact	Organizational impact
Short to medium term	Psychological contract broken Job insecurity Unfairness Distrust and sense of betrayal Depression, stress, fatigue Wanting it to be over Guilt Optimism	Reduced risk taking Reduced motivation Lack of management credibility Increased short-termism Dissatisfaction with planning and communication Anger over the process Sense of permanent change Continued commitment
Medium to long term	Insecurity Sadness Anxiety Fear Numbness Resignation Depression, stress, fatigue	Extra workload Decreased motivation Loyalty to job but not to company Increased self-reliance Sense of unfairness regarding top management pay and severance

Source: summarized from Noer (1993). Reprinted by permission of John Wiley & Sons, Inc.

Table 5.2 looks at the individual and organizational short to long-term impact that redundancy can produce. Many of these feelings are not necessarily disclosed: some are acted upon, others just experienced internally but having a clear effect on morale and motivation. Table 5.3 suggests a breakdown of what feelings are disclosed and undisclosed. You might notice that many of the feelings found amongst those going through this process are precisely the same ones that Kubler-Ross described in her work on the change curve (1969).

Table 5.3 Disclosed and undisclosed feelings about redundancy

Feelings	Disclosed	Undisclosed
Held in	Fear, insecurity and uncertainty. Easier to identify and found in every redundancy situation.	Sadness, depression and guilt. Often not acknowledged and hidden behind group bravado.
Acted out	Unfairness, betrayal and distrust. Often acted out through blaming others and constant requests for information.	Frustration, resentment and anger. Often not openly expressed but leak out in other ways.

Source: summarized from Noer (1993)

Dealing with redundancy: Noer's model

Noer sees interventions at four different levels when dealing with redundancy in an organizational context. Most managers only progress to level one, whereas Noer suggests that managers need to work with their people at all four levels. (See Figure 5.3.)

Level one: getting the implementation process right

Level one interventions are all about getting the process of change right. In any change process there needs to be a good level of efficient and effective management. This includes a communication strategy and a process that is in line with organizational values.

Noer suggests that once the decision is made to effect redundancies, it needs to be done cleanly and with compassion. This requires open communication – 'over communicating is better than under-communicating' – emotional honesty and authenticity.

Although this is just level one it is hard to get this one absolutely right!

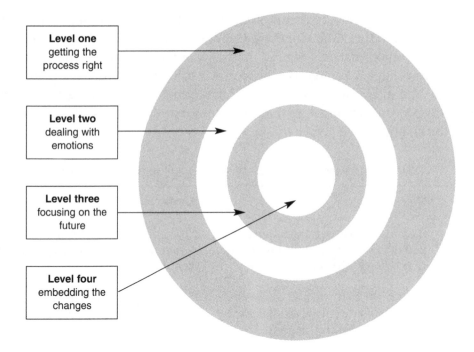

Figure 5.3   Noer's four-level redundancy intervention model
Source: Noer (1993)

Level two: dealing with emotions

Once you have attended to getting the task process right, the next level is getting the emotional process right. This involves dealing with the disclosed and undisclosed feelings mentioned above. Let us be frank: a lot of people are not very good at this. For many, allowing the release of emotions and negative thoughts about the situation feels like they are opening a hornet's nest. Managers need some support and a considerable amount of self-awareness if they are to handle this well.

There are many ways that managers can facilitate this process, with either one-to-one meetings or team meetings.

This level is about 'allowing time for expressions of feelings about situation plus implications for future and next steps for moving on'.

Level three: focusing on the future

The change curve indicates that a period of inner focus is followed by a period of outward focus. Noer's research suggests that once levels one and two have been dealt with, the organization now needs to focus on those surviving the redundancy.

This is aimed at 'recapturing' their sense of self-control, empowerment and self-esteem. In the same way that those who have been made redundant need to go through a process of regaining their self-worth and focusing on their strengths, those remaining need to do the same.

There should be plenty of organizational imperatives for this to happen! But once again, let it be a considered approach rather than haphazard. The organization would not have gone through the changes that it has, without a clear need to do so. It remains to those left to address that need – be it cost-efficiency, productivity, culture change or merger. The more that individuals and teams can be involved in shaping the organization's future, the greater will be the engagement and commitment, and the greater the chances of success.

Level four: embedding the changes

Level four interventions occur at a whole-system level. One option – the _laissez-faire_ or reactive one – is to pretend that nothing much has changed. In terms of Satir's model, as described by Weinberg, the organization can fail to really address or redress the situation. It could:

- try to reject foreign elements;

- try to accommodate foreign elements in its old model;

- try to transform the old model to receive foreign elements, but fail.

Any of these options creates a scenario in which the changes are not sustainable. Noer suggests embedding any changes made into the new way of working. This includes:

- creating structural systems and processes that treat and/or prevent survivor syndrome symptoms;

- redefining the psychological contract – being clear about what the new deal now is between employer and employee;

- enacting and embodying the new culture and its values if that is one of the stated objectives;

- ensuring all HR practices and management style are aligned with the espoused culture.

Key lessons that Noer teaches us are:

- to address change on both the task and people level;

- to pay attention, not only to what individuals and groups are going through now, but also the tasks necessary to move the organization along; to use these tasks to engage people as they come out of the more negative aspects of the change curve;

- to take the opportunity of the turbulence of the situation to embed into the organization those structures, systems and processes that will be necessary to sustain the changes in the longer term.

ENABLING TEAMS TO ADDRESS ORGANIZATIONAL CHANGE

Teams are often strongly impacted by restructuring processes. Their composition changes, or they have a new leader, or maybe they have a new purpose. There needs to be a process for quickly establishing individual and team roles, responsibilities and priorities.

Issues that teams and groups have to contend with during periods of organizational change brought about by restructuring include:

- loss of individual roles and jobs;

- new individual roles and jobs;

- loss of team members;

- new team members;

- new team purpose and objectives;

- new line manager;

- new organizational or departmental strategy.

Any of these can cause individual members of a team, or the team as a whole, to experience a range of emotions and new ways of thinking about their organization, their colleagues and their own career.

Teams need to develop so that their contribution to the organizational changes can be as good as possible as quickly as possible.

From our consultancy experience we find one particular framework useful for newly restructured teams. This framework encompasses a number of the issues we have highlighted. We encourage teams to work through the four-part framework in order to establish quickly the sense of team cohesion necessary for tasks to be accomplished in a meaningful and collaborative way. This is best done in a workshop format.

We have found that if a team spends the time to focus both on the people and task side of this process, it will be able to deal with the transition less turbulently than one that has not.

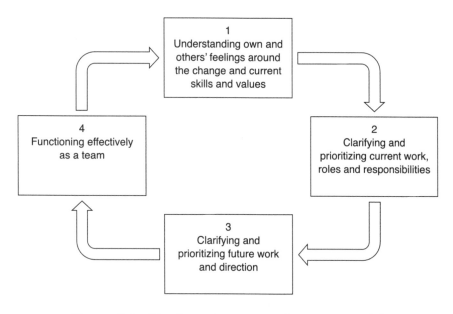

Figure 5.4 The four-stage team alignment model

Four-stage team alignment

1. Understanding one another's skills, feelings and values.

    It is useful for the team to acknowledge its own journey to where it is today. This means talking about the individuals, the team and other influential parts of the organization, and the processes of changes that have been gone through to arrive at the current situation. How much of this it is necessary to acknowledge will depend upon the scale of change and the story so far.

Table 5.4 Addressing team change during restructuring

	Forming		Storming	
	Task (orientation)	People (dependency)	Task (organization)	People (conflict)
Team purpose	Establish purpose of change and team objectives in relation to change	Ensure understanding and commitment from team around change purpose on an intellectual and emotional level	Ensure clarity around purpose of change and team objectives in relation to change	Check out individual engagement to purpose (enrolment, enlistment, compliance, resistance). Discuss differences.
Team roles	Establish roles and responsibilities of whole team and individual members	Ensure individuals understand their roles and those of others. Establish whether there are any overlaps or grey areas.	Ensure clarity of roles and responsibilities of whole team and individual members	Establish degree of comfort with individual roles and establish levels of support and challenge required. Highlight areas of team tension.
Team processes	Highlight the need for team processes	Establish groundrules for team working	Establish processes for decision making, problem solving, conflict resolution if not already in place	Check out levels of trust and agreement. Surface areas of team tension.
Team relations	Highlight the need for team processes	Establish groundrules for team working	Ensure team is agreed on purpose, objectives, roles and processes	Build safe environment for team to openly express thoughts and feelings
Inter-team relations	Establish dependencies on and with other organizational groupings	Highlight the need to establish protocols with key organizational groupings	Establish process for communicating with other organizational groupings	Engage with other groupings on how they will work together
MBTI*	Ensure balance between high level vision and more tangible and specific objectives	Balance between acknowledging the business case for the change and individuals' feelings about the change	Ensure balance between tying agreements down and keeping options open	Ensure that different types are understood and potential pitfalls and communication barriers
Key Belbin roles	Chair, shaper, plant, company worker	Chair, team worker	Chair, resource investigator	Chair, team worker, monitor-evaluator
Organizational focus	Ensure alignment of team goals to organizational change objectives	Ensure team members engage on an intellectual and emotional level with organizational goals	Ensure team structure, roles and responsibilities fit with proposed changes and organizational ethos	Ensure commitment to organizational goals and operating in line with values

	Norming		Performing	
	Task (open data flow)	People (cohesion)	Task (problem solving)	People (interdependence)
Team purpose	Review progress on team purpose and objectives; adjust as necessary	Review progress, recognize achievement	Review progress on team purpose and objectives; adjust as necessary	Review team performance against purpose, recommit as necessary
Team roles	Review roles and responsibilities; adjust as necessary	Review progress, recognize achievements and development areas	Review roles and responsibilities; adjust as necessary. Develop strategies for improving performance.	Review individual role performance and structure, recognize achievement and provide development
Team processes	Review team processes; adjust as necessary	Review team processes; adjust as necessary	Review team processes; adjust as necessary. Develop strategies for improving performance.	Review level of team efficiency; adjust as necessary. Develop strategies for improving performance.
Team relations	Review team relations; attend to if necessary	Review progress; recognize achievement	Review team relations; attend to if necessary. Develop strategies for improving performance.	Reflect upon level of team effectiveness. Develop strategies for improving performance.
Inter-team relations	Review level of inter-team working; plan negotiations if necessary	Review level of inter-team working; engage others in negotiating better relations if necessary	Implement actions from review if necessary. Develop strategies for improving performance.	Continue to foster good working relations with other organizational groupings
MBTI*	Review predominate team type, take appropriate managerial action, if necessary	Review team strengths and weaknesses and develop blind spots	Balance time between reviewing past performance and planning future changes	Balance time between individual and team needs, past performance and future planning
Key Belbin roles	Monitor-evaluator, shaper, company worker, completer-finisher	Chair, monitor-evaluator, team worker	Shaper, (plant), monitor-evaluator, completer-finisher	Chair, monitor-evaluator, team worker
Organizational focus	As team begins to experience less turbulence, review alignment with organizational goals and check team performance against milestones	Ensure team model values and espoused behaviours within and outside of team	Ensure team in all of its five elements is performing at an effective level	Ensure team is operating effectively across organizational boundaries

* MBTI = Myers Briggs Type Indicator

2. Clarifying and prioritizing current work.

    The team need to clarify the current level of demand, and must work together to satisfy current customer needs.

3. Clarifying and prioritizing future work and direction.

    If teams are facing a large change agenda, they can easily become overwhelmed unless activities are phased and planned. Do-ability must be convincing. Teams need to take stock of their current agenda, ensure it is understood, and agree priorities, responsibilities and timing.

4. Functioning effectively as a team.

    The impact of stages 1 to 3 can be extremely demanding on a team. The team needs to develop clarity about its roles, dynamics, practicalities of meetings, phasing of its development activities, communication and follow-through. Most teams will have deficiencies and development needs in one or more areas. Teams need to assess where they need to improve and focus on those areas as a priority.

The specific outcome of this process for individuals and teams is greater clarity about the practical changes that need to happen and how necessary transformations can be managed.

You will have seen from the chapters on individual and team change that all individuals and teams undergoing change will progress through various stages. The four-stage team alignment model above attempts to address some of the key points from those chapters. Table 5.4 on pages 190 and 191 brings all the key team factors together in one table as useful reference.

CONCLUSION

Restructuring is an ever-present phenomenon in today's organizations, and the process itself can be deeply unrewarding for those who initiate and those who experience it. We have drawn together ideas in Table 5.4, from both a task and a people perspective, which will increase the chances of achieving a smoother journey. However it must be emphasized that turbulence is one thing you will not avoid. How you manage it will be the test of how well you can lead change.

6

Mergers and acquisitions

This chapter addresses the specific change scenario of tackling a merger or an acquisition. We pose the following questions:

- Why do organizations get involved in mergers and acquisitions? Are there different aims, and therefore different tactics involved in making this type of activity work?

- Merger and acquisition activity has been very high over the last 10 years, and at a global scale. We must have learnt something from all this activity. What are the conclusions?

- Can the theory of change in individuals, groups and organizations be used to increase the success rate of mergers and acquisitions, and if so, how can it be applied?

The chapter has the following four sections:

- the purpose of merger and acquisition activity;

- lessons from research into successful and unsuccessful mergers and acquisitions;

- applying the change theory: guidelines for leaders;

- conclusions.

THE PURPOSE OF MERGER AND ACQUISITION ACTIVITY

We begin with a short history of mergers and acquisitions. It is useful to track the changes in direction that merger and acquisition activity have gone through over the last 100 years to achieve a sense of perspective on the different strategies employed. Gaughan (2002) refers to five waves of merger and acquisition activity since 1897 (see box), claiming that we are currently in the fifth wave of this ever-evolving field. However activity has slowed recently, with reported figures showing a 26 per cent reduction in global merger and acquisition activity in 2002.

THE FIVE WAVES OF MERGER AND ACQUISITION ACTIVITY

First wave (1897–1904): *horizontal* combinations and *consolidations* of several industries, US dominated.

Second wave (1916–29): mainly *horizontal* deals, but also many *vertical* deals, US dominated.

Third wave (1965–69): the *conglomerate* era involving acquisition of companies in different industries.

Fourth wave: (1981–89): the era of the *corporate raider*, financed by junk bonds.

Fifth wave: (1992–?): larger mega mergers, more activity in Europe and Asia. More *strategic* mergers designed to compliment company strategy.

Source: adapted from Gaughan (2002)

It is important to classify types of merger and acquisition to gain an understanding of the different motivations behind the activity. Gaughan (2002) points out that there are three types of merger or acquisition deal: a horizontal deal involves merging with or acquiring a competitor, a vertical deal involves merging with or acquiring a company with whom the firm has a supplier or customer relationship, and a conglomerate deal involves merging with or acquiring a company that is neither a competitor, nor a buyer nor a seller.

So why do companies embark on a merger or acquisition? The reasons are listed below.

Growth

Most mergers and acquisitions are about growth. Merging or acquiring another company provides a quick way of growing, which avoids the pain and uncertainty of internally generated growth. However, it brings with it the risks and challenges of realizing the intended benefits of this activity. The attractions of immediate revenue growth must be weighed up against the downsides of asking management to run an even larger company.

Growth normally involves acquiring new customers (for example, Vodafone and Airtouch), but can be about getting access to facilities, brands, trademarks, technology or even employees.

Synergy

Synergy is a familiar word in the mergers and acquisitions world. If two companies are thought to have synergy, this refers to the potential ability of the two organizations to be more successful when merged than they were apart (the whole is greater than the sum of the parts). This usually translates into:

- Growth in revenues through a newly created or strengthened product or service (hard to achieve).

- Cost reductions in core operating processes through economies of scale (easier to achieve).

- Financial synergies such as lowering the cost of capital (cost of borrowing, flotation costs).

However, there may be other gains. Some acquisitions can be motivated by the belief that the acquiring company has better management skills, and can therefore manage the acquired company's assets and employees more successfully in the long term and more profitably.

Mergers and acquisitions can also be about strengthening quite specific areas, such as boosting research capability, or strengthening the distribution network.

Diversification

Diversification is about growing business outside the company's traditional industry. This type of merger or acquisition was very popular during the third wave in the 1960s (see box). Although General Electric (GE) has flourished by following a strategy that embraced both diversification and divestiture, many companies following this course have been far less successful.

Diversification may result from a company's need to develop a portfolio through nervousness about the earning potential of its current markets, or through a desire to enter a more profitable line of business. The latter is a tough target, and economic theory suggests that a diversification strategy to gain entry into more profitable areas of business will not be successful in the long run (see Gaughan, 2002 for more explanation of this).

A classic recent example of this going wrong is Marconi, which tried to diversify by buying US telecoms businesses. Unfortunately, this was just before the whole telecoms market crashed, and Marconi suffered badly from this strategy.

Integration to achieve economic gains

Another motive for merger and acquisition activity is to achieve horizontal integration. A company may decide to merge with or acquire a competitor to gain market share and increase its marketing strength.

Vertical integration is also an attraction. A company may decide to merge with or acquire a customer or a supplier to achieve at least one of the following:

- a dependable source of supply;

- the ability to demand specialized supply;

- lower costs of supply;

- improved competitive position.

Pressure to do a deal, any deal

There is often tremendous pressure on the CEO to reinvest cash and grow reported earnings (Selden and Colvin, 2003). He or she may be being advised to make the deal quickly before a competitor does, so much so that the CEO's definition of success becomes completion of the deal rather than the longer-term programme of achieving intended benefits. This is dangerous because those merging or acquiring when in this frame of mind can easily overestimate potential revenue increases or costs savings. In short, they can get carried away.

Feldmann and Spratt (1999) warn of the seductive nature of merger and acquisition activity. 'Executives everywhere, but most particularly those in the world's largest corporations and institutions, have a knack for falling prey to their own hype and promotion.... Implementation is simply a detail and shareholder value is just around the corner. This is quite simply delusional thinking.'

Table 6.1 Comparison of reasons for embarking on a merger or acquisition

Reason for M&A activity	Advantages	Disadvantages	Organizational implications
Growth	Immediate revenue growth pleases shareholders. Reduction in competition (if other party is competitor). Good way of overcoming barriers to entry to specific areas of business.	More work for the top team. Hard to sustain the benefits once initial savings have been made. Cultural problems often hard to overcome, thus potential not realized.	Top team required to make a step change in performance. New arrivals in top team. Probably some administrative efficiencies. Integration in some areas if beneficial to results.
Synergy	May offer significant, easy cost-reduction benefits. Attractive concept for employees (unless they have 'heard it all before').	More subtle forms of synergy such as product or service gains may be difficult to realize without significant effort. Cultural issues may cause problems that are hard to overcome.	Top teams need to work closely together on key areas of synergy. Other areas left intact.
Diversification	May offer the possibility for entering new, inaccessible markets. Allows company to expand its portfolio if uncertain about current business levels.	Economic theory suggests that potential gains of entering more profitable profit streams may not be realized. May be hard for top team to agree strategy due to little understanding of each other's business areas.	Loosely coupled management teams, joint reporting, some administrative efficiencies, separate identities and logos
Integration	Buyer or supplier power automatically reduced if other party is buyer or supplier. More control of customer demands or supply chain respectively. Reduction in competition (if other party is competitor). Increase in market share/marketing strength.	More work for the top team. In the case of horizontal integration (other party is a competitor), cultural problems often hard to overcome, thus potential not realized.	Integrated top team, merged administrative systems, tightly coupled core processes, single corporate identity
Deal doing	Seductive and thrilling. Publicity surrounding the deal augments the CEO's and the company's profile.	The excitement of the deal may cloud the CEO's judgement.	Anyone's guess!

LESSONS FROM RESEARCH INTO SUCCESSFUL AND UNSUCCESSFUL MERGERS AND ACQUISITIONS

The following quote from Selden and Colvin (2003) gives us a starting point:

> 70% to 80% of acquisitions fail, meaning they create no wealth for the share owners of the acquiring company. Most often, in fact, they destroy wealth.... Deal volume during the historic M&A wave of 1995 to 2000 totalled more than $12 trillion. By an extremely conservative estimate, these deals annihilated at least $1 trillion of share-owner wealth.

Selden and Colvin put the problems down to companies failing to look beyond the lure of profits. They urge CEOs to examine the balance sheet, and say that M&As should be seen as a way to create shareholder value through customers, and should start with an analysis of customer profitability.

However, this contrasting quote from Alex Mandl, CEO of Teligent since 1996, in a *Harvard Business Review* interview (Carey, 2000) provides a different view:

> I would take issue with the idea that most mergers end up being failures. I know there are studies in the 1970s and 80's that will tell you that. But when I look at many companies today – particularly new economy companies like Cisco and WorldCom – I have a hard time dismissing the strategic power of M&A. In the last three years, growth through acquisition has been a critical part of the success of many companies operating in the new economy.

Carey's interview occurred before the collapse of Enron and WorldCom, so he did not know what we know now. The recent demise of both Enron and WorldCom due to major scandals over illegal accounting practices has considerably dampened enthusiasm for merger and acquisition activity worldwide. These events have raised big questions about companies that finance continuous acquisitions as a core business strategy. The use of what *BusinessWeek* describes as 'new era' accounting is making investors nervous, and causing companies to be very careful with their investments and their financial reporting.

The discussion about the overall success rate of merger and acquisition activity still continues. But what lessons can be learnt from previous experience of undertaking these types of organizational change?

CASE STUDY OF SUCCESS: ISPAT

Ispat is an international steel-making company which successfully pursues long-term acquisition strategies. It is one of the world's largest steel companies and its growth has come almost entirely through a decade-long series of acquisitions.

Ispat's acquisitions are strictly focused. It never goes outside its core business. It has a well-honed due diligence process which it uses to learn about the people who are running the target company and convince them that joining Ispat will give them an opportunity to grow.

The company works with the potential acquisition's management to develop a five-year business plan that will not only provide an acceptable return on investment, but chime with Ispat's overall strategy.

Ispat relies on a team of 12 to 14 professionals to manage its acquisitions. Based in London, the team's members have solid operational backgrounds and have worked together since 1991.

We have taken several different sources, all of which propose a set of rules for mergers and acquisitions, and distilled these into five learning points:

- Communicate constantly.

- Get the structure right.

- Tackle the cultural issues.

- Keep customers on board.

- Use a clear overall process.

Communicate constantly

In the excitement of the deal, company bosses often forget that the merger or acquisition is more than a financial deal or a strategic opportunity. It is a human transaction between people too. Top managers need to do more than simply state the facts and figures; they need to employ all sorts of methods of communication to enhance relationships, establish trust, get people to think and innovate together and build commitment to a joint future. They also need to use all the avenues available to them such as:

- company presentations;

- formal question and answer sessions;

- newsletters;

- team briefings;

- noticeboards;

- newsletters;

- e-mail communication;

- confidential helplines;

- Web sites with questions and answer session;

- conference calls.

COMMUNICATE CONSTANTLY

The top team had been working on the acquisition plans for over four months. Once the announcement was eventually made to all employees I just wanted to get on with things. I had so much enthusiasm for the deal. There was just endless business potential.

The difficulties came when I realized that not everyone shared my enthusiasm. My direct reports and their direct reports constantly asked me detailed questions about job roles and terms and conditions. It was beginning to really frustrate me that they couldn't see the big picture.

I found I had to talk about our visions for the future and our schedule for sorting out the structure at least five times a day, if not more. People needed to hear and see me say it, and needed me to keep on saying it. I learned to keep my cool when repeating myself for the fifth time that day.

MD of acquiring company

Devine (1999) of Roffey Park says that managers with merger and acquisition experience tend to agree that it is impossible to over-communicate during a merger. They advocate the use of specific opportunities for staff to discuss company communications. They also advise managers to encourage their people to read e-mails and attend communication meetings, watching out for those who might be inclined to stick their heads in the sand. Managers need to be prepared as regards formal communications:

- Develop your answers to tricky questions before you meet up with the team.

- Expect some negative reactions and decide how to handle these.

- Be prepared to be open about the extent of your own knowledge.

Carey (2000) says it is necessary to have constant communication to counteract rumours. He advises, 'When a company is acquired, people become extremely sensitive to every announcement. Managers need to constantly communicate to avoid the seizure that may come from over-reaction to badly delivered news.'

In company communications, it is very important to be clear on timescales, particularly when it comes to defining the new structure. People want to know how this merger or acquisition will affect them, and when. Carey (2000) says, 'Everyone will be focused on the question "what happens to me?" They will not hear presentations about vision or strategic plans. They need the basic question regarding their own fate to be answered. If this cannot be done, then the management team should at least publish a plan for when it will be done.'

PRODUCTIVITY LEVELS DURING TIMES OF CHANGE

A very interesting statistic I once read says that people are normally productive for about 5–7 hours in an eight-hour business day. But any time a change of control takes place, their productivity falls to less than an hour.

Dennis Kozlowski, CEO Tyco International, quoted in Carey (2000)

Get the structure right

THE IMPORTANCE OF DECISIONS ABOUT STRUCTURE

At the time we thought it best to keep everyone happy and productive. Both the merged companies had good production managers, so we decided to ask them to work alongside each other, to share skills and learn a bit about the other person's way of working.

We thought this was the best idea to keep production high, and to promote harmony and learning. However, in the end it turned out to be highly unproductive. It was a huge strain for the two individuals involved in both cases. They thought they were being set up to compete, despite protestations that this was not so. Both began to show signs of stress.

This structural decision (or rather indecision) also slowed the integration process down as people wanted to stay loyal to their original manager. They studiously avoided reporting at all to the new manager from the other company. Joint projects ended in stalemate and integration of working standards was almost impossible to achieve.

HR Director, involved in designing structure for merger

Structure is always a thorny issue for merging or acquiring companies. How do you create a structure that keeps the best of what is already there, while providing opportunities for the team to achieve the stretching targets that you aspire to?

Carey makes the point that it is essential to match the new company structure to the logic of the acquisition. If for example the intention was to fully integrate two sales teams to provide cost savings in administration and improve sales capability, then the structure should reflect this. It is tempting for senior managers to avoid conflict by appointing joint managers. Although this may work for the managers, it does not usually work for the teams. Integration becomes hard work as individuals prefer to keep reporting lines as they were.

Structure work should start early. Carey advises managers to begin working on the new structure before the deal is closed. Some companies use an integration team to work on this sort of planning. These people are in the ideal position to ask the CEO, 'What was the intended gain of this acquisition?' and 'How will this structure support our goals?'

It is important that promotion opportunities provided by merger or acquisition activity are seen as golden opportunities for communicating the goals and values of the new company. Feldmann and Spratt (1999) warn against 'putting turtles on fence posts'. They emphasize the importance of providing good role models, and encourage senior managers to promote only those who provide good examples of how they want things to be. They say 'do not compromise on selection by indulging in a quota system (two of theirs and two of ours)'. And do not be tempted to fudge roles so that both people think they have got the best deal. This will only result in arguments and friction further down the line.

Tackle the cultural issues

Issues of cultural incompatibility have often been cited as problem areas when implementing a merger or acquisition. Merging a US and a European company can be complicated because management styles are very different. For instance US companies are known to be more aggressive with cost cutting, while European companies may take a longer view. Reward strategy and degree of centralization are also areas of difference. Jan Leschly, CEO of SmithKline Beecham, says in 'Lessons for master acquirers' (in Carey, 2000), 'The British and American philosophies are so far apart on those subjects they're almost impossible to reconcile.'

David Komansky, CEO of Merrill Lynch, made over 18 acquisitions between 1996 and 2001. In the same _HBR_ article (Carey, 2000), he says:

> It's totally futile to impose a U.S.-centric culture on a global organization. We think of our business as a broad road within the bounds of our strategy and our principles of doing business. We don't expect them to march down the white line, and, frankly, we don't care too much if they are on the left-hand side of the road or the right-hand side of the road. You need to adapt to local ways of doing things.

The amount of cultural integration required depends on the reason for the merger or acquisition. If core processes are to be combined for economies of scale, then integration is important and needs to be given management time and attention. However, if the company acquires a portfolio of diverse businesses it is possible that culture integration will only be necessary at the senior management level.

The best way to integrate cultures is to get people working together on solving business problems and achieving results that could not have been achieved before the merger or acquisition. In 'Making the deal real' (Ashkenas, Demonaco and Francis, 1998), the authors have distilled their acquisition experiences at GE into four steps intended to bridge cultural gaps:

- Welcome and meet early with the new acquisition management team. Create a 100-day plan with their help.

- Communicate and keep the process going. Pay attention to audience, timing, mode and message. This does not just mean bulletins, but videos, memos, town meetings and visits from management.

- Address cultural issues head-on by running a focused, facilitated 'cultural workout' workshop with the new acquisition management team. This is grounded on analysis of cultural issues and focused on costs, brands, customers and technology.

- Cascade the integration process through, giving others access to a cultural workout.

Roffey Park research (Devine, 1999) confirms the need to tackle cultural issues. This research shows that culture clashes are the main source of merger failure and can cost as much as 25–30 per cent in lost performance. They identify some of the signs of a culture clash:

- People talk in terms of 'them and us'.

- People glorify the past, talking of the 'good old days'.

- Newcomers are vilified.

- There is obvious conflict – arguments, refusal to share information, forming coalitions.

- One party in the merger is portrayed as 'stronger' and the other as 'weaker'.

Therefore an examination of existing cultures is normally useful if there is even a small possibility that cultural issues will get in the way of the merger or acquisition being successful. This is a good exercise to carry out in workshop format with the teams themselves at all levels. The best time to look at cultural issues is when teams are forming right at the start of the integration. It breaks the ice for people and allows them to find out a bit about each other's history and company culture.

TACKLING THE CULTURAL ISSUES

The managers from company A described their culture as:
- fairly formal;
- courteous and caring;
- high standards;
- lots of team work;
- clear roles.

Company B added:
- precise;
- good reputation.

The managers from company B described their culture as:
- highly informal;
- a bit disorganized;
- relationships are important;
- customer focused;
- fast and fun.

Company A added:
- flexible roles;
- lack of hierarchy.

New culture – what did they need:
- role clarity;
- adaptability;

- high standards;
- customer focus;
- responsiveness;
- enjoyment;
- team work.

What might be the difficult areas:

- Balancing clarity of roles with adaptability – culture clash?
- Achieving high standards without getting too formal.
- Being responsive while keeping to high standards.
- Working as one team, rather than two teams.

Action plan:

1. Define flexible roles for all management team. Must be half page long.
2. Highlight areas where standards need to be reviewed.
3. Audit customer responsiveness and set targets.
4. Tackle each of the above by creating small task force with members from both companies.

Output from a management team meeting focusing on building a new culture.

Cultural differences can be looked at using a simple cultural model such as the one offered in *Riding the Waves of Culture: Understanding cultural diversity in business* by Fons Trompenaars and Charles Hampden-Turner (1997). See Figure 6.1 for our representation of the various scales. People from each merger partner mark themselves on these scales and openly compare scores. In the workshop it is useful to ask the team to predict what kind of difficulties they might have as they start to work together, and to make an action plan to address these. We have run several such workshops, and in these we strongly encourage people to try to work together to define the new culture. This can be challenging work, especially if the acquisition or merger is perceived as hostile, but necessary work if any sort of integration is desired.

Roffey Park's advice appears below:

- Identify the key tactics used by team members to adhere to their own cultures.

- Identify cultural 'hot-spots', highly obvious differences in working practices that generate tension and conflict.

- Using a cultural model, get team members to explore the traits of their cultures, ask them what was good or bad about their former cultures.

Cultural dimensions				
Rule versus relationships	Universalist Focus on rules		⟷	Particularist Focus on relationships
The group versus the individual	Individualism More use of "I"		⟷	Communitarianism More use of 'We'
The range of feelings expressed	Neutral Do not reveal thoughts and feelings		⟷	Affective Reveal thoughts and feelings
The range of involvement	Specific Direct		⟷	Diffuse Indirect
How status is accorded	Achievement oriented Use titles only when relevant to task		⟷	Ascription oriented Extensive use of titles

Figure 6.1 Trompenaars and Hampden-Turner's cultural dimensions
Source: Trompenaars and Hampden-Turner (1997).

- Get your people to identify cultural values of meanings that are important to them and that they wish to preserve.

- Challenge team members to identify a cluster of values that everyone can commit to and use as a foundation for working together.

Keep customers on board

> Customers feel the effects first.… They don't care about your internal problems, and they most certainly aren't going to pay you to fix them.
>
> (Feldmann and Spratt, 1999)

'It's very easy to be so focused on the deal that customers are forgotten. Early plans for who will control customer relationships after the merger or acquisition are essential,' says Carey (2000). Devine (1999) adds weight to this by commenting:

> Mergers are often highly charged and unpredictable experiences. It is all too easy to take your eye off the ball and to forget the very reason for your existence. Ensure that your team concentrates on work deliverables so that everyone remembers that there is a world outside and that it is still as competitive and pressurized as ever. Help everyone to realize that your competitors will be on the lookout for opportunities to exploit any weaknesses arising from the merger. You might find that in the face of an external threat, cultural differences shrink in importance.

Some of our experiences as consultants contradict the idea that increased focus on the customer can help a team to forget cultural differences. The opposite effect can happen, where teams and individuals from the two original merging companies use customer focus to further accentuate cultural difficulties:

- Sales people fight over customers and territory.

- Managers blame each other rather than help each other when accounts are lost.

- People from company A apologize to customers for the 'shortcomings' of people from company B rather than back them up.

This lesson accentuates the need to tackle cultural issues early, as well as to define clear groundrules for working with customers as one team.

HOW TO KEEP CUSTOMERS ON BOARD

One of our first actions was to embark on a series of customer visits that involved a senior sales person from both the merging companies. This allowed us to learn how to work together, and fast! It reassured customers and allowed us to deliver a clear message:

- _we were now one company;_
- _there would be a single point of contact going forward;_
- _the merger was amicable and well managed._

Sales Manager from merged retail company

AVOIDING THE SEVEN DEADLY SINS

Feldmann and Spratt (1999) identify seven deadly sins in implementing a merger or acquisition. Their book goes on to describe in detail how to ensure that you avoid these problems.

- **Sin 1: Obsessive list making.** Don't make lists of everything that needs to be done – it is exhausting and demoralizing. Instead, use the 80:20 rule. Focus on the 20 per cent of tasks that add the most value.

- **Sin 2: Content-free communications.** Don't send out communications that contain only hype and promotion. Employees, customers, suppliers and shareholders all have real questions, so answer them.

- **Sin 3: Creating a planning circus.** Use targeted task forces, rather than a hierarchy of slow-paced committees.

- **Sin 4: Barnyard behaviour.** Unless roles and relationships are clarified, feathers will fly in an attempt to establish pecking order. Simply labelling the hierarchy will not sort this one out.
- **Sin 5: Preaching vision and values.** If you want cultural change, you have to work at it. It will not happen through proclamation.
- **Sin 6: Putting turtles on fence posts.** Ensure that the role models you select for promotion provide good examples of how you want things to be. Do not compromise on selection by indulging in a quota system (two of theirs and two of ours).
- **Sin 7: Rewarding the wrong behaviours.** Sort out compensation and link it to the right behaviours.

Use a clear overall process

The pitfalls associated with planning and successfully executing a merger or acquisition imply that it is important to have an overarching process to work to. GE's Pathfinder Model is summarized in Table 6.2. It acts as a useful checklist for those involved in acquisition work (more in Ashkenas, Demonaco and Francis, 1998). This model, derived through internal discussion and review, forms the basis for GE's acquisitions programme.

Table 6.2 Adapted version of GE's Pathfinder Model

Preacquisition	• Assess cultural strengths and potential barriers to integration. • Appoint integration manager. • Rate key managers of core units. • Develop strategy for communicating intentions and progress.
Foundation building	• Induct new executives into acquiring company's core processes. • Jointly work on short and long-term business plans with new executives. • Visibly involve senior people. • Allocate the right resources and appoint the right people.
Rapid Integration	• Speed up integration by running cultural workshops and doing intensive joint process mapping. • Conduct process audits. • Pay attention to and learn from feedback as you go along. • Exchange managers for short-term learning opportunities.
Assimilation	• Keep on learning and developing shared tools, language, processes. • Continue longer-term management exchanges. • Make use of training and development facilities to keep the learning going. • Audit the integration process

Source: Ashkenas, Demonaco and Francis (1998)

USE A CLEAR PHASED PROCESS

It's easy to get sucked into mindless list generation. There is an extraordinary amount of stuff to be done when you merge with another company. The trouble is that list making is very tiring, and the lists have to be numbered and monitored which takes time and effort. We found that it was much simpler to develop a phased process than to list everything that needed to be done. We then created a timeline with obvious milestones such as 'structure chart delivered', or 'terms and conditions harmonized'. This helps people to keep on track without creating a circus of action planning and reporting.

Organization development manager talking about the merger
of two management consultancies

APPLYING THE CHANGE THEORY: GUIDELINES FOR LEADERS

Which elements of the theory discussed in earlier chapters can be used to inform those leading merger and acquisition activity? We make links with ideas about individual, team and organizational change to help leaders to channel their activities throughout this turbulent process. In addition, we refer to the previously mentioned research into successful mergers and acquisitions by Roffey Park Institute (Devine, 1999) which offers some useful guidelines for organizational leaders.

Managing the individuals

Mergers and acquisitions bring uncertainty, and uncertainty in turn brings anxiety. The question on every person's mind is, 'What happens to me in this?' Once this question is answered satisfactorily, each individual can then begin to address the important challenges ahead. Until that time, there will be anxiety. Some people will be more anxious than others depending on their personal style, personal history and proximity to the proposed changes. And if people do not like the look of the future, there will be a reaction.

The job of the leader in a merger or acquisition situation is firstly to ensure that the team know things will not be the same any more. Second, he or she needs to ensure people understand what will change, what will stay the same, and when all this will happen. Third, the leader needs to provide the right environment for people to try out new ways of doing things.

Schein (see Chapter 1) claims that healthy individual change happens when there is a good balance between anxiety about the future and anxiety about trying out new ways of working. The first anxiety must be greater than the second, but the first must not be too high, otherwise there will be paralysis or chaos.

In a merger or acquisition situation there is very little safety. People are anxious about their futures as well as uncertain about what new behaviours are required. This means the leader has to create psychological safety by:

- painting pictures of the future; visioning;

- acting as a strong role model of desired behaviours;

- being consistent about systems and structures.

But not by:

- avoiding the truth;

- saying that nothing will change;

- hiding from the team;

- putting off the delivery of bad news.

Chapter 1 addressed individual change by first introducing three schools of thought:

- behavioural;

- cognitive;

- psychodynamic.

The behavioural model is useful as a reminder that reward strategies form an important part of the merger and acquisition process and must be addressed reasonably early. The cognitive model is based on the premise that our thinking affects our behaviour. This means that goal setting and role modelling too are important.

However, the psychodynamic approach provides the most useful model to explain the process of individual change during the various stages of a merger or acquisition. In Table 6.3 we use the Kubler-Ross model from Chapter 1 to illustrate individual experiences of change and effective management interventions during this process of change.

Table 6.3 Stages of merger or acquisition process and how to manage reactions of staff

Stage	Employee experience	Management action
Merger or acquisition is announced	Shock. Disbelief. Relief that rumours are confirmed.	Give full and early communication of reasons behind, and aims of this merger or acquisition
Specific plans are announced	Denial – it's not really happening. Mixture of excitement and anxiety. Anger and blame – 'This is all about greed', If we'd won the ABC contract we wouldn't be in this position now.'	Discuss implications of the merger or acquisition with individuals and team. Give people a timescale for clarification of the new structure and when they will know what their role will be in the new company. Acknowledge people's needs and concerns even though you cannot solve them all. Be patient with people's concerns. Be clear about the future. Find out and get back to them about the details you do not know yet. Do not take their emotional outbursts personally.
Changes start to happen – new bosses, new customers, new colleagues, redundancies	Depression – finally letting go of two companies, and accepting the new company. Acceptance.	Acknowledge the ending of an era. Hold a wake for the old company and keep one or two bits of memorabilia (photos, T-shirts). Delegate new responsibilities to your team. Encourage experimentation, especially with building new relationships. Give positive feedback when people take risks. Create new joint goals. Discuss and agree new groundrules for the new team. Coach in new skills and behaviours.
New organization begins to take shape	Trying new things out. Finding new meaning. Optimism. New energy.	Encourage risk taking. Foster communication at all levels between the two parties. Create development opportunities, especially where people can learn from new colleagues. Discuss new values and ways of working. Reflect on experience, reviewing how much things have changed since the start. Celebrate successes as one group.

Managing the team

Endings and beginnings are important features of mergers and acquisitions, and these are most usefully addressed at the team level. The ideas of William Bridges (Chapter 3) provide a useful template for management activity during ending, the neutral zone and the new beginnings that occur during a merger or acquisition.

Managing endings

The endings are about saying goodbye to the old way of things. This might be specific ways of working, a familiar building, team mates, a high level of autonomy or some well-loved traditions. In the current era of belt-tightening and cost-cutting, there might be quite a lot of losses for people, similar to the effects of a restructuring exercise. (See Chapter 1 for more tips on handling redundancies.) Here is some advice for how managers can manage the ending phase (or how to get them to let go):

- Acknowledge that the old company is ending, or the old ways of doing things are ending.

- Give people time to grieve for the loss of familiar people if redundancies are made. Publish news of their progress in newsletters.

- Do something to mark the ending: for example have a team drink together specifically to acknowledge the last day of trading as the old company.

- Be respectful about the past. It is tempting to denigrate the old management team or the old ways of working to make the new company look more attractive. This will not work. It will just create resentment.

Managing the transition from old to new

This phase of a merger or acquisition, often known as integration, can be chaotic if it is not well managed. The 'barnyard behaviour' mentioned above combined with high anxiety about the future can lead to good people leaving and stress levels reaching all-time highs. Conflicts that are not nipped in the bud at this stage can lead to huge and permanent rifts between the two companies involved.

Tuckman's model of team development is useful to explain what goes on in a new merged management team, or a newly merged sales team. We have also added some suggestions for how to manage these phases. See Table 6.4.

Timing for this stage is also important. The integration stage should neither be squeezed into an impossible two-week period, nor be treated as an open-ended process that continues unaided for years. The need to squeeze this phase into a two-week

Table 6.4   How to manage the development of a merged team

Stage	Team activity	Advice for leaders
Forming	• Confusion • Uncertainty • Assessing situation • Testing ground rules • Feeling out others • Defining goals • Getting acquainted • Establishing rules	Be very clear about roles and responsibilities in the new company. Talk about where people have come from in terms of the structure, process and culture in their previous situation. Compare notes. Define key customers for the team and begin to agree new groundrules for how the team will work together.
Storming	• Disagreement over priorities • Struggle for leadership • Tension • Hostility • Clique formation	Make time for team to discuss important issues. Be patient. Be clear on direction and purpose of the team. Nip conflict between cultures and people in the bud by talking to those involved.
Norming	• Consensus • Leadership accepted • Trust established • Standards set • New stable roles • Cooperation	Develop decision-making process. Maintain flexibility by reviewing goals and process.
Performing	• Successful performance • Flexible task roles • Openness • Helpfulness	Delegate more. Stretch people. Encourage innovation.

period comes from management denial of the very existence of integration issues. Conversely, the need to let things take their course over time comes from a belief that time will solve all the issues and they cannot be hurried. Therefore they are allowed to drag on and possibly get worse, and more entrenched.

Bridges offers advice about managing the integration phase which we have adapted to be directly useful for mergers and acquisitions:

* Explain that the integration phase will be hard work and will need (and get) attention.

- Set short-range goals and checkpoints.

- Encourage experimentation and risk taking.

- Encourage people to brainstorm with members of the new company to find answers to both old and new problems.

Managing beginnings

It is important to recognize when the timing is right to celebrate a new beginning. Managers need to be careful not to declare victory too soon. Here are some ideas for this phase:

- Be really clear about the purpose of the merger or acquisition, and keep coming back to this as your bedrock.

- Paint a vision of the future for you and your team, describing an attractive future for those listening. (ROCE or ROI just doesn't do it for most people!)

- Act as a role model by integrating well at your own level, and being seen to be doing so.

- Do something specific to celebrate a new beginning.

Managing yourself

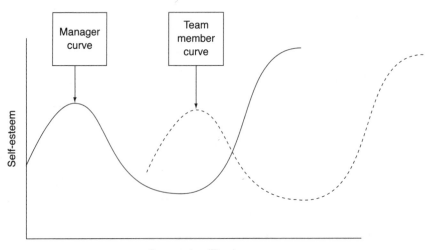

Figure 6.2 Change curve comparisons

There are many challenges ahead for managers as they enter a merger or acquisition. Managers may be uncertain about their own position, while attempting to reassure others about theirs. They may even be considering their options outside the organization while encouraging others to wait and see how things turn out.

Other difficulties include the overwhelming needs of team members for clarity, reassurance and management time. Managers find themselves repeating information again and again, and become frustrated with their team's inability to 'move on'. A glance at the Kubler-Ross curves pictured in Figure 6.2 will reveal that this problem comes from managers and their teams being out of 'sync' in terms of their emotional reactions. While the manager is accepting the situation and trying out new ideas, the team is going through shock, denial, anger and blame. This is quite a stark mis-match!

Devine (1999) offers a checklist for line managers:

- **Get involved.** Try to get in on the action and away from business as usual. Show you are capable of dealing with change.

- **Get informed.** Find out who is going up or down, especially among your sponsors or mentors. Have a 'replacement' boss you can turn to if your current one leaves.

- **Get to know people.** Network hard, get to know the people in the other company. Do not think of them as 'the enemy'.

- **Deal with your feelings.** Openly recognize feelings of anxiety and frustration. Form a support network and discuss these feelings with colleagues.

- **Actively manage your career.** Think carefully before moving function/role at the time of a merger. You are remembered for your current job, whatever your past experience. Do not necessarily accept the first role that is offered to you. Decide what you would like to do, prepare your CV and work towards it – everything is up for grabs!

- **Identify success criteria.** Often performance criteria have changed or become unclear. Re-benchmark yourself by talking to people involved in the merger. Get informal feedback from subordinates, peers and bosses.

- **Be positive.** Be philosophical and objective about what is under your control. Do not beat yourself up – you can't win 'em all.

Handling difficult appointment and exit decisions

Mergers and acquisitions often involve a restructuring process, which in turn involves managers in making difficult appointment and exit decisions. These decisions need to be fair, transparent, justified, swift and carried out with attention to people's dignity.

In one company that we know of, top management decided to reveal the newly merged company's structure chart in a formal town hall meeting of all staff. Those who did not appear on the chart had to make their own conclusions. You can imagine the resentment and lack of trust that this foolish and undignified process generated.

Devine advises:

- New appointments need to be seen to be fair. Try to ensure that selection criteria are objective, transparent and widely understood.

- Stick to company policy and processes. Do not take short-cuts as they are likely to backfire on you.

- Do not dither. This will cause resentment.

- Treat employees at every level with dignity.

Managing the organization

It is important to select and agree a change process that matches the challenges posed by the specific merger and acquisition. If the most important challenge is to achieve cost-cutting goals, then project management techniques can be applied and the changes made swiftly. This may mean the use of a task force to make recommendations, and the agreement of a linear process for delivering the cost-cutting goals. However, if the most important challenges are integration issues or cultural issues, then the ideas of both Bridges and Senge are relevant. Attention must be paid to managing endings, transitions and beginnings for specific teams involved in significant processes. Other teams may remain untouched.

We have used the Kotter model, introduced in Chapter 3, to illustrate the steps from initial news of the deal to full integration. This model is useful because it combines a range of different assumptions about change, so tackles the widest range of possible challenges.

1. **Establish a sense of urgency.** This is a tough balancing act for management. They must start to raise the issues that have led to the merger or acquisition without revealing the deal itself. For instance if the company is currently in a dwindling marketplace, then managers should highlight the need to do something about this, without necessarily revealing any intentions to buy or to merge. People will be suspicious and resentful of a deal that does not make any sense. 'Why are we diversifying now? I thought the plan was to buy the competition!'

2. **Form a powerful guiding coalition.** Managers of both companies need to begin working together as soon as they can. They need to spend time together and

build a bit of trust. When the deal is announced, managers will then be able to work together at speed.

3. **Create a new vision.** A top-level vision for the new company must be built by the new top management team. This vision will be used to guide the integration effort and to develop clear strategies for achieving this. The integration effort needs to be targeted in specific areas rather than be a blanket process, and clear timescales for implementation must be given.

   The new structure needs to be put quickly into place, a level at a time, ensuring that customers are well managed throughout. The new sales and customer service structure is therefore also a priority. New values and ways of working should also be discussed and identified.

4. **Communicate the vision.** Kotter emphasizes the need to communicate at least 10 times the amount you expect to have to communicate. In addition, all the research about mergers and acquisitions indicates that it is impossible to over-communicate. Managers need to be creative with their communication strategies, and remember to work hard at getting the two companies to build relationships at all levels.

   The vision and accompanying strategies and new behaviours will need to be communicated in a variety of different ways: formal communications, role modelling, recruitment decisions and promotion decisions. The guiding coalition should be the first to role model new behaviours.

5. **Empower others to act on the vision.** The management team now need to focus on removing obstacles to change such as structures that are not working, or cultural issues, or non-integrated systems. At this stage people are encouraged to experiment with new relationships and new ways of doing things.

6. **Plan for and create short-term wins.** Managers should look for and advertise short-term visible improvements such as joint innovation projects, or the day-to-day achievements of joint teams. Anything that demonstrates progress towards the initial aims of the merger or acquisition is newsworthy. It is important to reward people publicly for merger-related improvements.

7. **Consolidate improvements and produce still more change.** Top managers should make a point of promoting and rewarding those able to advocate and work towards the new vision. At this point it is important to energize the process of change with new joint projects, new resources, change agents.

8. **Institutionalize new approaches.** It is vital to ensure that people see the links between the merger or acquisition and success. If they have had to work hard to make this initiative happen, they need to see that it has all been worthwhile.

THE IMPORTANCE OF TRUST WHEN GOING THROUGH A MERGER

When we were acquired by ITSS we were full of trepidation. Our previous owners had stripped us of costs and then looked around for a buyer. We felt a bit used. So we were in no mood to start building trust.

ITSS kept calling this deal a merger, but we were hugely cynical about that. They had bought us after all. This was a case of vertical integration where a supplier buys its customer to gain access to primary clients and grow the business. We thought they would start to take our jobs and move the company to their own headquarters, around four hours down the motorway!

The whole thing came to a head one morning when some consultants were running an integration workshop for the new management team. ITSS were getting frustrated with our hostility. We were getting angry about their constant questioning about finances and account management and project costs. Someone from our company was brave enough to share his emotions.

The MD of ITSS, who is actually a pretty decent guy, sat down amidst us all and spoke quite calmly for about 10 minutes. He said, 'Look guys, I will do anything to make this company a success. Anything. But I need to know what I'm running here. I can't take that responsibility without knowing all the facts. I really want us to make this thing a success. But I need your help.'

After that we trusted him a bit more. Then things got better and better. That was four years ago. Things have improved every year since then. He kept his word, and that was really important to everyone.

Project Leader, acquired company

SUMMARY

There are five main reasons for undertaking a merger or acquisition:

- growth;
- synergy;
- diversification;
- integration;
- deal doing.

Recent research indicates that five golden rules should be followed during mergers and acquisitions:

- Communicate constantly.

- Get the structure right.

- Tackle the cultural issues.

- Keep customers on board.

- Use a clear overall process.

Individuals can be managed through the process using the Kubler-Ross curve as a basis for understanding how people are likely to react to the changes. Teams can be managed through endings, transitions and new beginnings using the advice of Bridges. Tuckman's forming, storming, norming, performing process also lends understanding to the sequences of activities that leaders of new joint teams need to take their teams through.

Managers need to manage themselves well through an integration process. Roffey Park's advice is:

- Get involved.

- Get informed.

- Get to know people.

- Deal with your feelings.

- Actively manage your career.

- Identify success criteria.

- Be positive.

Difficult appointment and exit decisions also need to be well managed using these principles:

- Be fair.

- Stick to the procedures.

- Do not dither.

- Remember people's dignity.

Kotter's model can be used to plan a merger and acquisition process as it combines several different assumptions about the change process, so provides adequate flexibility for the range of different purposes of merger or acquisition activity.

7

Cultural change

 If you were asked to give a new recruit some words of encouragement on how to be successful within your organization, what would you say? You might give some formal advice about carrying your ID at all times, but you might also make some of the following suggestions:

> Keep your head down.
> It's OK to make mistakes here, as long as you don't repeat them.
> The boss likes to see you working really hard at all times.
> We work hard but play hard. The people who get on here work long hours but enjoy themselves in the pub afterwards.
> It doesn't pay to ask too many questions.
> You'll find everyone pulls together here and will want to see you as part of the team.

With this helpful advice, you begin to educate the person about the way things get done around the organization. You also reveal what some of the required behaviours are, and thus you actively reinforce the prevailing culture.

As Schein (1990) says, culture is the 'the pattern of basic assumptions that a given group has invented, discovered or developed in learning to cope with its problems of external adaptation and internal integration, and that have worked well enough to be considered valid and, therefore, to be taught to new members as the correct way to perceive, think, and feel in relation to those problems.'

Culture is not just about induction programmes, it is everywhere in organizational life. Culture is vitally important for the organization because of its impact on performance. Molenaar *et al* (2002), quoting leading writers in the field, say:

> [T]o truly understand corporate culture, its characteristics must also be understood. The following is a compilation of the most prevalent cultural characteristics:
>
>> Corporate culture represents behaviors that new employees are encouraged to follow (Kotter and Heskett, 1992)
>> It creates norms for acceptable behavior (Hai, 1986)
>> Corporate culture reinforces ideas and feelings that are consistent with the corporation's beliefs (Hampden-Turner, 1990)
>> It influences the external relations of the corporation, as well as the internal relations of the employees (Hai, 1986)
>> Culture can have a powerful effect on individuals and performance (Kotter and Heskett, 1992)
>> It affects worker motivation and goals (Hai, 1986)
>> Behaviors such as innovation, decision making, communication, organizing, measuring success and rewarding achievement are affected by corporate culture (Hai, 1986).

If we want to learn about how to change culture, we need to understand how it is created. Schein (1999) suggests that there are six different ways in which culture evolves. Some of these can be influenced by leaders and some cannot:

- A general evolution in which the organization naturally adapts to its environment.

- A specific evolution of teams or sub-groups within the organization to their different environments.

- A guided evolution resulting from cultural 'insights' on the part of leaders.

- A guided evolution through encouraging teams to learn from each other, and empowering selected hybrids from sub-cultures that are better adapted to current realities.

- A planned and managed culture change through creation of parallel systems of steering committees and project-oriented task forces.

- A partial or total cultural destruction through new leadership that eliminates the carriers of the former culture (turnarounds, bankruptcies, etc).

Schein underscores the fact that organizations will not successfully change culture if they begin with that specific idea in mind. The starting point should always be the business issues that the organization faces. Additionally he suggests that you do not begin with the idea that the existing culture is somehow totally 'bad'. He urges leaders to always begin with the premise that an organization's culture is a source of strength. Some of the cultural habits may seem dysfunctional but it is more viable to build on the existing cultural strengths rather than to focus on changing those elements that may be considered weaknesses.

This chapter focuses on culture in the context of managing change. We have chosen not to discuss concepts and theories of organizational culture as this is done so well elsewhere (see the reference list to get you started). We have instead decided to share our tips and guidelines on achieving culture change. These are derived from a variety of experiences of working within organizations, helping teams and individuals to make significant cultural shifts. We have also selected three case studies to illustrate the range of ways in which culture change can be tackled. The structure of this chapter is:

- Guidelines for achieving successful cultural change.

- Case study one: aligning the organization.

- Case study two: rebranding the organization.

- Case study three: creating an employer brand.

We wish to introduce the concept of 'rebranding' as a way of exploring cultural change. Our three case studies each take a slightly different approach to the process of rebranding. The first concerns the challenge of aligning the organization more closely to customer needs, the second is about reflecting the brand in everyday employee interactions with customers, and the third is about creating an employer brand to enable the organization to attract and retain the best staff, and to engage the energy and motivation of all employees.

Extensive academic research in the 1990s (see for instance Kohli and Jaworski, 1990) has consistently found that organizations with a strong market focus and brand presence experience better performance, based on measures such as sales revenue, profitability, growth rates and return on investment. Additionally a strong market focus has a number of related benefits including developing strong organizational culture, success in developing new products and services, sales force job satisfaction and offering a source of competitive advantage. This approach also aligns with our view that any culture change initiative must have sound customer-focused objectives at its core.

Internal rebranding is sometimes referred to as internal marketing. Greene, Walls and Schrest (1994) define internal marketing as 'the promoting of the firm and its product(s) or product lines to the firm's employees'. Berry and Parasuraman's (1991) definition is 'internal marketing is attracting, developing, motivating, and retaining qualified employees through job-products that satisfy their needs. Internal marketing is the philosophy of treating employees as customers.' However, although these definitions both point us in the right direction, the important end goal is to ensure that the key components of the brand are communicated to customers and the wider external audience. The brand must therefore be understood, believed and exemplified by customer-facing staff, supported by the rest of the organization.

Crosby and Johnson (2001) conclude:

> The strongest brands are those that elicit emotional attachment from customers. When interacting with your company, customers and prospects may have feelings of safety, pride, excitement, comfort, confidence, caring, or trust. These interactions activate feelings and build strong brand commitment.
>
> … it's important not to overlook the effects of brand on the employees of the firm. Employees often have a large role to play in managing customer relationships, and the brand can help guide their behaviour. In effect, the brand is a promise to customers of how they can expect to be treated by the company. To the extent employees understand the expectations being created by the brand, and are motivated and trained to live up to those expectations, then the firm can have a truly integrated customer relationship management strategy.

GUIDELINES FOR ACHIEVING SUCCESSFUL CULTURAL CHANGE

Here we draw together some of the key themes arising from our experience which we hope will help you to address the issues of culture change in your own organization. Specific themes are reflected in the three chosen case studies, and we pick these out in the separate introductions to each one later in the chapter.

Always link to organizational vision, mission and objectives

Culture change as an isolated objective is meaningless. Organizations should only involve themselves in culture change if the current culture does not adequately support the achievement of strategic objectives. Start from the business strategy to determine what organization capability or core competencies need to be developed. Ensure that there is a clear vision and a real need to change. People need to be convinced by a compelling vision rather than compelled in a coercive way. They need to see the overwhelming logic of the proposed changes. The more people are drawn towards the vision the better.

Create a sense of urgency and continually reinforce the need to change

The introduction of a foreign element into the organizational system is a good way of making change happen (see Satir's model in Chapter 1). This can come from an external or internal source. Whatever it is, it needs to have the force to kick-start the culture change process. And there need to be plans and processes in place which keep the momentum going.

Attend to stakeholder issues

When you want culture to change you have to put yourself into the shoes of the stakeholders. Address the issues of the people who need to change by involving them as much as possible. Change brought in a crass or unthoughtful way will rebound on management. Whether change is being proposed for positive or negative reasons the organization's future success is dependent on engaging staff to enter into the new way of doing things. How will the proposed changes benefit stakeholders? Will customers, partners, staff and suppliers really feel a positive difference? If some parties are going to lose out, how will you handle this?

Remember that the how is as important as the what

Culture is about the way you do things around the organization. So if your organization has a set of core values, and of course it does explicitly or implicitly, then you need to be managing the cultural change in line with these values. If you say one thing but do another then you might as well give up now. For instance, a stated value of 'integrity' is rather hollow if senior managers do not keep their promises, or fail to explain why the plan has changed.

Build on the old, and step into the new

If you want to shift the organization from one way of doing things to a new way of doing things then you will need to see and do things from a variety of perspectives. Any current culture, like any person, will have positive and negative features. You will need to retain and build on the current strengths and ensure that you do not throw the baby out with the bathwater. You will also need to start right now in modelling aspects of the new culture – if you want a coaching culture then start coaching; if you want people to be empowered then start empowering! Now is also the opportunity to step outside of the bubble that you're in. No one ever changed a culture by simply drawing up plans and listing required behaviours, so now is the time to be creative, do things in different ways and learn from people outside of the system.

Generate enabling mechanisms

It is important to generate enabling mechanisms such as reward systems and planning and performance management systems that support the objectives and preferred behaviours of the new culture. For example, this means ensuring that teams have clear objectives that are closely aligned to organizational objectives.

Act as role models

Managers need to act as role models. They will need to model the new values but also support individuals and teams through a period of upheaval. This can be done through using some of the strategies outlined in Chapters 1 and 2, such as working with teams through the stages of forming and storming, and working with individuals as they adjust to the new ways of doing things.

Create a community of focused and flexible leaders

On the one hand many people want clear, confident and focused leadership during periods of change; on the other hand people also want leaders who will reflect upon what is happening 'on the ground' and adjust their plans accordingly. Leadership of cultural change requires clarity of end vision together with the ability to manage and cope with emergent issues. All six of Goleman's leadership styles might be called for during a period of cultural change (see Chapter 4). However, it would be a mistake to believe that any one individual could carry this off by him or herself. Chapter 4 also describes a number of ways that leadership can be dispersed throughout the organization to make change happen.

Insist on collective ownership of the changes

One common trap is to make the HR department the owners of cultural change, while the CEO and the senior management team own the changes in business strategy. This type of functional decomposition of a change initiative is doomed to failure. This generally leads to senior managers becoming detached from the cultural issues, and thus neglecting their role modelling responsibilities. Employee cynicism grows (quite rightly!), and this can become a very powerful force for resisting change. This division of labour also leads to HR people being lumbered with programmes and initiatives that look like unnecessary overheads to the local line leaders, which HR people end up having to 'push' and 'sell'. This can be a very disheartening outcome, especially when the initial ideas are often entirely sound.

CASE STUDY ONE: ALIGNING THE ORGANIZATION

This case study sets out our analysis and recommendations for an organization facing major strategic and cultural change. Some of these recommendations were taken up, and some withered on the vine, but the process of analysing and recommending is thought-provoking in itself and we felt worthy of inclusion here.

Summary of key points arising from the case study

- Even if employees sense the need to change, and want to change, this is not always enough. In this case study, people were asking for a clear sense of direction. A clear vision is often required to catalyse action, especially if it translates well into specific tasks.

- The greater the depth and breadth of people involved in diagnosing the current state, developing a vision of where the organization needs to be heading, and generating solutions to bridge the gap, then the more chance the organization has of gaining sufficient momentum for change. In this case study, many people were engaged in the analysis, which led to increased interest and energy in making things happen.

- The greater the clarity of focus (towards the end user) the greater the chance one has of aligning people, processes, systems and structures to this end. Business-as-usual and change initiatives have to be dovetailed. It is no use if there are 101 initiatives that are not joined up and working with one another.

- Processes and standards must support the desired behaviours. An organization cannot strive for a quality service, for instance, if the culture does not support people doing quality things. It is of little value if the customer services assistant is exceedingly pleasant but not empowered to take decisions when the customer needs a decision.

- Managers and staff need to be supported through the transition process with the necessary coaching and training. For the organization to become more focused, efficient and effective people have to be doing something different. Speedier rubbish collection will not impress the public if a trail of litter is left after each collection. Not only do these changes have to be communicated clearly, they also have to be followed by the necessary skills development and induction.

- Organizations do not change by themselves – not at the speed that is normally required in this world of ever-increasing demands. The momentum is generated first by leadership and then by followership. Leaders at all levels within the organization have to have clarity of purpose, the relevant leadership skills and knowledge to deploy and to see themselves as leading from the middle, with the organization and its stakeholders all around them. Top team alignment is also crucial in times of change.

Case study description

A large local authority was not functioning as efficiently or as effectively as it wanted. It was not being fully responsive to the needs of its citizens or its various communities of interest. We conducted an organizational analysis of the city council to find out what was helping the council achieve its stated outcomes and what was getting in the way of this. The analysis consisted of interviews with directors and strategic managers, and focus groups with middle managers and front-line staff. Leading politicians of all political persuasions were interviewed. A number of key stakeholders such as citizens' panels, partnerships and the trade unions were also involved. Our report highlighted six interrelated areas in which the council needed to significantly improve its overall effectiveness and thereby reduce internal and external pressure.

The commitment, talent and effort of all those we met were impressive. Many people from front-line workers to the most senior politicians and officers were enthusiastic about the city and what the council might contribute to its life and development. There were clearly many very good services being offered to the city. However, at the same time there was a strong feeling at all levels of untapped potential. The council's energies were being dissipated through not having a true focus.

The emerging themes are outlined below and illustrated in Figure 7.1

Continually increasing customer and citizen focus

The passion to deliver the best possible service to both external and internal customers, colleagues and partners was variable, with many parts of the organization moving forward, but at an uneven pace. The various self-inspection and external inspection processes were prompting the council to streamline systems and procedures for service delivery. However there were many instances cited where 'customer care' just was not part of the mindset and where systems, policies and procedures conspired to hinder the achievement in this area.

The interface between front-line services and the centre required particular attention, specifically on how best to commission the providers. Service level agreements, for example, were not fully used, and other mechanisms needed to be installed to ensure there was both a psychological and a written commitment to achieve excellent service delivery across directorates and to the end user.

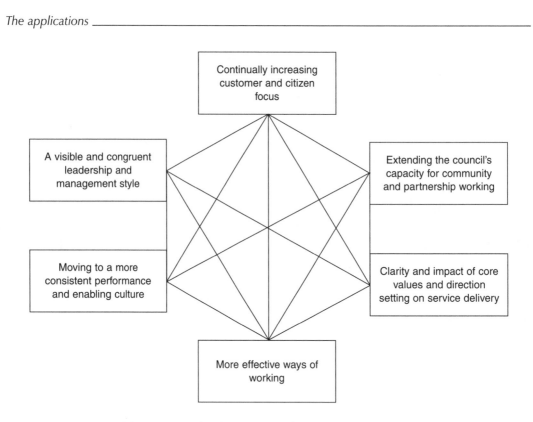

Figure 7.1 Six key points from case study one

Clarity and impact of core values and direction setting on service delivery

Everyone had accepted the council's core values, but that was perhaps because they were commonsensical and there was nothing in them that anyone could contest. However there was scope for them to be revisited, made more specifically demanding and directed towards action in order to realize their potential. There were too many values, and these were neither meaningfully translated into ways of working nor explicitly linked to preferred outcomes or any performance management system. They had been launched with a fanfare some time before, and no investment had been put into their continued dissemination and implementation.

Everyone in the council had a mix of agendas to work to: various corporate policy priorities, service delivery priorities, inter-agency working and development initiatives. Greater clarity was needed throughout the council about what outcomes were being sought and how they could come together at every level. All managers and service heads felt the tension of multiple demands and needed an effective process for balancing these demands and setting personal and team targets.

The corporate policy priorities had a tremendously varied degree of ownership, due partly to the lack of clarity around what they actually meant, and also to a suspicion whether the political leadership and corporate managerial leadership were really committed to driving them through. They did not translate easily into a vision for a better city that employees could rally behind, and therefore the result was confusion and a growing cynicism, rather than commitment.

There was little evidence that people were rewarded or recognized for moving the corporate agenda on, and the lack of ongoing budget provision for these corporate initiatives also indicated a hesitancy when it came to putting money where the mouth was.

A visible and congruent leadership and management style

At all levels, but notably at middle and front line, there were requests for clearer, bolder and consistent leadership. This was seen as particularly being the challenge for political leaders and senior officers in managing the council's myriad conflicting demands.

Clarity of vision and articulation of the council's true direction and the way it was to be achieved were needed to minimize confusion and focus people's minds and resources.

Clearer, bolder and consistent leadership needed to include:

- a consistent and congruent set of priorities;

- processes for managing conflicts of priority and pressure which inevitably occur within complex organizations;

- a demonstrable commitment and accountability for driving the priorities through;

- a set of values embodied throughout the leadership, and used as a reference point for decision making;

- minimization, at the very least, of cross-party destructive tensions.

Corporate leadership was most needed for tackling conflicts between front-line services and the centre. It was also needed for harmonizing corporate policy and the service/functional agenda, and for improving the way change was managed across the organization.

Good management of change was lacking. This was seen as particularly necessary with regards to the major modernizing agenda facing the council. Management needed to start to communicate these changes so that staff felt engaged in the co-creation of their futures, and so that the feeling of initiative overload, where change is endured rather than embraced, was reduced.

It was also noticeable that the roles of different management teams and groups were not always clear. The senior management team and the service heads needed to begin to take a more strategic role, at least part of the time.

Moving to a more consistent performance and enabling culture

There was wide recognition that the council was improving its ability to manage performance, but many wished to see greater consistency and general improvement. This meant a need to establish realistic targets for everyone across all their work, and to review progress regularly against these, ensuring that any changes to plan were discussed and incorporated.

The organization was already moving towards a performance management and competency based framework. Some areas were beginning to experiment with a development process that linked to service plans, team plans and individual plans. This was successfully helping people to clarify key outcomes and contributions from individuals and teams, and this approach promoted greater ownership of the service and the council's agenda.

For the organization to embrace performance management more fully, the organization needed to begin to address a number of cultural issues that were hindering progress:

- the lack of direction and multiple priorities;

- the overwhelming feeling of organizational complexity;

- the uncertainty of what the city council actually stood for;

- the lack of understanding (in both senses of the word) between the constituent parts of the organization;

- the 'political' nature of many of the transactions and relationships;

- the tendency towards a blame culture where valuing, appreciating and recognizing the contribution of others is kept to a minimum;

- the 'closedness' of the culture (inability to look outside for new ideas);

- the lack of focus on developing people.

More effective ways of working

There were many ways to improve council working, from making meetings more productive and less time-consuming, through to mastering the complexities of matrix management and having effective information management systems. With the complexity of the council's task, with demands coming from all directions at all levels, there needed to be a clear (or as clear as possible) way of working a matrix structure to cope with the specialist, cross-cutting and geographical dimensions of service delivery.

There was a real need to accelerate the business planning process, to ensure a performance management system was delivered in a consistent way across the organization and to reduce conflict at the myriad of boundaries within the organization.

Extending the council's capacity for community and partnership working

Increasingly the role for all staff required greater community engagement and partnership working. Although this was demanding both on workload and skills it also offered greater learning, and interestingly for some was preferable to internal working.

Most managers when prompted could cite examples of good partnership working that had been developed over the previous few years. This was one of a number of areas that the organization could be justifiably proud of. The challenge was for people to have the confidence to communicate this to all the stakeholders and be able to applaud and celebrate success.

The competencies in this new area of effective partnership were real nuggets of success. These competencies needed to be transferred not only to other areas of partnership working but also to where different parts of the council could work more effectively with each other.

CASE STUDY TWO: REBRANDING THE ORGANIZATION

This case study describes one organization's journey as it worked towards reinvigorating its brand. The process chosen and the choices made along the way make interesting reading.

Summary of key points arising from case study

- It is important to create a sense of urgency and momentum when a major cultural change is required. In this case study, the senior management team made a strong start, and put in the effort to keep things going. This required many people to be involved and energized, and for the number of people involved to keep growing.

- Commitment to culture change cannot be developed by e-mail, or by memo. It has to be done face to face and in real time. Cultural change is achieved through action rather than words, so people need to see their managers doing it as well as talking about it. In this case study there was a lot of face-to-face straight talking.

- Breaking the mould is hard work! It involves planning and thinking and role modelling, plus developing and implementing supporting processes and policies.

- New teams provide new opportunities. Bridges (see Chapter 4) describes the neutral zone as a time of tremendous creative opportunities. Similarly we have noticed that new senior management teams such as the one featured in this case study are more likely to be able to change an organizational culture because they themselves are changing.

- Supporting individuals is not soft! The hard work involved in facing the real issues one to one with people pays off. It builds trust and ensures understanding. But it takes courage, especially when change involves the communication of unwelcome and painful news. Even when change appears to offer hope for a brighter and better future, some may not see it that way.

Case study description

The case study concerns a financial services organization that undertook a strategic review and decided that it needed to reinvigorate the brand. With the previous case study we focused on gaining internal alignment to the organizational service. This case study takes a different perspective. The key focus of this rebranding exercise was the external marketing of the products and services on offer, and the way that customer-facing staff represented the brand. This is best illustrated by Wasmer and Bruner's research (1991) which maps the relationship flows between the customer, the organization and the customer service provider (see Figure 7.2). They saw the major constituents of their brand as:

- marketing communications;

- products on offer;

- speed of service;

- quality of service.

As a result of the strategic review the organization decided that the key to its competitive advantage was the way in which its customer-facing employees transacted with

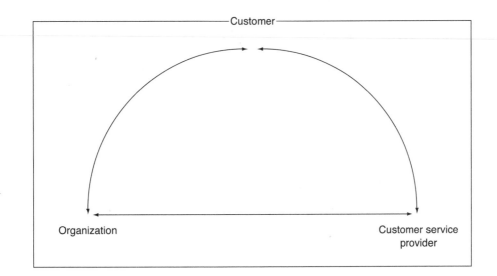

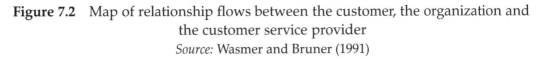

Figure 7.2 Map of relationship flows between the customer, the organization and the customer service provider
Source: Wasmer and Bruner (1991)

customers and potential customers. They were referring to not just the usual types of customer service behaviour such as greeting, courtesy and complaint handling but also the ways that the brand itself was being portrayed. The customer does not just receive communication from the organization in terms of its marketing and its goods. It also receives information via the customer service providers.

To focus more clearly on its target audience, the organization segmented its potential customer market into four quadrants based on their interest in financial services and their level of self-knowledge of financial needs and potential solutions. One quadrant of the market was generally knowledgeable and sophisticated. Another quadrant had a high interest in the financial area of their lives but relatively little knowledge. The third quadrant had a reasonable knowledge base but this was not accompanied by any great level of interest. The final quadrant had little interest and little knowledge (see Figure 7.3).

This segmentation generated a number of questions:

- What type of advice was best suited to each quadrant?

- Did the organization want to deliver that sort of advice?

- What was the organizational capability to deliver that advice (profitably)?

- Could the organization be developed to bridge any gaps?

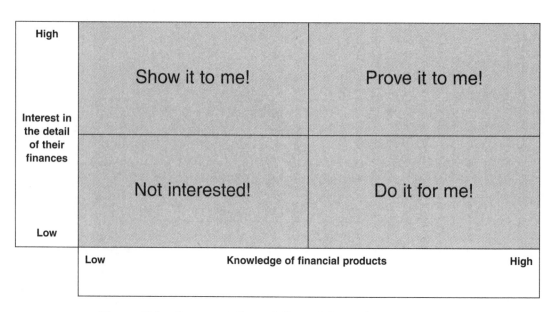

Figure 7.3 Segmentation of financial services customers

The areas that showed most promise were those potential customers who either were interested in investing in their financial future but needed help in negotiating their way through the financial maze, or did not have the interest but wanted someone to do it for them, and do it well. These were the 'Show it to me!' and 'Do it for me!' customers.

Although those in the High–High quadrant were generally high net worth individuals, the people who fell into that category wanted a high level of service but were also more liable to shift their savings and investments from one financial institution to another fairly frequently. The Low–Low quadrant likewise required a high level of support but did not necessarily have the available funds to warrant that level of investment from the organization.

Once the primary focus for business development opportunities had been established, the next stage was to decide what sorts of things needed to happen for customer needs to be satisfied. This included outlining the behaviours and attitudes that customer-facing staff (and those back-office staff supporting them) needed to exhibit. Key areas included the ability to generate interest, to establish credibility, to have clarity of communication and to be proactive to customer needs.

The reorientation of the company to this particular strategy included the generation of a new set of company values. These values were not just a list of slogans but were translated into behavioural statements. These statements defined the preferred way of operating in the business and indeed also became part of the recruitment process.

The values were not only 'nice-to-have' or 'motherhood and apple pie', but were designed to align people within the organization to the company strategy and the preferred behaviours. So for example a value of 'treat people well' was translated into making people feel they are your number one priority, and treating all customers and each other with respect. The value of 'say it as it is' was translated into talking to customers and colleagues in a straightforward manner. These behaviours could be verified by observation or customer feedback. They could also be learnt.

Of course to get to the stage where frontline staff behaved in accordance with company strategy required other enabling actions, which were drawn from best practice and appropriate models of individual, team and organizational change.

Getting started

The whole change started with a comprehensive strategy review and the generation of a programme plan with specific projects covering areas such as brand development, systems development, business lead generation and defining the customer experience. This was kick started by the senior management team with some input from relevant stakeholders. However initially it was a 'top-down' process which drew a lot from the machine metaphor. Using Kotter's terminology a sense of urgency was created ('with the market as it is we cannot carry on as we have been doing') and an overarching vision developed.

The next layer of managers below the senior management team were enlisted to form part of the guiding collation. A change management team was formed, tasked with managing the transition from both a task and people perspective, with sponsorship from and direct reporting line into the senior management team. Quite soon however the changes picked up their own momentum.

Gaining commitment

It became apparent that not everyone was dissatisfied with the status quo. People were a little unclear about the desirability of some of the changes, and some of the more impractical aspects of the proposed changes were accentuated. The senior management team by now had extended the members of the guiding coalition to involve a critical mass of 85 'strategy leaders'. It was their task to reinforce the need to change, and to develop a clarity of vision that could be translated into tangible objectives and behaviours throughout the organization.

This translation process occurred over several months, and became an iterative process with all staff. Conversations were had, which set out what the managers wanted to see but involved staff at the front line talking through the practicalities. This process raised some points about the original thinking which needed amending, and enabled staff to get a much better idea of what was required of them.

Breaking the mould

The transition from the old to the new was effectively dealt with by the good use of programme management, led by the senior management team, and supported by a specially constituted change management team. Feedback loops to and from key stakeholders including staff were an integrated part of the process.

The generation of a set of values which were translated into behavioural imperatives, coupled with values workshops with all staff, set a benchmark for the organizational culture. The values helped to minimize organizational politics by encouraging 'straight talk'. This was impressively role modelled by the senior management team and the change management team, who were open and honest with both good news and bad.

A key aspect of the new way of doing things was the openness to ideas wherever they came from and the development of an enabling and empowering culture. Creativity, risk-taking and learning were encouraged through the co-option of diagonal slices of staff onto change initiative working groups and by scheduled reviews throughout the transition period.

Self-esteem and performance can drop during periods of change. In a sense this is unavoidable – a natural and normal reaction to change affecting individuals (see Chapter 1). Key interventions here included demonstrable listening to staff concerns and many examples of staff issues being dealt with in a way that satisfied them but did not compromise the general business direction. In addition objective third-party consultants were used as additional support for individuals and groups of individuals who were most affected by the changes. Line managers were prepared with full communication of the changes to pass on, and open access was given to more senior managers to tap into their knowledge and experience. Greater emphasis was put on coaching through the line, which quickly enabled managers to tackle performance issues arising from the change.

Building new teams

The realignment of the organization as a result of the new strategy had a number of knock-on effects on different teams. The senior team was a newly configured team at the beginning of the strategy review process, and acquired a new sales director part-way through the process. An important component of the time its members spent together was attending to their team development process. The development process was focused on the tasks in hand – strategy review and strategy implementation – but on a regular basis members took the time out to look at where they were as a team, and how they were performing and inter-relating.

The generation of the values was both a real and a symbolic act for the senior management team. Having generated the values, they translated them into actions for themselves. They offered this to the rest of the organization as a guideline, but wanted different parts of the organization to discover what the values meant for them personally as a part of a team. This, together with the senior management team role modelling the values, was seen as a crucial part of the process.

The realignment within the organization meant that other teams and groups throughout the organization were affected to a greater or lesser degree. For example, the increased focus on savings, investments and mortgages led to a division of labour and separate reporting lines for staff within the branch network. In addition the centralized contact centre was required to develop greater links and better lines of communication with the national advisor salesforce. Both these examples necessitated a breaking down of old groupings and the development of a new set of teams and consequent relationships.

Supporting individuals

People processes formed a large part of the change plan. This included a communication strategy that was in line with the new values of openness, honesty and straight talk. Processes were put in place to ensure that individuals displaced had clarity around their situation and guidelines as to how things would progress. Selection to new posts was made using an equitable process, and the new reward scheme was aligned to the new strategy and values.

Outplacement was provided for those leaving the organization and counselling provided for those who needed to talk their situation through in a confidential setting. Coaching and mentoring were provided for more senior managers who had to take up new roles and needed to make sense of the changes and make their own adjustments within themselves.

CASE STUDY THREE: CREATING AN EMPLOYER BRAND

Summary of key points arising from case study

- Start from the business strategy. An employer brand only has meaning when it is presented in the context of an overarching company strategy.

- Lead change from within the business to enhance success. In the case study, the trap of HR owning the culture change was studiously avoided. This enhanced the acceptability of the new brand.

- Do not over plan the change process – stay flexible. Things change as organizations move through a change process. This case study illustrates how to plan phase by phase, ensuring that feedback is incorporated into future plans.

- Be creative – do things in new ways. Culture change can only be achieved by doing things differently. In this case, the organization incorporated some radically new ways of doing things by using the principle of marketing to engage employees in the desired changes.

- Build on the current cultural strengths rather than attack current habits or try to break things down. The employer brand was derived from conversations with a wide cross-section of employees, so there was a 'rightness' about the brand values, which impressed people.

Case study description

This third case study illustrates the challenges and opportunities offered by creating an employer brand. The organization in this case study is a highly successful and dynamic global spirits and wine business which has grown steadily through merger and acquisition over the last 10 years. The steady progress of industry consolidation worldwide led this business to consider its future as either an acquiring or an acquired company. This contemplation led to a desire to strengthen various aspects of the business, resulting in three interrelated aims:

- To be fit and ready to take opportunities as they arise, whether they come from industry consolidation, acquisition or new ventures.

- To achieve quality growth by:
  - generating volume and share growth on specific existing key brands;
  - encouraging innovation and launching new products;
  - integrating newly acquired brands and businesses.

- To enable the above to happen smoothly by implementing simple and flexible systems and processes such as those delivered by SAP.

In order to encourage full engagement and involvement in the new strategy, the organization decided to launch an employer brand which challenged all business units to get full commitment of all employees, so that each person could become part of a unified winning team, connecting with consumers and taking the business to new levels of growth. The top team wanted everyone to be engaged in the action, committed to the goal and confident of their part in achieving it. Everyone was expected to take an active role individually, and work with others as part of the team.

One of the significant pieces of data that informed this employer brand strategy was the following quote from the Collins and Porras survey, *Built to Last* (1994): 'Companies with strong positive core vision and core values have outperformed the general stock market by a factor of 12 since 1925.'

The employer brand

The employer brand arose from the existing culture. It was worked on by both internal and external people through eliciting current views of the company ethos, and gathering aspirations of current employees.

The concept of the brand wheel was used to define the brand. This is encapsulated in Figure 7.4. The brand wheel idea, developed by Bates North America, is used to define the functional and emotional components of a brand. Bates North America has developed an impressive reputation for reinvigorating brands. The brand wheel is based on various concepts that go into creating a brand such as essence, values and personality. The brand essence is heart or spirit of the brand. The brand values are about how the brand makes a person feel and what it says about them if they become associated with the brand. The brand personality is a way of talking about the brand as if it were a person, to get to the emotional content of the brand itself.

Out of the brand wheel came a concise definition of the six key brand values together with their associated behaviours. See box.

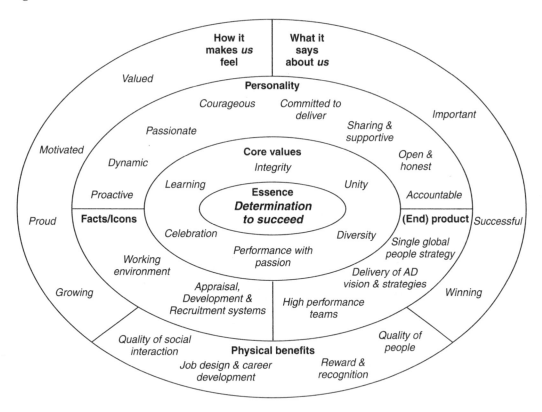

Figure 7.4 Brand wheel for employer brand

THE SIX EMPLOYER BRAND VALUES

Value: integrity

Behaviours:

- Expressing views and opinions in an open, honest and constructive way.
- Consistently delivering on their promises and commitments.
- Taking accountability for decisions and actions.

Value: unity

Behaviours:

- Contributing enthusiastically to team goals, sharing and aligning own objectives with team(s).
- Supporting and encouraging players on their own team and other teams.
- Building personal success on team success and contributing to other teams' success.

Value: diversity

Behaviours:

- Treating diverse views, cultures and communities with respect.
- Learning from the variety of different cultures, countries, functions and teams within the organization.
- Acknowledging different approaches and seeking win–win solutions.

Value: performance with passion

Behaviours:

- Setting and exceeding stretching targets, individually and in teams.
- Demonstrating high levels of pace, energy and commitment in achieving goals.
- Finding new opportunities to improve their game and being courageous by trying them.

Value: celebration

Behaviours:

- Sharing success, recognizing and rewarding achievement of other players.
- Encouraging the celebration of success and building a 'success leads to more success' culture.
- Having a can-do mentality and encouraging others to do the same.

Value: learning

Behaviours:

- Being proactive in professional and personal development.
- Sharing learning and supporting the development of other players.
- Going outside the 'comfort-zone', challenging the status quo, and learning from mistakes.

The process

The organization devised a three-stage process to move from this definition of six core values to a position of full involvement with the new strategy. The three stages were awareness, adoption and advocacy (see Figure 7.5), with only the first stage planned in detail. The second and third stages were give a broad brush plan, but awaited the results of the first stage to enable sensible planning.

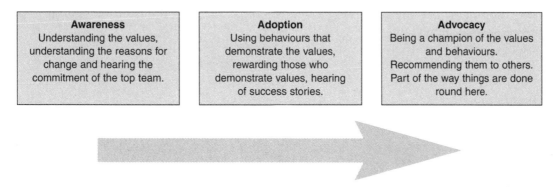

Awareness	**Adoption**	**Advocacy**
Understanding the values, understanding the reasons for change and hearing the commitment of the top team.	Using behaviours that demonstrate the values, rewarding those who demonstrate values, hearing of success stories.	Being a champion of the values and behaviours. Recommending them to others. Part of the way things are done round here.

Figure 7.5   Financial service quadrants

The awareness stage involved three main activities:

- A video was circulated to all managers, which identified the values in an exciting way.

- Senior managers were asked to introduce the values at any business meetings they were already running within a six-month period (special meetings were not held, and HR people did not run the process alone).

- The six values were integrated into the performance review process. They became key performance measures for each individual.

The Adoption stage is going on at the time of writing, and was preceded by a question-naire which tested the success of the awareness stage. Adoption in this context is about implementation, so this stage of the process is very practical and involves lots of 'hands-on' activities. A brand director was appointed at the end of the awareness stage to look after and promote the employer brand, and interestingly, this person has a marketing rather than an HR background. Planned activities so far include a newsletter circulating stories of success and the creation of a Web site on the company intranet that allows exchange of views and offers team exercises and thought-provoking resources to help people to get to grips with the values. Employer brand items and gifts such as mugs, sweatshirts and hats will also be available for those who want to promote the brand locally, or wish to have themed celebrations.

Advocacy is already appearing in pockets around the organization. Various managers have been selected as brand champions, but this process is seen as emergent rather than one that needs to be closely managed.

The planning team also used the Beckhard change formula to guide their actions (see Chapter 3). This meant having a clear vision, explaining the need for change and devising some first steps.

8

IT-based process change

IT has become a significant part of every person's working life. According to US economic analysis figures, companies are now spending an average of 30 per cent of their capital expenditures on information technology compared with 5 per cent in the 1960s. It is viewed as a critical resource.

However, despite the sophistication of the IT equipment available and the range of IT tools and techniques that have been devised and in many cases heavily promoted, organizations are still failing to gain the business value they hope for when they embark on IT-based change. It seems that while the promise of IT is high, the reality of what we actually experience is disappointing. It is as if the capacity of IT to deliver great things has overtaken our ability to use it effectively within our organizations.

Data gathered by Wharton Management School in 1996 reinforces this gap between expectation and reality. The research indicates that although 72 per cent of company executives asked say that it is critical for their organization to use high-tech tools such as IT to be competitive, only 17 per cent of respondents say that the benefits of these tools are being realized.

So what goes wrong in the process of realizing the benefits? Why do organizations have trouble with IT-based change? This chapter looks at the particular difficulties of achieving successful IT-based change and offers advice on how to overcome particular obstacles associated with this type of endeavour. The topics addressed are:

- strategy and IT;
- the role of IT management;
- the need for IT change managers;
- achieving process change;
- changing the information culture;
- new rules for a new age.

The potential gains of successfully implementing IT-based change are many and varied. Organizations are attracted by the idea that they will gain the capability to do a range of highly desirable things. Some of the potential gains concern innovation and development:

- to achieve flexible responsive production of customized goods;
- to segment the market place in new ways through analysing information, and then create new products for those segments;
- to serve customers in new ways by creating access via the Internet;
- to create new forms of partnership and new types of organization.

But many of the potential gains concern achieving efficiencies to:

- reduce the need for agents and intermediaries by providing employee or customer self-service facilities over the Internet or intranet;
- achieve sophisticated functionality at reasonable cost (for instance by introducing standard packages such as ERP);
- allow globalization of operations;
- enable choices to be made about how the company is structured while retaining the necessary level of central control;
- produce better information, with a greater level of detail than was possible before, and make it available faster to allow better decisions to be made;

- enable 24-hour working to maximize the ability to serve the globe and make best use of resources;

- encourage greater staff involvement by making information available to more people in the company;

- increase the opportunity for flexible working on the road or at home;

- reduce staff costs;

- increase the value of skills and knowledge by sharing information well.

Consider the growth in the use of SAP systems as an example of how companies are responding to the need to realize some of the potential gains listed above. SAP is a company that provides enterprise-wide applications that can satisfy most of a business's activities. SAP global sales have seen phenomenal growth from US$500 million in 1991 to US$2,400 million in 1996. Companies are obviously impressed by the powerful system, but there are many stories of the painful struggles that people have to go through before they achieve optimum usage of the software. It is certainly not an easy ride to move from strategy to implementation.

IMPLEMENTING IT WORLDWIDE – WHAT'S IN IT FOR THEM?

It all started in the Head Office in the United States. We developed a strict plan of action. We had a very clear timetable for the coming 18 months. A series of conference calls with the financial directors in each region made it clear what the time frame was for rolling out the system, and what needed to be done in preparation for this. However, when the moment came, they just were not ready, despite continuous reassurances that it would be done in time.

At the last minute we had to call in some consultants to work through the readiness check-list with the various regional teams. This cost us quite a bit of extra money that we had not budgeted for.

I don't think I have ever met such silent resistance. Until then, the regional offices had been allowed to report financial information in their own way. To them, the requirement to use the new system seemed very intrusive, and of no practical value. I guess we had only really seen and explained the advantages from a central point of view. If I did the same process again, I would take more time to go through the 'What's in it for them?' angle.

Financial projects manager, IT company

STRATEGY AND IT

It used to be that managers could delegate IT decisions to the organization's resident computer experts and they would simply go away and decide how to design and build a solution. But now, the decisions being made can affect the whole business in terms of service and product possibilities, smooth running of day-to-day operations and opportunities for sharing information. Is it sensible to leave these decisions up to technical experts who do not always have a full understanding of the organization's vision and purpose? Companies can and frequently do end up with a range of incompatible systems that may never achieve an optimum configuration. This can take years to sort out. Or even worse, a significant component system may be unable to fulfil management's long-term plans for organizational change, which may necessitate being able to segment data in different ways.

But there is a problem with senior management getting closer to the IT decision-making process. Davenport (1994) says, 'General managers ... usually don't know much about computers. They may like the idea of using information technology strategically.... But they seldom know how to translate their wishes into specific IT investments.' How can this situation be managed?

IT strategic grid

First, it is important to decide what sort of contribution IT makes to the organization's strategy. This enables the senior management team to gauge how much and what sort of attention the development and running of IT systems should be given by themselves and by others.

To make this decision it is necessary to look at two factors: strategic impact of application development and strategic impact of existing systems. For some organizations, the development of new innovative IT systems has a significant strategic impact; for others, they are more focused on installing off the shelf packages to enhance some aspect of internal performance. Similarly, some organizations are 100 per cent dependent on IT to maintain operational performance, such as manufacturing organizations. For others, it might take quite a period of time before a disruption in IT services would create a significant performance dip.

The grid in Figure 8.1 is useful for assessing the organization's current IT strategic position and thus deciding how much senior management attention needs to be spent on IT issues, and how IT should be managed. It is worth noting that the organization may change its position on the grid over a number of years.

'Support' organizations may spend a lot of money on IT, but they are not totally dependent on IT systems for operational success day to day, minute to minute.

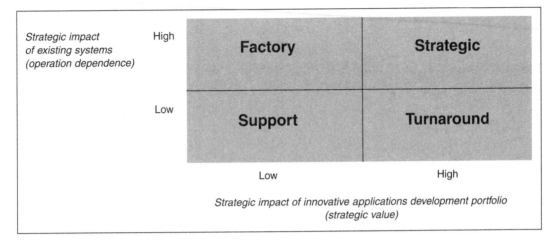

Figure 8.1   IT strategic grid
Source: adapted from Cash *et al* (1992)

Neither do they gain strategic advantage from innovative application developments. A doctor's surgery would qualify here. In this case, senior management can be quite distant from the IT planning process.

'Factory' organizations are completely dependent on the smooth running of their IT systems. For instance, a manufacturing unit might grind to a halt if the IT systems were to fail. However, with this type of organization, innovative applications developments, although important, are not crucial to the organization's ability to be competitive, except when its performance starts to lag behind competitors, and a move to the 'strategic' quadrant occurs.

'Turnaround' organizations are those in which innovative applications developments are crucial to the firm's strategic success, but the day-to-day running of IT systems is not so critical. This might for example be an organization developing e-learning packages. The other classic examples are DHL, UPS and Fedex, who all offered customers the ability to go online and check the status of packages that were being dispatched. This gave them tremendous strategic advantage. In this case IT planning needs substantial effort, and needs to be linked closely to organizational strategy.

'Strategic' organizations such as banks and insurance companies are those in which innovative applications development brings significant competitive advantage and day-to-day processes are highly dependent on the smooth running of IT systems. In these types of organization, there is a very tight link between business strategy and IT strategy, and the head of IT normally sits on the board of directors.

Developing guiding principles

How do senior managers ensure that IT investment decisions are in line with the organization's long-term strategy? The answer may be to develop a set of guiding principles which govern IT investment decisions.

The 'principles' approach to IT is advocated by Davenport. He recommends that a task force is set up comprising from 5 to 10 senior managers, including a senior information systems person, together with a small group of IS managers. This group should begin to devise a set of guiding principles that link strategy to IT investment decisions. The senior managers act as sponsors later in the process, endorsing the principles devised by the group.

The IS managers create the initial set of principles which convey the basic attitudes of the company towards technology, the overall direction the business is taking and the use to be made of existing technologies. These principles should be good for two or three years, or until there is a major shift in strategy. They should cover infrastructure, applications, data and organization. Examples of such principles are given by Davenport:

On infrastructure: *We are committed to a single vendor environment.*

On applications: *IS will provide applications that support cross-functional integration of business processes.*

On data: *Data created or obtained within the company belongs to the corporation – not to any particular function, unit, or individual. It is available to any user in the company who can demonstrate a need for it.*

On organization: *The user-sponsor of a systems project will be responsible for the business success of the system.*

Once this amount of time and effort is spent aligning the thinking between senior business managers and IT managers, the strategic course for IT progress is set, and decision making becomes much easier.

THE ROLE OF IT MANAGEMENT

IT management skills are critical to an organization's ability to incorporate the technologies that are 'out there' and use them to best advantage. However, IT staff are often left out of the core decision-making processes and treated as implementers rather than strategists. The solution, we believe, is to ensure that IT management skills are present not only with IT departments, but all over the organization (see box).

Sambamurthy and Zmud (in Sauer and Yetton, 1997) say:

> In our experience the most valued IT management skills tend to require lengthy development periods as they are heavily dependent on local – for example organization-specific – knowledge. We have also found that not all firms are equally endowed with the most valuable IT management skills. Furthermore, in order to be effectively applied, a firm's IT management skills must be intricately woven into the complex milieu of an organization's structures, roles, processes, culture, and the many relationships among a firm's business and IT managers.

In today's organizations the responsibility for managing IT is widely dispersed. It no longer sits solely with the IT director, but is shared amongst group-level IT people, business-level IT people, business line management, vendors, partners, consultants and contractors. This web of interconnected individuals somehow needs to sustain the organization's ability to innovate, plan, design, develop, implement, integrate and maintain IT systems.

So what are the unique skills and knowledge areas required by an organization collectively to ensure that IT is used to improve business processes, enable changes in organizational structure, add value to its knowledge base and create or support the development of new products and services? Sambamurthy and Zmud carried out a four-year research programme in the early 1990s, out of which emerged seven categories of IT management competencies:

- **Business deployment.** The key competences in this area are the ability to examine, visualize and communicate the value offered by emerging IT. This needs to be coupled with the use of multi-disciplinary teams, with a good shared understanding of IT, to rapidly implement innovative IT solutions.

- **External networks.** This area of competence refers to the need for the organization to develop close partnerships with external parties to increase their awareness of emerging IT.

- **Line technology leadership.** Users such as line managers and senior managers need to participate actively in championing IT initiatives. This area of competence concerns the ability to take technical leadership, which line managers may delegate rather too quickly to IT people through lack of understanding of the technology.

- **Process adaptiveness.** This competence refers to the ability of all employees to relate to IT and the way it can transform business processes. It is also about the organization's track record in restructuring its processes, and the existence of an environment where employees can discover and explore the functionality of IT systems. This means anything from the existence of a help desk, to online tutorials, to devoting time to training. For instance Deloitte and Touche has an innovation centre where employees can experiment with new technologies such as Web services to decide whether or not they could be useful.

- **IT planning.** This competence concerns the ability of managers within the organization to link strategic plans with IT plans, and to plan and execute individual projects.

- **IT infrastructure.** This competence is about the appropriateness and flexibility of the underlying infrastructure which allows innovative IT practices to emerge and to be capitalized upon.

- **Data centre utility.** This competence concerns the ability of those within the organization to build, maintain and secure fundamental information processing services.

We would add one competence to this list, as many organizations have completely outsourced IT operations and development, just leaving themselves with project managers and business analysts:

- **Managing outsourced services.** This concerns the ability to evaluate potential service options, manage the transition to outsourced IT services and manage service levels and service evaluation.

Sambamurthy and Zmud asked 230 senior IT executives to assess the levels of these competencies in their own organizations and to rate their organization's success in deploying IT successfully. This research revealed a strong link between the level of these competencies and the organization's level of success with deploying IT in support of its business strategy and work processes. The organizations in the group of respondents characterized by the highest level of IT management competency were also those demonstrating the highest success rate in deploying IT.

We offer the following three-stage process for moving towards better IT management.

Step one

Bring together a task force including senior management, line management and IT people. Start a discussion about how IT strategy will link to organizational strategy over the next five years. Select the IT management competencies that you think will be most important.

Step two

Conduct an audit of the key IT management competencies, involving as many people as possible. Use internal (good development for them) or external (better access to benchmarking data) consultants for this process. Feed back the results and identify hot spots where competence is low, but importance is high.

Step three

Plan how to raise the level of the most significant competences, allocating resources, responsibility and defining a specific timescale.

IT MANAGEMENT COMPETENCIES

- Business deployment:
  - examination of the potential business value of new, emerging IT;
  - utilization of multi-disciplinary teams throughout the organization;
  - effective working relationships among line managers and IT staff;
  - technology transfer, where appropriate, of successful IT applications, platforms and services;
  - adequacy of IT-related knowledge of line managers throughout the organization;
  - visualizing the value of IT investments throughout the organization;
  - appropriateness of IT policies;
  - appropriateness of IT sourcing decisions;
  - effectiveness of IT measurement systems.
- External networks:
  - existence of electronic links with the organization's customers;
  - existence of electronic links with the organization's suppliers;
  - collaborative alliances with external partners (vendors, systems integrators, competitors) to develop IT-based products and processes.
- Line technology leadership:
  - line managers' ownership of IT projects within their domains of business responsibility;
  - propensity of employees throughout the organization to serve as 'project champions'.
- Process adaptiveness:
  - propensity of employees throughout the organization to learn about and subsequently explore the functionality of installed IT tools and applications;
  - restructuring of business processes, where appropriate, throughout the organization;
  - visualizing organizational activities throughout the organization.

- IT planning
  - integration of business strategic planning and IT strategic planning;
  - clarity of vision regarding how IT contributes to business value;
  - effectiveness of IT planning throughout the organization;
  - effectiveness of project management practices.
- IT infrastructure
  - restructuring of IT work processes, where appropriate;
  - appropriateness of data architecture;
  - appropriateness of network architecture;
  - knowledge of and adequacy of the organization's IT skill base;
  - consistency of object (data, process, rules) definitions;
  - effectiveness of software development practices.
- Data centre utility:
  - appropriateness of processor architecture;
  - adequacy of quality assurance and security controls.

Source: Sambamurthy and Zmud in Sauer and Yetton (1997)
Copyright © 1997. Reprinted by permission of John Wiley and Sons, Inc

THE NEED FOR IT CHANGE MANAGERS

The days of the highly specialized in-house technical IT expert or 'geek' are probably numbered. Many IT solutions are off-the-shelf, and the teams of analysts and developers which used to occupy in-house IT departments are shrinking, or being outsourced, or simply not required. IT people with change management skills are needed now more than ever. Those IT people who can understand technology, be aware of what is 'out there' and what it can do for organizations, plus grasp how to create the changes desired by the organization are highly valuable.

IT courses and literature both tend to focus on the acquisition of IT skills and knowledge, or on the importance of good project management. The goal of IT work has traditionally been to deliver a piece of finished software to timescale and to budget,

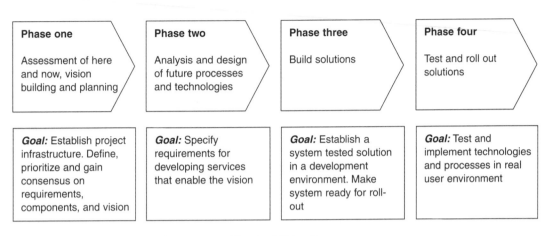

Phase one	Phase two	Phase three	Phase four
Assessment of here and now, vision building and planning	Analysis and design of future processes and technologies	Build solutions	Test and roll out solutions
Goal: Establish project infrastructure. Define, prioritize and gain consensus on requirements, components, and vision	**_Goal:_** Specify requirements for developing services that enable the vision	**_Goal:_** Establish a system tested solution in a development environment. Make system ready for roll-out	**_Goal:_** Test and implement technologies and processes in real user environment

Figure 8.2 Typical IT roll-out process

according to the specification. Much emphasis is made on getting the specification right, getting the right skills in place and controlling changes along the way. See Figure 8.2 which illustrates a typical IT roll-out process. There is precious little reference to stakeholder management or business user involvement, although it may be implicit.

The emergence of rapid development techniques allows for real-time updating of software and flexible scoping of a project, but this approach involves a new way of specifying and managing development of IT systems which can be hard to establish and keep going.

IT people tend not to learn about change management. They learn to see their job as ending when the system is delivered. This is beginning to change in more forward-looking organizations, but is still an issue in many IT departments, and in many software development companies and consultancies too. IT people need to improve their skills in influencing and managing change, as well as their understanding of how organizational change works, and the nature of motivation and resistance in organizational systems.

The first aspect of the way the IT people work in organizations is the role that they tend to assume when working with business clients. Block (2000) offers a useful way of describing the three types of role that a consultant can have when dealing with a client. This is helpful when considering the ways in which IT people can choose to work with their clients. The three types of role are:

- expert role;
- pair of hands role;
- collaborative role.

The expert role

The consultant is the expert. The client has fully delegated the authority to plan and implement changes to the consultant. Decisions on how to proceed are made by the consultant on the basis of his or her expert judgement. The client elects to play an inactive role, and is responsive only when required by the consultant to respond. The client's role is to judge and evaluate after the fact. The consultant's goal is to solve the immediate problem.

When IT people choose this role (as they very often do) it means that they have the space to get on with the job in hand without interruption or interference, but it means that they can hide behind their expertise when things go wrong, much to the frustration of business managers. The other problem with this approach is that the client's commitment to the technical solution is often rather thin. This means that when the client gets the end product, he or she is not always happy, having taken little interest until the finished item hits his or her desk.

The pair of hands role

Here the client sees the consultant as an extra pair of hands. The client retains full control. The consultant is expected to apply specialized knowledge to implement action plans towards achievement of goals defined by the client.

The consultant takes a passive role and does not question the client's plans. Decisions on how to proceed are made by the client. The consultant may prepare recommendations for the client's review and approval.

Collaboration is not really necessary and two-way communication is limited. The client initiates and the consultant responds. The client's role is to judge and evaluate from a close distance.

When IT people take this type of role with their clients, problems occur because the manager may not have selected the best solution, and the consultant did not feel that he or she could question what he or she was told to do.

The collaborative role

In this case problem solving is a joint undertaking. Consultants working in this mode apply their special skills to help clients solve problems; they don't solve problems for the client. The consultant and client work to become interdependent. They share responsibility 50/50 for action planning, implementation and results. Control issues become matters for discussion and negotiation. Disagreement is expected and seen as a source of new ideas.

The consultant's goal is to solve problems so that they stay solved. Next time the client will have the skills to solve the problem.

In this mode, the relationship between consultant and client is creative, productive and responsibility is shared. This is the most appropriate role for IT people to take with clients in today's complex organizations. However, it demands that IT people acquire skills beyond the technical. Some clients will see this type of relationship as slow, and may interpret collaboration as some form of obstruction. They will want to gain access to the quick results that the 'experts' used to give them, which will lead them to the problems highlighted above with the expert role.

What skills and knowledge might be required to enhance an IT person's ability to work collaboratively with business managers? The intended outcome is to increase the possibility of implemented IT systems resulting in the intended behaviour change. We suggest that IT people involved in large-scale change initiatives need to acquire the following skills and knowledge if they are to become better agents of change:

- Knowledge:
    - How does organizational change happen?
    - What motivates people and how can that motivation be activated?
    - Where does resistance to change come from, and how can it be handled?
    - What change processes and what leadership styles are there to choose from, and what are the effects of each?
    - Wide understanding of different business processes.
    - Good understanding of organizational culture and its impact on change.

- Skills:
    - Coaching managers to solve change issues.
    - Facilitating multidisciplinary team workshops.
    - Influencing those outside your direct control.
    - Client and stakeholder management (saying no as much as you say yes)!!
    - Collaborative process mapping.
    - Ability to speak the client's language (using their terminology).

If you are an IT person reading this, then your irritation level may now have reached an all-time high! You may be thinking, 'I am already doing all this!' We congratulate you, and offer our additional thoughts on the role of HR people in IT-based change. HR people suffer this syndrome in reverse. While they might focus on all the people-related aspects of desired changes, they often fail to grasp the nature of the technology involved. Again this is changing, but slowly.

Enterprise-wide applications such as PeopleSoft are now taking hold in many organizations, replacing many of the tasks that HR people have traditionally called their own (promotion, recruitment, arrangement of training). HR people need to be ready to understand and explore the possibilities offered by these systems so that they can think through how people will be affected, and orientate their internal structures and skills accordingly. This might mean setting up some quite different structures. Some central HR departments that we have worked with are now providing help desks and supporting users of IT, while offering HR policy guidance rather than taking on a full HR management role.

ACHIEVING PROCESS CHANGE

IT-based change is about process change. It involves people doing different things in different ways with different inputs and different outputs. New or improved IT systems are brought in to either increase efficiency or to allow innovation to occur, not to simply automate what is already there, so process change almost always occurs. But how is this best achieved?

In this section we compare two different approaches to process change. These are BPR (business process re-engineering) and socio-technical design. We look at the pros and cons of these two approaches, and investigate how these two approaches can be combined to offer a new way of successfully improving processes using IT as a lever.

BPR

BPR is one of the best known approaches to achieving IT-based change in organizations. It was first set out in a book by Hammer and Champy in 1993, entitled *Reengineering the Corporation: A manifesto for business revolution,* and was received with much enthusiasm from the business community, appearing to offer the answer to how to achieve radical change and maximize effectiveness. The tenets of this approach are:

- Rigorous focus on business processes that deliver value to the customer.

- Radical process redesign from scratch, leading to radical transformation.

- All unnecessary process detail is eliminated.

- Old processes are obliterated.

- Redesign produces processes that give significant strategic improvements in competitive performance.

- Enabled by IT.

AN EXAMPLE OF BPR

A car leasing organization in the UK decided to completely redesign its customer service processes, with the goal of gaining competitive advantage over other car leasing companies by being much faster and much more responsive. It also intended to offer some self-service operations to customers via the Internet. A task force was selected from the existing customer service team, and these people worked alongside a team of specialized BPR consultants to radically redesign the customer service processes over a period of three to four months.

The new process designs looked excellent, but problems came in the form of resistance when teams had to work on implementing processes that were obviously going to lead to staff redundancies. The roll-out was done over an intensive six-month period, which was very stressful for managers and staff alike. Customers noticed a significant dip in service, so much so that two key accounts were lost during the roll-out period. Things are better now, with new teams in place and improved processes, but if anyone was brave enough to do a cost–benefit analysis, the results would probably not look good.

Unfortunately the number of BPR successes where expectations have been fully realized is said to be quite small. Advocates of BPR take some pride in this. They claim that the potential gains of this approach are so great, it is bound to be risky. However, Sauer and Yetton (1997) say, 'Not only is the risk [of BPR] substantial, but the stakes are unusually high. The cost of failure for a project that involves organizational transformation is likely to be much greater than the simple loss of investment. The time lost in undertaking a project that fails may give competitors a lead that cannot be recovered.'

This is a mechanistic approach that spends little effort on the social or organizational side of the process. A typical BPR approach follows the steps seen in Figure 8.3. There might be some team work, some multi-skilling and some group problem solving; there is usually quite a strong prescriptive element to the IT solution. Also, although the impact on structures, skills, culture and standards is thought about, it is often not acted upon until the later phases of the programme of change, as an add-on. Many believe that this approach is not the most effective way of engaging people in defining what process improvements are needed, and in making them happen. Resistance may be encountered, which will waste effort, or cause the initiative to fail.

BPR therefore offers the very attractive prospect of radically transforming key processes by starting from a totally blank sheet. The downside comes during implementation, when resistance from those who have not been involved may be encountered. Radical process improvements which lead to staff redundancies are difficult to manage, and team performance will dip during the implementation period. Staff read the signs of a new systems implementation where redundancies will result, and are demotivated at an early stage in the lifecycle.

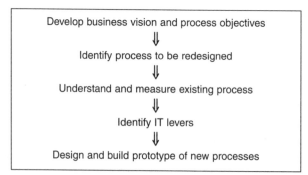

Figure 8.3   A typical BPR approach
Source: adapted from Davenport and Short (1990)

Socio-technical design

The principles of socio-technical design are concerned with getting a balance between:

- the strategic vision of the organization;

- the technology and the tasks needed to provide the product or service;

- the needs of the staff.

This school of thought stems from a systems view of organizations, based in the organism metaphor (see Senge in Chapter 3), and is a much more incremental, evolutionary approach. The approach is less widely used than BPR, and seems more cautious and humanistic than traditional BPR processes, which have a rather macho feel to them, advocating throwing everything out and starting again.

The underlying principles of socio-technical design are identified in Mumford and Beekman (1994). These principles were originally developed by the Tavistock Institute of Human Relations in London in the late 1960s, but still appear to hold good today:

- **The principle of minimum critical specification:** tell people what to do but not how to do it.

- **The principle of variance control:** problems must be corrected as close to the point of origin as possible, and preferably by the group that caused them.

- **The principle of multiskilling:** give individuals a range of tasks including some routine and some challenging.

- **The principle of boundary management:** identify boundaries between groups or functions and ensure that these are well managed and that the people on them have the necessary information to pass the product smoothly to its next transformation stage.

- **The principle of information flow:** information systems should be designed so that information goes directly to the place where action is to be taken, or to the source that originated it.

- **The principle of design and human values:** an important objective of organizational design should be to provide a high quality of working life for employees, for instance to fulfil the need to feel the job leads to a desirable future.

- **The principle of incompletion:** the need to recognize that design is an ongoing and iterative process.

Socio-technical design involves more forethought, planning and incremental change than BPR, which is faster, more risky and more exciting. As defined by the Tavistock Group, this process was facilitated by either a consultant or a manager, and followed the steps below. Some of these activities may look a bit quaint these days. When compared with BPR, the focus might appear rather 'fluffy' as much attention is given to the psychological needs of the workforce. See Figure 8.4.

Socio-technical design is still alive and well in some companies, but has been rather overtaken by the speed and promise of BPR. Although the incremental, developmental approach is seen to work well, it is often too slow for many environments where big results are sought quickly, without taking people off the job to do the research and take action.

Combination approach: PROGRESS methodology

The PROGRESS methodology for process improvement is also offered by Mumford and Beekman (1994), and brings together the principles of socio-technical design and the technology focus and efficiency emphasis of BPR (see Figure 8.5). Key to this method is the belief that the future users of a system must play a major role in its design. Cross-group design teams must be set up, sponsored by senior management and facilitated by a skilled facilitator to achieve their goals.

It is useful to illustrate the PROGRESS approach using a case study.

Initial scanning
(description of existing system – inputs, outputs, work flow, organization, environment – compiled by consultant)

Identification of unit operations
(identification of the main stages of the production process)

Identification of variances
(identification of weak links in the systems where it becomes difficult to achieve required standard)

Analysis of social system
(handling of variances, relationship needed for optimum working of the system, extent of flexibility between roles, pay relationships, staff psychological needs)

How workers see their roles
(do roles meet psychological needs?)

The maintenance and supply systems
(how do these processes affect production?)

The corporate environment
(how do development plans affect the future operation of the department?)

Proposals for change
(actions are suggested after discussion and feedback with all those involved. Proposals for change must contribute both to the improvement of the production systems and to the social systems. Proposals normally involve some level of self-management by the production team)

Figure 8.4   The socio-technical design process
Source: Mumford and Beekman (1994)

County planning office case study

The county planning department was overstretched and 'in crisis'. Plans were stacking up, and a three-month delay was the normal experience of those submitting plans for approval. This was starting to become untenable, as people in the community wanted to get on with building work and could not do so without planning approval.

A consultancy firm using the PROGRESS approach was called in to work with the planning team. The planning process itself was identified by the team as being cumbersome and slow, but although they could see the problems, they had never had the time to sort them out. The consultants planned in some intensive half-day sessions with the planning team to map out the process and identify weak links. Although the impact of spending time in the workshop sessions caused even more backlog to build up for the team, they were confident that they could reduce the planning cycle time (from arrival of the application to sending out of approval) by 30 per cent if they focused on it for long enough and drew out some simple agreed actions.

Step one	Identify the process you wish to redesign	
Step two	Define the mission, efficiency objectives, critical success factors and major problems (variances)	
Step three	Describe the environment in which the process takes place (pressure from outside, market conditions etc)	
Step four	Describe the process as it is at present (often missed out in BPRI): tasks, variances, value chain, structure	
Step five	List the variances (weak links in the system, where standards are hard to achieve consistently)	
Step six	List and rank value adding activities	
Step seven	Analyse the social system – who works with whom and how, required relationships, knowledge of each other's roles	
Step eight	Job satisfaction analysis – good fits and bad fits	
Step nine	Probable or possible new developments	
Step ten	Future strategy of the organization	
Step eleven	Proposals for change – based on above information, and in discussion with the team	

Figure 8.5   The PROGRESS methodology for process improvement
Source: Mumford and Beekman (1994)

Various core problems were identified:

- Seating arrangements were not optimal. The department was split between two buildings for historical reasons. Time was being wasted going to and fro, looking for people and searching for things.

- Lack of knowledge of different roles in the team was causing misunderstanding and friction.

- One administrator was particularly overloaded with tasks that she was finding extremely boring.

- Lack of a cataloguing system meant that time was wasted searching for paper-based items.

- The planning officers were often out of the office, but were not accessible. It was impossible to get messages to them, which was in turn holding up decision-making processes.

The following actions were agreed:

- The team was moved so that they could all sit in the same office.

- Four people were asked to learn more about each other's roles by spending two hours a week together on joint projects.

- The administrator shared out her 'boring' tasks on a weekly basis.

- A simple computer-based cataloguing system was introduced.

- Planning officers were given a shared mobile phone, which they used to check every half-day for messages.

These simple measures resulted in a 27 per cent reduction in cycle time of the planning process. The department started to reduce the backlog, and life became less stressful for everyone.

CHANGING THE INFORMATION CULTURE

One of the difficulties with implementing new IT systems is getting people to use them in the manner intended. There are many horror stories of expensive IT investments that are never fully incorporated into daily organizational life.

Does the introduction of technology automatically change behaviour? Our experience says that this does not happen. In the worst case the new technology reinforces the habits and attitudes already present. (See the example in the box.) Organizations need to do more than simply change the IT equipment and systems available if they want to experience a radical shift in behaviour. A culture change may be required to create the shifts in information sharing required, because the introduction of new IT systems alone will not achieve this, suggests Davenport (1994). He says, 'It shouldn't surprise anyone that human nature can throw a wrench into the best-laid IT plans, yet technocrats are constantly caught off-guard by the "irrational" behaviour of "end-users"'. He says that what is important is how people use information, not how they use technology.

IMPROVING THE SALES PROCESS THROUGH THE USE OF IT?

We recruited George in January. He was a dynamic salesman, brought in to boost our capacity to develop major accounts. George had used this great IT system in his old company, and encouraged us all to come to a presentation about what this type of system could offer.

The proposed system would allow salespeople to share information about customers and contacts. He said this would boost our capacity to plan our sales visits, and partner with each other to work more creatively with existing and potential clients. It sounded good.

We bought the system in June. It was pretty simple to use, and everyone seemed in favour, so there should have been no issues. After two months, only George and two other salespeople were using the system and updating it regularly. This was out of a team of 12 of us. People just weren't used to sharing information in this way, and as we were still measured on our individual sales targets, there was no incentive to help others by revealing our contacts.

George got really frustrated, and accepted another job by the end of November.

Sales executive in electronics company

Perhaps we need to forget about technology for the moment, and look at existing information sharing habits and develop some goals for behaviour change. But what are the rules governing information sharing behaviour? Davenport states the information facts of life:

- Most of the information in organizations – and most of the information people really care about – is not on computers.

- Managers prefer to get information from people rather than computers; people add value to raw information by interpreting it and adding context.

- The more complex and detailed an information management approach, the less likely it is to change anyone's behaviour.

- All information does not have to be common; an element of flexibility and disorder is desirable.

- The more a company knows and cares about its core business area, the less likely employees will be to agree on a common definition of it.

- If information is power and money, people will not share it easily.

- The willingness of individuals to use a specified information format is directly proportional to how much they have participated in defining it, or trust others who did.

- To make the most of electronic communications, employees must first learn to communicate face to face.

- Since people are important sources and integrators of information, any maps of information should include people.

- There is no such thing as information overload; if information is really useful, our appetite for it is insatiable.

IT systems such as Lotus Notes and other forms of groupware are often readily taken up by employees because of the range of ways of sharing information offered. However, people need to have time to explore and learn about the possibilities of these systems so that they can make best use of them. E-mail is now taken for granted, but also has downsides such as 'non-information overload' rather than information overload. Non-relevant e-mails take time to scan, process and delete. It is almost too easy to share information via e-mail, and people will do it for their own reasons (such as covering their backs, making themselves look good, bringing network power into play and making others look bad) rather than for the benefit of the recipient.

IT systems are expensive to implement. Therefore, it would be beneficial if executives could start to see the difference between deciding to implement an IT system, and deciding to change the company's information-sharing habits. Experience shows us that the first will certainly not guarantee the second, and the second often requires a culture change which requires energy, commitment, sponsorship and clear direction (see Chapter 8).

NEW RULES FOR A NEW AGE

As we were writing this chapter, we noticed an interesting article in the *Harvard Business Review* entitled 'IT doesn't matter' (Carr, 2003). The writer suggested that IT is an infrastructure technology, rather than a leading edge one. This means that it is no longer a scarce resource that can give an organization an important competitive edge. It is now readily available at less cost, but companies are still investing.

For the last 25 years companies have been investing in IT systems to the point where they are now firmly built into the infrastructure of commerce. Compare this with the progress of the railway, or the electricity generator. At certain points during this progression there have been moments when companies have gained a competitive advantage from being the first to implement a particular technology; however this is now starting to level off, and so should investment plans.

The three new rules for IT management offered by Carr give some guidelines for those ready to review their IT investment strategy:

- **Spend less.** Carr says that companies with the biggest IT investments rarely post the best financial results. The focus should now be on ensuring that you do not put your company at a cost disadvantage, because the competitive gains will be minimal.

- **Follow, don't lead.** The longer you wait to buy IT systems, the more you will get for your money. Carr says that it is unwise to be on the cutting edge, with the possibility that software or hardware is unproven.

- **Focus on vulnerabilities, not opportunities.** Companies need to pay more attention to security and network vulnerabilities, as well as systems reliability and minimizing downtime. IT spend should be carefully controlled, and resources managed in an economic way.

SUMMARY AND CONCLUSIONS

It is difficult to align organizational strategy with IT strategy, but unless this is done the two strategies can drift apart, causing the organization major problems, especially if strategy changes, or enterprise-wide approaches are sought. Organizations need to assess where they are on the strategic grid (factory, strategic, support, turnaround) to decide how closely linked these strategies need to be, and to decide how and what sort of senior management attention IT deserves.

Strategy and IT decision making can become dangerously decoupled through lack of communication and understanding between business managers and IT managers. IT systems begin to drift away from their original purpose, and may actually begin to limit the company's possibilities for information sharing and therefore damage its future. In this case it may be beneficial to generate a list of 'guiding principles' to enable clear decision making by all managers.

IT management needs to be taken more seriously. IT managers are often left out of the decision-making loop and excluded from the core decision-making process in an organization. They become mere 'implementers' of other people's solutions. IT management skills need to be present not only within IT departments, but all over the organization.

IT people need to learn more about organizational change processes. IT people have been traditionally uninterested in anything except technology, which has led to a division between designing the IT system (IT's responsibility) and realizing the benefits by getting people to use it well (business managers' responsibility). This is changing, but not fast enough. IT people now need to shift their competency from being technical experts, to being specialists with change management skills.

Human-oriented processes for implementing IT systems work better than processes that have a purely technical focus, and incremental process change has a better record of success than radical process change. Excitement about 'radical' process change has led to a belief that only radical changes bring radical results. BPR (business process re-engineering) has not brought all the hoped-for benefits, because of its lack of focus on people and the inherently risky nature of radical process transformation. It is highly probable that incremental, more human-oriented solutions such as those based on socio-technical design actually work better.

If a change in information-sharing habits is required, this means addressing the change as you would a cultural change. Problems come when senior managers and IT people believe that technology will automatically change behaviour. Often the reverse happens: the new technology reinforces the habits and attitudes already present. A culture change may be required to create the shifts in information sharing required, because the introduction of new IT systems alone will not achieve this.

Chief executives have started to over-value the power of IT, beyond the strategic gains it can really offer. IT is not now a scarce resource, but a fact of life. Some say that IT's importance has diminished, and that organizations need to approach IT investment and management in a very different way, allowing others to experiment with new systems before deciding to buy, and only investing where there is vulnerability.

Conclusion

So what did we set out to do, and what did we achieve here? We wanted to write a book that allowed leaders of all persuasions to dip into the rich casket of theory on change, and to come out with their own jewels of learning. We most of all wanted to help to create the time and space for people to reflect on the changes facing them in the past, now and in the future by making the theory accessible, asking the right questions and providing practical glimpses of our experiences. We hope all of this will stimulate new thoughts and new connections.

Two significant messages are ringing in our ears as the ink begins to dry on the first edition of this book. These are explained below. We also want two-way communication with our readers, and want to make that possible through this section.

THE IMPORTANCE OF PERIPHERAL VISION

The first message we want to convey is about the importance for leaders of being awake and being aware. The notion of peripheral vision is a key one to keep in mind. Leaders need to wake up to what is going on around them. This means noticing more than the obvious, the loud or the directly visible. It means having an awareness of what is going on at the edges, and being observant about motion and change. Whichever assumptions a leader employs about the nature of change (machine, political system, organism or flux and transformation) there is a need to be extremely observant about what is going on in and around the organization.

We see theories and models as helpful in the process of gaining clearer peripheral vision. If leaders have a language and a framework for noticing things, they begin to notice more. As a young student of music, I can remember studying sonata form, which seemed only mildly interesting as a piece of theory. However, it led to increased enjoyment of musical shapes and I began to notice more, and listen with a sharper ear.

How do leaders achieve peripheral vision? Well, it does take time. But it means talking and listening to a wide cross-section of people. It means asking good questions and maintaining open relationships. It means making sure that enough time is given to leadership as well as management. And, most painfully for some, it means spending more time gathering information and spending less time making decisions.

FINDING THE SPACE TO REFLECT

The second message is about the importance of reflection time. Leaders benefit greatly from taking regular, focused time to reflect on what is going on around them (the fruits of their peripheral vision), what is happening right now, what the options are and where they are personally in all this. Their organizations benefit too because leadership action is considered, rather than knee-jerk.

Can this reflection be done alone in the car, or in the bath? Well, to some extent. However, it is easy to avoid anxieties by making quick decisions when you are alone. It is only when we are with other people we respect and trust that we really begin to consider other options and look difficulties in the eye.

We recommend coaching or action learning if you are serious about developing yourself as a leader. This can range from a regular meeting with a close colleague to a longer-term commitment to working with a group of leaders, or it can involve a series of one to one sessions with a professional leadership coach. Happily, this is becoming more acceptable in many organizations and seen less as a sign of weakness.

HOW TO GET IN TOUCH WITH THE AUTHORS OF THIS BOOK

Comments

We are interested to hear from you if you have enjoyed the book or if you have any suggestions or ideas that would improve it. Please send your thoughts to us via the contact details below.

Credits

We have made strenuous efforts to get in touch with and acknowledge those responsible for the ideas and theories contained in this book. However we realize that we may have unintentionally neglected to mention some people. If you are aware of any piece of work contained here that has not been properly credited, please do let us know so that we can make amends in future editions of this book.

Coaching and consultancy

If you would like any information about our coaching and consultancy work in connection with managing change and leadership development, we would be delighted to hear from you.

Contact us at:

www.makingsenseofchange.com

or e-mail us using estherandmike@makingsenseofchange.co.uk

References

Adams, J, Hayes, J and Hopson, B (1976) *Transitions: Understanding and Managing Personal Change*, Martin Robertson, London

Aiello, R J and Watkins, M D (2000) The fine art of friendly acquisition, *Harvard Business Review* (Nov–Dec), pp 101–07

Ashkenas, R N, Demonaco, L J and Francis, S C (1998) Making the Deal Real, *Harvard Business Review* (Jan–Feb), pp 165–78

Bandler, R and Grinder, J (1979), *Frogs into Princes*, Real People Press, Utah

Beck, A (1970) Cognitive therapy: nature of relationship to behaviour therapy, *Behaviour Therapy*, **1**, pp 184–200

Beckhard, R F and Harris, R T (1987) *Organizational Transitions: Managing complex change*, Addison-Wesley, Reading, MA

Belbin, M (1981) *Management Teams: Why they succeed or fail*, Butterworth-Heinemann, London

Bell, B and Kozlowski, S (2002) A typology of virtual teams: implications for effective leadership, *Group and Organization Management* (March), pp 14–49

Bennis, W (1994) *On Becoming a Leader*, Addison-Wesley, Reading, MA

Berry, L and Parasuraman, A (1991) *Marketing Services: Competing through quality*, Free Press, New York

Bion, W R (1961) *Experiences in Groups and Other Papers*, Tavistock Publications, London

Block, P (2000) *Flawless Consulting*, 2nd edn, Jossey Bass Pfeiffer, San Francisco, CA

Bridges, W (1991) *Managing Transitions*, Perseus, Reading, MA

Bridges, W and Mitchell, S (2002) Leading transition: a new model for change, in *On Leading Change*, ed F Hesselbein and R Johnston, pp 47–59, Jossey-Bass, New York

Brown, S L and Eisenhardt, K M (1995) Product development: past research, present findings, and future directions, *Academy of Management Review*, **20** (2), pp 343–78

Bryman, A (1992) *Charisma and Leadership in Organizations*, Sage, London

Buber M (1961) *Tales of the Hasidim*, (2 volumes) Schocken, New York

Buchanan, D and Huczynski, A (1985) *Organizational Behaviour*, Prentice Hall, London

Bullock, R J and Batten, D (1985) It's just a phase we're going through, *Group and Organization Studies*, **10** (Dec), pp 383–412

Burns, T and Stalker, G M (1961) *The Management of Innovation*, Tavistock, London

Carey, D (2000) Lessons from master acquirers, *Harvard Business Review* (May–Jun), pp 145–54

Carnall, C A (1990) *Managing Change in Organizations*, Prentice Hall, London

Carr, N G (2003) IT doesn't matter, *Harvard Business Review* (May)

Casey, D (1993) *Managing Learning in Organizations*, Open University Press, Buckingham

Cash, J I Jr, McFarlan, F W and McKenney, J (1992) *Corporate Information Systems Management: The issues facing senior executives*, 3rd edn, Irwin, Illinois

CIPD [accessed 2003] Organising for Success in the 21st Century [Online] www.cipd.org.uk

Cohen, S G. and Bailey, D E (1997) What makes teams work: group effectiveness research from the shop floor to the executive suite, *Journal of Management*, **23**, pp 239–90

Collins, J C and Porras, J I (1994) *Built to Last: Successful Habits of Visionary Companies*, HarperBusiness, New York

Covey, S (1989) *The Seven Habits of Highly Effective People*, Simon and Schuster, London

Covey, S (1992) *Principle-Centred Leadership*, Simon and Schuster, London

Crosby, L and Johnson, S (2001) Branding and your CRM strategy, *Marketing Management* (Jul/Aug)

Davenport, T H (1994) Saving IT's soul, *Harvard Business Review* (Mar–Apr), pp 11–27

Davenport, T H and Short, J E (1990) The new industrial engineering: information technology and business process redesign, *Sloan Management Review* (Summer)

Deal, T and Kennedy, A (1999) *The New Corporate Cultures*, Texere, London

Devine, M (1999) *Mergers and Acquisitions: The Roffey Park mergers and acquisitions checklist*, Roffey Park Management Institute, West Sussex, UK

Ellis, A and Grieger, R (eds) (1977) *Handbook of Rational-Emotive Therapy*, Springer, New York

Evans, P (2000) Chapter 5 in *Management 21st Century: Someday we'll all manage this way*, ed S Chowdbury, Financial Times/Prentice Hall, London

Feldmann, M L and Spratt, M F (1999) *Five Frogs on a Log*, Wiley, Chichester

Gardner, H (1996) *Leading Minds: An anatomy of leadership*, HarperCollins, London

Gaughan, P A (2002) *Mergers, Acquisitions, and Corporate Restructurings*, Wiley, New York

Glaser, R and Glaser, C (1992) *Team Effectiveness Profile*, Organization Design and Development, King of Prussia, PA

Goffee, R and Jones, G (1998) *The Character of a Corporation*, HarperCollins, London

Goleman, D (1998) *Working with Emotional Intelligence*, Bloomsbury, London

Goleman, D (2000) Leadership that gets results, *Harvard Business Review*, **78** (2) (Mar), pp 78–90

Green, M [accessed 2001] What makes a premier performer? [Online] www.transitionalspace.co.uk

Greene, W, Walls, G and Schrest, L (1994) Internal marketing: the key to external marketing success, *Journal of Services Marketing*, **8** (4), pp 5–13

Griffin E (1991) *First Look at Communication Theory*, McGraw-Hill, New York

Hai, D M (ed) (1986) *Organizational Behavior: Experiences and cases*, West Publishing, St Paul, MN

Hailey, V H and Balogun, J (2002) Devising context sensitive approaches to change: the example of Glaxo Wellcome, *Long Range Planning*, **35** (2) (Apr), pp 153–79

Hammer, M and Champy, J (1993) *Reengineering the Corporation: A Manifesto for Business Revolution*, HarperBusiness, New York

Hampden-Turner, C (1990) *Creating Corporate Culture*, Addison-Wesley, Reading, MA

Handy, C (1993) *Understanding Organizations*, Penguin, London

Heifetz, R and Laurie, D (1997) The work of leadership, *Harvard Business Review*, **75** (1) (Jan–Feb), pp 124–34

Henrik, R (1980) *The Psychotherapy Handbook*, New American Library, New York

Herzberg, F (1968) One more time: how do you motivate employees? *Harvard Business Review* (Jan/Feb), pp 53–62

Hesselbein, F and Johnston, R (2002) *On Leading Change*, Jossey-Bass, New York

Hill, W F and Gruner, L (1973) A study of development in open and closed groups, *Small Group Behavior*, **4**, pp 355–82

Hirsh, S and Kummerow, J (2000) *Introduction to Type in Organisations*, Consulting Psychologists Press, Palo Alto, CA

Hoyt, F and Beverlyn, K (1987) Services marketing: a conceptual model, *Journal of Midwest Marketing*, **2**, pp 195–99

Jaworski, B and Kohli, A (1993) Market orientation: antecedents and consequences, *Journal of Marketing*, **57** (Jul), pp 53–70

Jones, J and Bearley, W L (1986) *Group Development Assessment*, Organization Design and Development, King of Prussia, PA

Kanter, R (2002) The enduring skills of change leaders, in *On Leading Change*, ed F Hesselbein and R Johnston, pp 47–59, Jossey-Bass, New York

Keidal, R W (1984) Baseball, football, and basketball: models for business, *Organizational Dynamics* (Winter)

Kerr, S (1995) On the folly of rewarding A while hoping for B, *Academy of Management Executive*, **9** (1), pp 7–14

Kohli, A and Jaworski, B (1990) Marketing orientation: the construct, research propositions and managerial implication, *Journal of Marketing*, **54** (Apr), pp 1–18

Kolb, D (1984) *Experiential Learning*, Prentice Hall, New York

Kotter, J P (1990) What leaders really do, *Harvard Business Review*, **68** (3) (May), pp 101–11

Kotter, J and Heskett, J (1992) *Corporate Culture and Performance*, Free Press, New York

Kotter, J P (1995) Leading change: why transformation efforts fail, *Harvard Business Review*, **73** (2), pp 59–67

Kotter, J P (1996) *Leading Change*, Harvard Business School Press, Boston, MA

Kubler-Ross, E (1969) *On Death and Dying*, Macmillan, New York

Larson, C and LaFasto, F (1989) *Teamwork: What must go right, what can go wrong*, Sage, Newbury Park, CA

Lewin, K (1951) *Field Theory in Social Science*, Harper and Row, New York

Lewin, K (1952) *Field Theory in Social Science*, Tavistock, London

Lipman-Blumen, J (2002) The age of connective leadership, in *On Leading Change*, ed F Hesselbein and R Johnston, pp 89–101, Jossey-Bass, New York

Locke E A and Latham G P (1984) *Goal Setting: A motivational technique that works!* Prentice Hall, Englewood Cliffs, NJ

Maslow, A (1970) *Motivation and Personality*, Harper & Row, New York

McCaulley, M (1975) How individual differences affect health care teams, *Health Team News*, **1** (8), pp 1–4

McGregor, D (1960) *The Human Side of Enterprise*, McGraw-Hill, Maidenhead

Meredith, J R and Mantel, S J Jr (2000), *Project Management. A managerial approach*, Wiley, New York

Miles, R E and Snow, C C (1984) Fit, failure and the hall of fame, *California Management Review*, **26** (3), pp 10–28

Modlin, H and Faris, M (1956), Group adaptation and interaction on psychiatric team practice, *Psychiatry*, **19**, pp 97–103

Mohrman, S A, Cohen, S G and Morhman, A M (1995) *Designing Team-Based Organizations: New forms for knowledge work*, Jossey-Bass, San Francisco

Molenaar, K, Brown, H, Caile, S and Smith, R (2002) Corporate culture, *Professional Safety*, Park Ridge, Jul 2002

Morgan, B B, Glickman, A S, Woodward, E A, Blaiwes, A S and Salas, E (1986) *Measurement of Team Behaviors in a Navy Environment* (Tech. Rep no 86–014), p 3, Naval Training Systems Center, Orlando, FL

Morgan, B and Salas, E (1993) An analysis of team evolution and maturation, *Journal of General Psychology*, **120** (3), p 277

Morgan, G (1986) *Images of Organization*, Sage, Thousand Oaks, CA

Mumford, E and Beekman, G (1994), *Tools for Change and Progress*, CSG, Leiden

Nadler, D A and Tushman, M L (ed Nadler M B) (1997) *Competing by Design: The power of organizational architecture*, Oxford University Press, New York

Nevis, E (1998) *Organizational Consulting: A Gestalt approach*, Gestalt Institute of Cleveland Press, Ohio

Noer, D (1993) *Healing the Wounds: Overcoming the trauma of layoffs and revitalizing downsized organizations,* Jossey-Bass, San Francisco, CA

Obholzer, A and Roberts, V (eds) (1994) *The Unconscious at Work*, Routledge, London

O'Neill, M (2000) *Executive Coaching with Backbone and Heart*, Jossey-Bass, San Francisco, CA

Pascale, R (1990) *Managing on the Edge*, Penguin, London

Pavlov, I P (trans 1928) *Lectures on Conditioned Reflexes*, International, New York

Perls, F (1976) *The Gestalt Approach and Eyewitness to Therapy*, Bantam, New York

Perls, F, Hefferline, R and Goodman, P (1951) *Gestalt Therapy*, Dell, New York

Pfeiffer, J (1992) *Managing with Power: Politics and influence in organizations*, Harvard Business School Press, Boston, MA

Porter, L and Tanner, S (1998) *Assessing Business Excellence*, Butterworth Heinemann, Oxford

Pugh, D S (ed) (1990) *Organization Theory*, Penguin, London

Quinn, J (1980) *Strategies for Change: Logical incrementalism*, Irwin, New York

Rogers, C (1967) *On Becoming a Person*, Constable, London

Rokeach, M (1968) *Benefits, Attitudes and Values*, Jossey-Bass, San Francisco

Rowan, J (1983) *The Reality Game*, Routledge and Kegan Paul, London

Royce, W (1998) *Software Project Management*, Addison Wesley, Reading, MA

St John of the Cross (2003*) Dark Night of the Soul*, Riverhead Books, New York

Satir, V, Banmen, J, Gerber, J and Gomori, M (1991) *The Satir Model: Family therapy and beyond*, Science and Behavior Books, California

Sauer, C and Yetton, P W (1997) *Steps to the Future: Fresh thinking on the management of IT-based organizational transformation*, Jossey-Bass, San Francisco, CA

Shein E (1969) *Process Consultation: Its Role in Organization Development*, Addison Wesley Publishing Company, Reading, MA

Schein, E (1990) Organisational culture, *American Psychologist*, **45** (2)

Shein, E (1992) *Organizational Culture and Leadership* (2nd ed), Jossey-Bass, San Francisco

Schein, E (1999) *Corporate Culture Survival Guide*, Jossey-Bass, San Francisco, CA

Schein, E and Bennis, W (1965) *Personal and Organizational Change through Group Methods*, Wiley, New York

Schutz, W (1982) *Elements of Encounter*, Irvington Publishers, New York

Scott Peck, M (1990) *The Different Drum, Community-making and peace*, Arrow, London

Selden, L and Colvin, G (2003) M&A needn't be a loser's game, _Harvard Business Review_ (Jun), pp 70–79

Senge, P (1993) _The Fifth Discipline_, Century Business, London

Senge, P, Keliner, A, Roberts, C, Ross, R, Roth, G and Smith, B (1999) _The Dance of Change_, Nicholas Brealey, London

Shaw, P (2002) _Changing Conversations in Organizations_, Routledge, London

Skinner, B F (1953) _Science and Human Behaviour_, Macmillan, London

Stacey, R (1993) _Strategic Management and Organisational Dynamics_, Pitman, London

Stacey, R D (2001) _Complex Responsive Processes in Organizations: Learning and knowledge creation_, Routledge, London

Sundstrom, E, de Meuse, K P and Futrell, D (1990) Work teams: applications and effectiveness, _American Psychologist_, **45**, pp 120–33

Thompson, J (2001) _Strategic Management_, Thomson, London

Townsend, A M, DeMarie, S M and Hendrickson, A R (1998) Virtual teams: technology and the workplace of the future, _Academy of Management Executive_, **12**, pp 17–29

Trompenaars, F and Hampden-Turner, C (1997) _Riding the Waves of Culture: Understanding cultural diversity in business_, Nicholas Brealey, London

Tuckman, B (1965) Development sequences in small groups, _Psychological Bulletin_, **63**, pp 384–99

Turquet, P M (1974) Leadership: the individual and the group, in _Group Relations Reader 2_, ed A D Colman and M H Geller, pp 71–87, A K Rice Institute, Washington, DC

Wasmer, D and Bruner II, G (1991) Using organizational culture to design internal marketing strategies, _Journal of Services Marketing_, **5** (1) (Winter)

Weinberg, G (1997) _Quality Software Management: Volume 4, Anticipating Change_, Dorset House, New York

Whelan-Berry, K and Gordon, J (2000) Effective organizational change: new insights from multi-level analysis of the organizational change process, _Academy of Management Proceedings_, p 1

Whittaker, J (1970) Models of group development: implications for social group work practice, _Social Science Review_, **44** (3)

Wind, J Y and Main, J (1998) _Driving Change_, Kogan Page, London

Index